Rethinking Child Welfare
in Canada

Rethinking Child Welfare in Canada

edited by

Brian Wharf

OXFORD
UNIVERSITY PRESS

OXFORD
UNIVERSITY PRESS

70 Wynford Drive, Don Mills, Ontario M3C 1J9
www.oupcan.com

Oxford University Press is a department of the University of Oxford.
It furthers the University's objective of excellence in research, scholarship,
and education by publishing worldwide in

Oxford New York

Athens Auckland Bangkok Bogotá Buenos Aires Calcutta
Cape Town Chennai Dar es Salaam Delhi Florence Hong Kong Istanbul
Karachi Kuala Lumpur Madrid Melbourne Mexico City Mumbai
Nairobi Paris São Paulo Shanghai Singapore Taipei Tokyo Toronto Warsaw

with associated companies in Berlin Ibadan

Oxford is a trade mark of Oxford University Press
in the UK and in certain other countries

Published in Canada
by Oxford University Press

Copyright © 1993 by Brian Wharf

Canadian Cataloguing in Publication Data

Main entry under title:
Rethinking child welfare in Canada
Includes bibliographical references and index.

ISBN 0-19-541451-9

1. Child welfare – Canada. I. Wharf, Brian.

HV745.A6R48 1998   362.7'0971   C98-932384-6

3 4 5 6 - 03 02 01 00

This book is printed on permanent (acid-free) paper ∞.
Printed in Canada

Contents

Preface

Rethinking Child Welfare in Canada was initiated out of a profound sense of dissatisfaction with child welfare policy and practice in this country. While our awareness of policy and practice has been shaped by our knowledge of and research into child welfare in British Columbia, (Armitage, 1989; Callahan, 1988, 1989; and Wharf, 1985), we are sufficiently cognizant of the national child welfare scene to recognize that child welfare programs in other provinces are far from satisfactory. Our appraisal is supported by the Laidlaw Foundation's review of child welfare practice, which concluded that innovative developments in child welfare were to be found in voluntary agencies and were conspicuously lacking in provincial ministries of child welfare and children's aid societies (Laidlaw Foundation, 1991).

When we began this book we wondered if the insights from feminist, First Nation, and community-based approaches could suggest some new directions for child welfare. But at the outset we had little idea whether these insights would withstand a critical review or whether they would add up to a coherent bundle. In particular we did not foresee that consideration of these insights would lead to rethinking not just the policy and practice of child welfare but also some larger social policies. During the process of writing the book we have become aware that child welfare reforms are typically directed at improving the co-ordination of services by rearranging departmental and agency structures, or at increasing the number and adequacy of services and occasionally increasing the priority of preventive programs. This preoccupation with the adequacy and co-ordination of services has diverted attention from the assumptions that underpin child welfare and from the larger social policies that effectively set the context for child welfare. *Rethinking Child Welfare in Canada* eschews this traditional path of reform and gives attention to both the "ordinary" issues of child welfare and "the grand issues of social policy," such as the distribution of income and wealth (Lindblom, 1979: 523).

While the conceptualization of the book was not fully formed at the outset, it became more sharply drawn during the writing. From a methodological point of view we have reviewed child welfare from feminist, First Nations, and community-based perspectives and have inquired what child welfare would look like if these perspectives shaped policy and practice. We have merged these perspectives to argue that child welfare as currently shaped in legislation and policy and carried out in practice represents a severe instance of cultural lag and does not meet the needs of the families and children it purports to serve. We argue that changes in child welfare require complementary and supportive changes in the grand issues of social policy. In effect, then, the book represents a bottom-up view from a neglected and abused corner of society and suggests that the insights obtained from this view can not only reshape child welfare but alter some fundamental aspects of Canadian society.

Rethinking Child Welfare in Canada confronts the assumptions that lie behind the prevailing residual approach to child welfare. The first of these is that caring for children is not work and that a wage, therefore, is not justified unless the caring is done by other than the natural parent. In the latter case the work is poorly paid and given low status. A second assumption is that caring for children is a family matter untroubled by issues of income and other resources, and a complementary third assumption is that the state should not intervene in the private affairs of the family until the ability of parents to care for their children is exhausted. A fourth assumption has been that child welfare services can best be handled by departments of provincial governments without any attachment to local communities and without any need to adapt services to meet cultural needs.

The work at hand challenges these assumptions. It argues that caring for children is work of the highest priority. Whether in the home or in some other venue, caring for children is an important social concern and justifies the payment of a parental wage from the public purse. We contend, as well, that the circumstance of neglect should no longer be a reason for investigating and apprehending children and that the entire resources of child welfare agencies should be devoted to assisting and supporting parents. Further, child abuse should be reclassified as a criminal offence and handled by the criminal justice system. Violence against children is no different from other violent acts and must be treated in the same fashion.

Finally, in regard to the provision of services to consumers, the book suggests that community ownership of child welfare is important in order to provide an opportunity for social learning – for citizens at large to learn about and become involved in child welfare. From this essential tenet, it is argued that provincial departments of child welfare should no longer provide services but should retain responsibility for establishing legislation for overall policy, and setting standards and budgets. However, in contrast to recent suggestions calling for the integration of child welfare with other human services, we urge a policy of diversity and pluralism. Rather than one type of agency or structure being imposed on all communities, a variety of auspices should be tried and evaluated. Thus women's centres, First Nation band councils, and other constituencies committed to child welfare should be considered as appropriate auspices for providing child welfare services.

In short, the present work confronts the assumptions that govern child welfare and suggests some alternative assumptions. We recognize that some readers will disagree with our challenges and with our suggestions for redirecting the child welfare enterprise. Indeed, we will be disappointed if the book does not stir up some controversy among readers. Our hope is that *Rethinking Child Welfare in Canada* will push students, practitioners, and policymakers to think again about the care and welfare of children and not to be content with reforms that simply recluster existing services into new administrative arrangements.

A note about the content of the book is in order at this point. As Brad McKenzie pointed out in his review of the manuscript, *Rethinking Child Welfare* is "not a book about practice in child welfare in the ways this is traditionally defined. It does not address themes such as foster family care, family preservation, and treatment of child sexual abuse in any direct sense" (McKenzie, 1992: 1). Readers who are interested in and committed to improving practice modalities, be they mutual aid or professional interventions, will not find much assistance in the chapters that follow. Rather, they will find a critical review of the entire child welfare enterprise and some beginning suggestions for change.

The book is organized in the following fashion. Chapter 1 presents an historical review of child welfare in Canada. Chapter 2 describes the legislative and policy context that largely determines the practice world of child welfare. Chapter 3 portrays this world from the perspective of the front-line professional. Chapter 4 completes the discussion of the existing scene by describing the community and constituency context of child welfare.

The chapters in the second section take on the responsibility of rethinking child welfare. Chapter 5 presents information about both the past and current experiences of First Nations with child welfare. Chapter 6 provides a detailed account of feminist theories and their application to child welfare. Chapter 7 combines the insights emerging from the previous chapters and suggests several ways to reconstruct child welfare in Canada.

Part I

The Context of Child Welfare

Chapter 1

The Historical Context
of Child Welfare in Canada

Ewan Macintyre

The child welfare policy of a government is a very sensitive matter as the state and its agents are dealing with the privacy of its members and the shaping of the lives of the future adults of the society. The independence and privacy of the family are safeguarded in our society as a bulwark against oppression and as a place of personal freedom. But just as the family provides us with an opportunity to be our best, in terms of love and care, it also provides us with a private opportunity to be our worst towards family members in terms of violence and oppression. When and how the state should use its powers to attempt to modify the relationship of parents (and other adults) to their children is the subject of child welfare policy.

McCall (1990:347) defines child welfare as a field of social service practice in which the state, operating through specific statutory law, takes over "functions normally carried out by parents for their children." Child welfare programs that replace the "functions of parents" have been developed over the last 100 years and now form a common part of social service provision in all Western welfare states. In each country, and in each Canadian province, the policies governing child welfare reflect both assumptions about the obligations of parents and the view held by the government of when and how the state should be involved.

Many divergent themes inform child welfare policies and programs in Canada as we approach the twenty-first century. Some of these are historical, some ideological, some legal, and some professional. Some themes appear and reappear over time;

others are replaced with different ways of attempting to understand the special relationship of the child in the family within Canadian society.

After a discussion of the late nineteenth-century family and the emergence of the concept of childhood, this chapter reviews some of the social conditions that led to concern being raised about the welfare of children and considers important contributions to social reform made by private philanthropic organizations, including the Women's Missionary Societies and the National Council of Women in the late nineteenth and early twentieth centuries. The leadership role in developing child welfare services in Ontario and other provinces in the 1890s by members of the child-saving movement, including J.J. Kelso, and the important role played by the Canadian Council on Child Welfare's Charlotte Whitton in the 1920s and 1930s in developing child welfare standards of practice are described. The concept of *parens patriae*, which allows the state to act as substitute parent to protect the child's "best interests," is introduced. The experiences of four provinces – Nova Scotia, Quebec, Ontario, and British Columbia – are used to show some of the differences that emerged when children were seen as not the exclusive responsibility of their parents.

How this responsibility was assumed is described: some provinces established provincial child welfare departments; others, local Children's Aid Societies; yet others relied on religious or other private organizations to deliver services to children and their families. The Canadian child welfare system grew out of a concern to protect neglected, or orphaned, poor city street children and save them from becoming criminal or dependent adults.

THE FAMILY IN THE LATE NINETEENTH CENTURY

With urbanization and all family members no longer working as a productive unit for their own livelihood, the structure and function of the family changed. Unlike the rural family, which might have children working the land along with their parents and non-family members living in the home, the new urban family was more likely to be similar to our conception of the "traditional family," with the mother at home, the father in the labour force, and children at school or working out of the home. This traditional family is

characterized by a very strong sex-role differentiation that affects all other dimensions. The roles of wives and husbands, fathers and mothers, are clearly distinguished and largely non-overlapping. This differentiation is manifested in the assignment of economic responsibility and household management as well as in the responsibility for personal care. The father/husband is seen as responsible for the economic well-being of the entire family, while the mother/wife is seen as responsible for the physical, emotional, and overall well-being of family members. Her role includes providing care to family members in need of care. . . . By corollary, the father/husband is not seen as responsible except in economic terms, while the mother/wife is not seen as responsible for the economic well-being of the family. (Eichler, 1989: 59)

Wives and children in the traditional family, then, are conceptualized as economic dependants of the man who is husband and father. The caring work that wives perform in the home for their family members tends to be unrecognized and unrewarded; neither is it seen as having any economic value. The washing, cooking, cleaning, and nursing that women do for men and their children is not valued economically. Women in traditional families are viewed as social subordinates to the adult men in the family by virtue of their gender and their work; they are defined in relation to the work they perform for other family members.

In the traditional family, the husband/father is the family patriarch. This "resulted from a hierarchical social structure, whereby the chain of authority of the state was extended to the 'paterfamilias', whose responsibility it was to ensure the law-abiding behaviour of the family members, servants, apprentices, and employees within his household" (Walker, 1990: 105). Social reformers in the late nineteenth and early twentieth centuries wished to protect this traditional family. As a new understanding of childhood developed, this family type was viewed as best for children.

EMERGENCE OF THE CONCEPT OF "CHILDHOOD"

The concept of childhood changed dramatically in the latter part of the nineteenth century. Before that time, childhood

as a separate entity did not exist and children were treated in much the same manner as adults. Parents did not invest emotionally in children. With the advent of industrialization, children worked alongside adults in factories . . . they were not considered to be vulnerable or in need of special nurturing. Children were considered to be adults by age seven and were held accountable for their actions. Child-rearing was characterized by lack of parental affection, physical and emotional remoteness, and severe physical punishments. (Peikoff and Brickey, 1990)

By the end of the nineteenth century, children were no longer perceived as miniature adults. Childhood had begun to be seen "as a stage of life in which greater protection, sheltering, training and education were necessary" (Sutherland, 1985: 332). If the needs of the child could not be met by his or her own family, then other ways had to be found, including enacting laws "not just to stamp out individual injustices, but rather to protect and enhance the general quality of life within the continuum of childhood" (Bala and Clarke, 1981: 7).

Previously, children were treated no differently from adults with respect to the criminal law, nor were they treated any differently within the penal system. But in 1894 children were permitted trials in private to avoid the stigma of criminal proceedings, and if convicted of criminal activity and imprisoned, they were segregated from adults. The federal Act Respecting Juvenile Delinquents (1908) "underlines the philosophy that a child brought before the court as an alleged juvenile delinquent is to be treated as a misguided and misdirected child, one needing help and assistance," rather than as a criminal (*ibid.*).

In the latter half of the nineteenth century orphanages and training schools were established to remove children from almshouses, poor houses, and workhouses, first by religious and charitable groups, then by municipal governments as a result of provincial legislation spurred on by middle- and upper-class men and women who formed the child saving movement. These individuals wished to protect society from social unrest, to avoid present and future expenditures on public welfare, and to rescue city children and youth of the uneducated, lower class living in undesirable circumstances. They "blamed the parents of the children for the problem, but at the same time they ideologically reinforced the moral and social value of the family" (Albert, 1985: 330). Rather than focusing on the social and economic conditions that led children to be on the streets (lack of work for their parents, poor housing, poverty, etc.), they focused on the families, emphasizing the individual moral shortcomings of the parents and the need to control the behaviour of those who were now viewed as dependent, neglected, or delinquent children.

THE ROLE OF PRIVATE PHILANTHROPIC ORGANIZATIONS

Private philanthropy and volunteer efforts played an important role in the establishment of social services in Canada. Guest (1985: 14) notes that "the Catholic-Protestant dichotomy in private charity organizations was particularly evident in Eastern Canada from the 1830's on." Public-spirited citizens in many parts of Canada banded together to make the necessities of life available for the "worthy poor" to save them from the embarrassment of accepting public relief or to help those faced with a family or personal catastrophe. Fraternal organizations were established as an early form of self-help so that members and their families might avoid the stigma of having to accept charity. As well, during the late nineteenth century numerous charitable societies and agencies were established.

Volunteer middle-class home visitors were used by these societies to determine if help really was needed and if the applicants were worthy and thereby deserving. When there was doubt, the presence of children in the home often made the difference, and financial or other assistance was forthcoming. These visitors made moral judgements and "attempted to instil habits of industry and thrift and to promote self-respect and self-reliance" (Pitsula, 1979: 36). However, the "ideal of voluntary charity, though abstractly refined and uplifting, was not tenable" as Canada's cities swelled in size (*ibid.*: 37). Toronto, for example, grew from 44,800 in 1861 to 86,400 in 1881, to 208,000 in 1901. Not only did the size of cities increase, but the number of adults and children who were the victims of expanding industrialization also increased. This led to concern among the middle classes that society needed to be protected from a possible massive social upheaval and the belief that friendship between members of different classes working toward a common goal would serve to avert such an occurrence.

With the motto "Not alms, but a friend," middle-class volunteers served as "friendly visitors" to the poor, and by their example and guidance they hoped to demonstrate to lower-class families the way out of their poverty. However, by the turn of the century these representatives "realized that the causes of poverty were social, economic, and psychological rather than the result of personal moral failure. If moral failure was not the cause of poverty, then friendly visiting was not the solution" (Popple, 1983: 75), and concern began to be paid to social reform and changing environmental conditions.

Besides the "intensity of the processes of industrialization during the 1880s and 1890s [that] produced conditions of homelessness and exploitation for many Canadian children of the working class," thousands of homeless children were sent to Canada from orphanages, workhouses, and rescue homes in the United Kingdom to be placed in farming apprenticeships. Some of these placements were unsuccessful, and many young people "made their way to urban centres, especially Toronto, where their poverty became a visible problem," raising public concern that they were adding to the criminal class (Swift, 1991: 237).

At the same time that industrialization was resulting in more obvious poverty in the cities, a new middle class was emerging whose members experienced a rapid increase in their standard of living. "The social climate for this group, especially for women with increased leisure, provided time and energy for [them to work toward] social change" (*ibid.*).

In the early part of the nineteenth century, women became involved in social reform through participation in local charitable endeavours. By the end of the century, this involvement had increased tremendously with the founding of women's organizations that were reformist in orientation and national in scope. Women formed groups at the local, provincial, and national levels to promote cultural and patriotic nation-building activities. Of particular interest are four organizations that typified Canadian women's wishes to express their social concern about urban poverty and industrialization.

(1) The churches were the most important social institution in Canada at the turn of the century. Their Women's Missionary Societies "were the most important of the first great female alliances . . . intended originally for evangelical work . . . [members] responded to the urgent need for urban charity" (Strong-Boag, 1977: 88). Not only concerned with saving the heathen overseas, Women's Missionary Societies were concerned with issues at home, including the needs of women and children, the plight of Native peoples, new immigrants, and victims of alcohol abuse. The churches, concerned with saving and serving all people, not just the worthy, played an important role in shaping the movement for social reform and permitted the entrance of women into the public arena.

(2) The Young Women's Christian Association was formed with special concern for the young urban working woman's needs for a safe and wholesome place to live; she "had to be protected because she represented a future mother, the guardian of a household"

(*ibid.*, 92). The national association was established in 1893, and by the following year fourteen local YWCAs were in operation.

(3) The Woman's Christian Temperance Union, founded in 1874, had prohibition of the sale of alcohol as its major goal; abuse of alcohol was early identified as a cause of poverty and other sources of urban misery. Other goals of the WCTU included "advocating for higher education for women, the employment of women as factory inspectors, doctors, and teachers, child protection legislation, reformatories for juveniles, a hospital for women, and the establishment of cottage homes for children rather than large barrack-style institutions" (Baines, 1991: 48).

(4) The National Council of Women was formed in 1893 to expand the efforts of the many women's groups that were already concerned with issues such as "working girls, urban housing, public creches, children's recreation, cultural improvement, and social purity" (Strong-Boag, 1977: 95). Lady Aberdeen, the founder and first president believed that the mission of the NCW was, "in one word, mothering." She saw a relationship between mothering and family life and social reform, and recognized a need for women to work together to improve the lot of women and children in society. The Council had no denominational affiliation and brought together women's groups with the belief that they could work co-operatively for an improved Canada by co-ordinating feminine policies at the national level.

The reform work of these and other women's groups in the late nineteenth and early twentieth centuries, which was a type of Christian social action, had the following characteristics:

> (1) women enacted their caring mission not as individuals but as members of women's organizations – women were able to do in concert things that would be difficult to do alone; (2) women instituted new services and careers for women; (3) the targets of their reform efforts were typically poor women and children; and (4) women accepted subordinate and traditional roles under the aegis of the clergy. (Baines, 1991: 42)

In these ways, women's private mothering, maintenance, and caring for their own family members were transferred, through moral reform and rescue work, to "mothering on a national scale" (Ursel, 1992: 71) that included public caring for the poor, the disadvantaged, and the neglected. Protection of the family, however, included reproduction, the promotion of motherhood, and the defence of a patriarchal sexual code. Ursel believes that members of the social reform movement, with their shared patriarchal conception of the family, were the architects of social patriarchy. Their work helped to prepare the way for public support of the government legislation and social programs that were to follow. State intervention and regulation of family life, according to Ursel, supported the traditional familial patriarchy, and the transition of the locus of power from the family patriarch to the patriarchal state "can be understood as an adaptation for the preservation of family patriarchy" (*ibid.*: 55). She defines family patriarchy as power and authority over women and children exercised by men in the home. Social patriarchy is support for and control over women and children as a result of laws, regulations, and institutions of the state. Both types of patriarchy serve to subordinate women.

STATE INTERVENTION

The concept of *parens patriae* is fundamental in any discussion of law respecting children. The term, Latin for "protector" or "father of the country," may be defined as the "inherent jurisdiction of a court to look after the best interests of a child" (Bala and Clarke, 1981: 6). The court, under the authority of this doctrine, may act as a substitute benevolent parent on behalf of the state. In so doing, the court interferes with usual parental custody and other rights if such action is deemed in the best interests of the child(ren) involved. The grounds for such action have changed and expanded since the term was first used in Europe in the 1760s.

The best interests concept was first used to protect

the property and personhood of vulnerable persons. [It] . . . initially stressed the preservation of the property of lunatics, idiots and young persons. Eventually, some provision for the sustenance and education of these groups of people, as well as for the prevention of improper marriages of young wards, was subsumed into the protection principle as another royal and parental obligation. (Reitsma-Street, 1986: 9)

Later, *parens patriae* was expanded to include "active promotion of the opportunities that enhanced the physical, religious, social, and educational development of a young person" (*ibid.*). This expansion provided the state in the last decades of the nineteenth century with a rationale for removing neglected or delinquent children from their guardians, including parents, and placing them elsewhere: primarily, apprenticeships for the neglected and training institutions for the delinquent.

The state, it should be noted, focused its intervention more on the controlling and enforcing of standards of care and on aspects of parenthood that included "limiting and directing their environments, opportunities and activities," rather than on the caring aspects, leaving responsibility for financial maintenance and discipline with the child's own parents (*ibid.*: 20). If, for example, a child was removed from his or her own home and placed in a foster home, parents of that child were expected to make a financial contribution toward their child's maintenance.

The principles of best interests and need of protection within the *parens patriae* framework informed both Ontario's 1893 Act for the Prevention of Cruelty to and Better Protection of Children and the 1908 federal Juvenile Delinquents Act to justify state intervention into the lives of young persons and their families. For this to happen, however, the delinquent had to be convicted of a crime and the neglected child had to be in serious peril.

The Juvenile Delinquents Act was designed to protect children from their own "evil tendencies," or from such tendencies on the part of others, by establishing that representatives of the state should offer guidance and assistance. To protect young people, "private, speedy and informal trials by special judges who had the discretion to give the young person indeterminate dispositions" were established. The 1908 Act also gave probation officers the power to "supervise the activities and training of the young delinquent in his/her own home as an alternative to institutionalization, a fine, or suspended sentence" (*ibid.*: 14).

Juvenile and family court judges were given responsibility in "assessing situations in which a child's welfare is at stake . . . that it is what is in the best interests of the child which must be the preeminent consideration of the court" (Bala and Clarke, 1981: 11). The judge, acting in the role of benevolent parent on behalf of the state, had to attempt to see the situation through the eyes and mind of the young person before him and make his decision accordingly. Decisions were not based on what the parent might wish but on what the judge believed was in the child's best interests.

The amendments to both provincial child welfare and federal juvenile delinquent acts throughout most of the twentieth century were based on the principle of *parens patriae*. These "legislative changes enlarged and consolidated the discretionary powers of state representatives acting as benevolent parents protecting the best interests of more types of delinquent or neglected young persons and their family groups for longer periods of time" (Reitsma-Street, 1986: 27). These acts:

authorized a wide group of persons, including members of the social welfare community, to act as wise and benevolent parents to protect and promote the best interests of young people who were without parents or property to provide for their upkeep, or who lived with ill-treating, immoral parents, or who were delinquent because of an unfavourable environment. Family groups no longer completely owned their offspring to do with them as they wished; delinquents were no longer like adult criminals; and the state no longer ignored how family groups discharged their care and control responsibilities to young persons. (*ibid.*: 19-20)

Within the framework of *parens patriae* the state has the right, in the best interests of the child and for that child's protection, to remove some authority from the family through its legislative and court systems, to define good and bad parents' behaviour, to enunciate safe living conditions for children, to propose possible outcomes for the young persons involved, and to establish services on behalf of children believed in need of state intervention. This framework continues to provide the rationale for state intervention into family life. The principle was used first as a result of concern for deprived children who had been orphaned or abandoned, then for children living within their own families. That such intervention inevitably is in the child's best interest is a topic of continuing debate.

PROVINCIAL RESPONSIBILITY FOR CHILD WELFARE

In Canada, child welfare is a provincial matter. The enactment of legislation beginning in the last decade of the nineteenth century enabled the establishment and growth of children's aid societies and provincial departments of child welfare, so that each province could ensure that the safe and stable living conditions needed by children were provided. Swift reminds us "that the first responsibility of the state is not that of supplying care for children but of enforcing needed care through the medium of the family." The administrative arms of the law were charged with enforcing standards of child care and parental behaviour with a focus "from the beginning organized around the case-by-case supervision of particular families." Built into legislation and organizational policy "was the idea that the family was primarily responsible for its own destiny and the state was responsible for the enforcement of this ideal" (Swift, 1991: 238-39). Early provincial child welfare legislation was not concerned with poverty, exploitation of children, or other social issues that led them to be neglected, abandoned, or abused; it did mean that parents no longer had the right to absolute power over their children.

The experience of four provinces highlights these early developments. These particular provinces were chosen because of their different approaches and philosophies to the development of services, which in turn led to the establishment of different structures to administer child welfare services.

Nova Scotia

Before the mid-1880s orphaned or destitute children and families "were forced into workhouses where they were treated as chattels and subjected to much abuse. Many did not survive; those who did were often scarred for life" (Nova Scotia Department of Social Services, 1987: xi). In the 1830s, Joseph Howe, the owner and editor of the *Novascotian*, concerned with the plight of children in these workhouses, began a campaign for better conditions. During the next fifty years, many separate institutions for children in need were established, most often under religious auspices because the churches wanted to rescue children from moral decadence or saw such work as part of their Christian duty. These institutions included St. Mary's Convent Orphanage (1849), the Halifax Protestant Orphan's Home (1857), the Halifax Industrial School (1865), St. Paul's Home for Girls (1867), Halifax Infants Home (1875), and the Good Shepherd Industrial Refuge (1890) (*ibid.*).

The first legislation pertaining to the protection of children under sixteen years of age from neglect and abuse in their own homes in Nova Scotia came into effect in 1880. Records "show that by 1888, two-thirds of the . . . caseload concerned the abused children of needy families" (*ibid.*).

The Children's Protection Act, passed in 1906, enabled private children's aid societies to be established in Nova Scotia. These new "agencies were empowered to bring neglected boys (under fourteen) and neglected girls (under sixteen) before the Court, to act as their guardians, to place them in temporary shelters or private institutions, and to indenture them to suitable homes" (*ibid.*: xi-xii). Similar to the experience in other provinces, Children's Aid Societies in Nova Scotia experienced financial difficulties because their funding base depended on meagre municipal contributions.

Although Children's Aid Societies were established in many parts of the province between 1912 and 1931, not until 1940 did the provincial government provide direct grants, thus allowing them to develop and expand their services. At about the same time, a unique joint system of administration of local voluntary agencies and provincial social services offices was begun when the first joint service agreement was signed. Under these agreements, the regional administrator or district supervisor of the provincial Department of Social Services also acted as the executive director of the local Children's Aid Society. This pattern continues in most Nova Scotia communities. Where there are no local Children's Aid Societies, the provincial government is directly responsible for child welfare services.

Quebec

French Canada drew the bulk of its original non-Native population from the urban and semi-rural centres of continental France during the 1640-1730 period. In France, the family and the Roman Catholic Church exercised "a virtual monopoly of responsibility for assistance in the realms of both welfare and health." This traditional system came with the settlers of New France, who expected to continue to look to family members or the Church for assistance when it was needed. In France, unlike England and Germany, the state, embodied in the King, was not seen as having any direct responsibility for its citizens; rather, needy individuals turned to the Church when families were unable to help. "Traditionally, the sovereign, the nobility, the great landowners, and the bourgeoisie, which only then was beginning to emerge as a distinct social class, acquitted themselves of their charitable duties in the form of very substantial gifts to diocesan bodies and religious communities (Guillemette, 1961: 1).

As was the practice in France, the King made large grants of land to religious communities that had immigrated to New France or that were founded in the new North American colony. Revenues from these landholdings made possible the establishment and maintenance of hospitals, institutions for the aged and orphaned, and crèches for children born out of wedlock.

From the earliest days of the French colony along the St. Lawrence River the welfare system, including services for children, tended to be under the exclusive care of the Catholic Church. The welfare institutions that developed were private (personnel and policies depended entirely on private rather than state initiative), denominational (under the auspices of the Catholic Church and adhering to its doctrinal base), and institutional (the religious communities undertook, often within the confines of their own institutional community, to build and maintain institutions into which needy individuals might be admitted for care).

By the early 1760s the ample financial resources of the religious communities were sufficient to meet the needs of the people, and this welfare system was well entrenched in the social fabric of life in Quebec. Although the British after 1763 attempted to introduce radical changes more in keeping with their tradition of state (or at least local community) responsibility, welfare services provided out of taxes, and other principles found in the Elizabethan Poor Law of 1601, the French-speaking Catholic population resisted such changes, adamantly maintaining the service auspices and service delivery they were accustomed to.

At the time of Confederation in 1867, Quebec was not at all well equipped to move into the industrial revolution. While Montreal had some 90,000 inhabitants, the second largest city, Quebec City, had fewer than 60,000. The latter part of the nineteenth century was one of the saddest periods in Quebec's history. Between 1850 and 1900, half a million Quebecers left for the United States; many others moved to the western provinces. The new provincial government relied heavily on the federal government for financial assistance because its own financial resources were limited. Much farming was marginal and there were few manufacturing companies. Since the provincial government was not able to handle effectively its responsibilities regarding education and health services, the Church continued to offer them. In 1869, however, the Quebec legislature adopted the first Canadian law relating to the protection of the rights of children and youth, the Acte concernant les écoles d'industrie, a modified version of which remained in place until 1950. This Act allowed destitute or abandoned children to attend industrial schools for academic and industrial training (Christenson, 1989: 34).

As in other parts of Canada, industrialization in Quebec was accompanied by increasing urbanization in the early years of the twentieth century. Montreal tripled in size in the two decades from 1901 to 1921. The new city population, at a time of stress, found itself less able than the former rural society to cope with its welfare and assistance needs. At the same time, the Church was more concerned with maintaining its privileged position than with helping Quebecers enter the twentieth century – it extolled the virtues of rural life, cautioned against the evils of the city and the dangers of education, and preached the need to accept one's lot in life (Latouche, 1985: 1523).

When the existing private institutions were unable to meet the needs of those who came to their attention, they approached the public authorities for financial assistance to enable them to continue their work. The provincial government response was the Quebec Public Charities Act of 1921. This Act, despite its title, was designed to confirm the province's traditional system of private services. It provided a means for the government to give direct financial assistance to private religious institutions so that they might give services to those in need but unable to pay. The new legislation acknowledged a place for the provincial government in health and welfare services and laid the foundation for government involvement in social welfare by tying public assistance to welfare institutions. The Act did not provide for direct financial assistance to those in need; rather, it refunded institutions part of their costs in giving services to the poor.

Later, the growing English-speaking Protestant population of Quebec established private parallel services to those already in place to serve the French-speaking Catholic population. Quebec, thus, has a tradition of two systems and two points of view concerning its social welfare programs. The non-Catholic community established social agencies with lay personnel and voluntary boards of directors. The 1921 Act benefited only Catholic institutions, and non-Catholic agencies did not qualify for public assistance funds. However, when agencies were conceptualized as "institutions without walls" in the 1930s, both new Catholic agencies and non-Catholic ones came to be recognized as able to benefit from the Act (Guillemette, 1961: 4). Since the 1930s, a network of social agencies has been established, working alongside the traditional service institutions in Quebec.

Ontario

In Upper Canada, from the time of the passage of The Orphan's Act in 1799 until The Apprentices and Minors Act of 1851, the only alternatives for deserted or orphaned children who could not be informally adopted were apprenticeship and living in an almshouse. By the mid-1850s "many reformers recognized the need for separate children's institutions and devoted their efforts to the establishment and management of orphans' homes" (Bullen, 1990). The 1849 Municipal Act created local levels of government that allowed relief-giving by local authorities; services for children depended solely on local initiative and financing.

Adoption and institutional care as alternatives to apprenticeship became possible after 1874, when charitable societies were given the legal authority to prevent the maltreatment of apprentices. An 1884 amendment to the Industrial Schools Act (1874) "allowed school trustees to delegate responsibility for the establishment of residential schools for children under age 14 to any incorporated philanthropic society, subject to Provincial approval of the society's by-laws" (Ministry of Community and Social Services, 1979). Children were sent to industrial schools "by the courts if vagrant or delinquent, by parents because of their unmanageability or by the state because of parental neglect" (Ministry of Community and Social Services, 1990a: 1). Although industrial schools were seen as an improvement over almshouses for children, social reformers did not consider them as able to meet the needs of children before the court for three major reasons: there were too few spaces available in the schools; the issue of how to determine parental inadequacy was not addressed in the legislation; and an industrial school environment was inappropriate for growing children (*ibid.*).

J.J. Kelso, a newspaper reporter and social reformer concerned about the poor in his community, founded the Toronto Humane Society in 1887 for the prevention of cruelty to both children and animals. He was the spokesman for a new group of child savers who "generated a number of fresh ideas pertaining to child welfare, including a wider definition of needy children, an expanded role for the State, and an emphasis on the home as the proper environment for growing children" (Bullen, 1990: 15).

The Children's Protection Act (1888), or, to give it its full title, An Act for the Protection and Reformation of Neglected Children, gave courts the right to make neglected children wards of institutions and charitable societies. This Act had neither investigative nor interventive functions; it was meant only to protect children from further neglect rather than prevent them from being neglected in the first place. The local government was held responsible for assuming the cost of maintaining these wards.

In 1891 Kelso became the founding president of the Toronto Children's Aid Society, which was established "to provide a temporary refuge for the care and protection of neglected children" over four years of age; an already existing Infants Home in Toronto cared for younger children. Kelso and his colleagues believed that the Society could save neglected children from the streets and thus prevent them from becoming adult criminals. He viewed the Society as being in a position to place these children in "good," preferably rural, homes. Homes were preferred over institutions so that children might experience "normal" family environments.

A new Act for the Prevention of Cruelty to and Better Protection of Children was passed in 1893, establishing new principles of child care, laying the groundwork of legal authority for child welfare in Ontario, and serving as the prototype for similar legislation in other provinces. The Act was meant to protect children from wilful ill treatment and neglect, prostitution and taking part in night-time entertainments, poverty and homelessness, and immoral, depraved family life (Reitsma-Street 1986: 14). The Act made abuse of children an indictable offence and gave voluntary charitable societies broad powers to protect children, "including the right to remove children from their own homes, responsibility for the 'supervision and management' of children in municipal shelters, and the status and prerogatives of legal guardians. . . . [They] were empowered to collect a 'reasonable sum' from their municipalities for maintenance of wards" (Ministry of Community and Social Services, 1979: 10).

The Toronto Society received its first municipal grant of $2,000 in 1894 despite its concern about government involvement in its affairs. Later, in 1906, the Society refused a provincial government offer of a daily rate for each child in care because the board of directors believed this might lead to a lessening of private donations. In fact, no provincial funds were accepted by the Toronto Society until 1925 (*ibid.*).

The 1893 Act enabled the establishment of Children's Visiting Committees in each electoral district and additional Children's Aid Societies in Ontario as semi-public organizations with a legal mandate, each with a private board of directors. Concerned with cruelty to children and wishing to protect them from becoming immoral adults, Children's Aid Societies either supervised families found wanting or removed children from "evil" situations and placed them in foster homes with moral families where they could learn the value of work and discipline. The Act served to promote the foster home model of care as "an efficient, humane and economical alternative to institutionalization" (Bullen, 1990: 15). Within foster homes, mostly volunteer, "opportunities for education, training, and 'kind and proper treatment as members of the family where placed' were expected" (Reitsma-Street, 1986: 15). Wherever possible, the child's parents were expected to be responsible for the cost of foster home care, although parents of "neglected or abused children were seen as having forfeited their parental rights, and were to have no future access to or influence on them" (Ministry of Community and Social Services, 1990a: 2).

Bullen, in his paper examining the early motives and methods of the Children's Aid Societies, cautions that

> the unbending faith in the social value of work and discipline . . . created a hazy atmosphere that clouded the distinction between industrious habits and child exploitation . . . as . . . many foster parents and employers abused this belief and took more from the children in the way of work than they returned in the form of affection, education, opportunity and material rewards . . . [so that] many foster children found themselves condemned to a working-class world that offered few opportunities for personal development and social mobility. (Bullen, 1990: 15)

In 1893, Kelso was appointed the first Provincial Superintendent of Neglected and Dependent Children in Ontario, a position he held until his retirement in 1934. He was instrumental in establishing Children's Aid Societies throughout Ontario – sixty by 1907 – and in British Columbia, Manitoba, Prince Edward Island, and Nova Scotia during the first two decades of the twentieth century.

British Columbia

British Columbia became part of the Dominion of Canada in 1871 when its 12,000 white residents agreed to join the new confederation of eastern provinces with the understanding that a railroad would be constructed to link it with the East. By 1881 the white population had increased to 24,000 while the estimated Native population was 25,000. Until the late 1880s, the Native Indian population was "the dominant people of the Pacific Northwest" (Clague *et al.*, 1984: 3).

The rise of cities at the end of the nineteenth and beginning of the twentieth centuries in other parts of Canada was mirrored in B.C., and by 1901 Vancouver had 30,000 residents, Victoria, 21,000. The population of B.C. remains clustered along the coasts and interior valleys, as was the case when Natives were a clear majority. Today, the population of just under three million persons is 80 per cent urban, 20 per cent rural. Unlike other parts of Canada, B.C. does not have township and county or regional administrative units that have responsibility for service delivery. Although some 80 per cent of British Columbians live in communities with local government, most areas of the province have neither population nor local governments. The statutory social services, including child welfare, are administered by the provincial ministry of social services.

Concern for neglected children in Vancouver at the turn of the century led to the first child welfare legislation in British Columbia, the Infants Act of 1901. This Act provided for the legal transfer of guardianship of orphaned or neglected children to the state or to Children's Aid Societies, which were allowed to incorporate under this Act for the purpose of giving care to such children. The Act permitted police and Children's Aid Societies to apprehend children. Only two urban areas, however, Vancouver and Victoria, formed Societies. Until 1924, Societies in these two communities were the only organizations providing child welfare services in British Columbia.

Originally, children from throughout the province were viewed as the responsibility of the Vancouver CAS and committed to that agency. However, there was no statutory obligation for the provincial government or the municipality within which the child had previously lived to assist with paying maintenance costs for these children. In addition to children committed under the Childrens' Protection Act, other "non-committed" children were admitted into the care of the CAS at the request of their parents. This latter group of children, although admitted into care on a temporary basis, often stayed for extended periods of time as no assistance was given to their parents.

For many years the Vancouver CAS pressured the provincial government for funds, maintaining that if the state had the right under statute to remove children from their own homes, the state should also assume responsibility for their support. It was many years, however, before the provincial government agreed to pay full maintenance for all CAS wards, whether they were under the guardianship of the state or a private Children's Aid Society, and whether they were from Vancouver or another part of the province.

The year 1905 witnessed the establishment of the Catholic Children's Aid Society in Vancouver to meet the special needs of Catholic children to receive "proper religious training" throughout the province. This became the third, and last, Children's Aid Society to be formed in British Columbia.

The problem of neglected children became acute enough in 1919 to warrant the appointment of a Superintendent of Neglected Children by the provincial government to give greater force to the Infants Act. The superintendent's duties included the inspection of children's institutions receiving provincial grants. The two Children's Aid Societies in Vancouver were paid on a per diem per capita basis for children in their care from unorganized territories whose guardianship had been transferred to the provincial government. Cities and municipalities continued to be responsible for investigating charges of neglect in the first instance. However, the Superintendent became involved when the child was actually proved to be neglected as a result of a court hearing and was responsible for placement of the child in an institution in communities other than Vancouver and Victoria.

The early 1920s in Vancouver

> were rather stormy, unsettled ones for the two voluntary children's aid societies and the government officials whose responsibility it was to offer services to families and children throughout the province. The numbers requiring help increased every year, the resources and facilities to meet their needs were limited by small funds and virtually no trained personnel . . . the pressure of work and the heavy responsibilities it placed on the small, inexperienced and untrained staffs was becoming overwhelming . . . there were also hints of disagreements as to methods of management of agencies in addition to complaints of serious overcrowding in the children's institutions. (Watson, 1960: 6)

In 1925 the Rotary Club decided to assist with the building of a Preventorium, an institution for children unable to live with their own parents. The Rotary Club report of community service needs indicated that child welfare conditions should be studied further, for the child-care institutions in Vancouver were

> crowded to capacity, with almost daily demands being made for more admissions. Practically no work was being done with the child's own family group to remove the necessity of taking him into care. If he were separated from his family, there was no emphasis placed on substituting for his own home the next best thing, another family home. Almost the only type of service provided for the child in danger of neglect or dependency was institutional care. Such family homes as were being utilized were almost entirely "free work" homes, where the child was "earning his keep", or free adoptive homes. (*ibid.*: 7)

The Rotary Club recommended that a further study of child welfare in Vancouver should be conducted by people who were experienced and technically equipped to handle such a task.

At the same time that the issues of overcrowding and poor conditions in children's institutions were being raised by the Rotary Club, the provincial government was becoming concerned about the management of the Vancouver Children's Aid Society and the costs being incurred by the Society on behalf of non-committed children in its care, although provincial legislation covered only reimbursement for children committed to the care of the CAS. These concerns led to the B.C. child welfare study of 1927 conducted by Charlotte Whitton, which will be discussed below.

THE PROFESSIONALIZATION OF CHILD WELFARE SERVICES

As these four provincial examples indicate, the child-saving movement led to the establishment of Children's Aid Societies in many of Canada's urban centres. The success of this reform movement was a result of an alliance among the following loosely defined groups and interests.

(1) Some members of the social and economic elite of the community were drawn to the cause by humanitarian reasons and provided financial support. (2) The middle class provided volunteers and "the model for child rearing and proper moral behaviour," together with a concern to impose their views on others in order to protect children and to protect society from turmoil. (3) The middle class also provided the recruits for the growing profession of social work, a career and salaried extension of the volunteers' interests. (4) The Government empowered voluntary societies with the statutory authority to achieve their goals, supervised the societies' use of authority, and became the source of funds where voluntary contributions proved inadequate to the task (Jones and Rutman, 1981: 181-82).

The use of volunteers as board members and visitors was a well-entrenched practice when Children's Aid Societies were organized. Likewise, Children's Visiting Committees were composed of volunteers, three of whom were expected to be women. Members of such committees had to select and monitor foster homes for children in that society's care and were responsible for promoting within their communities "philanthropic sentiment on behalf of neglected, abandoned and destitute children" (*ibid.*: 65). With foster parents largely unpaid as well, early child welfare services were very much voluntary, often undertaken by women whose labour, while valued, was certainly not rewarded financially.

By the end of the nineteenth century, the volunteer system of giving help to individuals and families was gradually replaced by the employment of staff members, sometimes university-educated social workers, who arranged and supervised foster home placements. Like their volunteer predecessors, they "tended to reinforce the earlier approach of focusing on the family and its problems rather than on detrimental social conditions" (Albert, 1985: 330). One difference, however, was that the salaried caseworkers did not classify clients as deserving or undeserving. The moral shortcomings of clients were not part of the professional's investigative process.

Although social workers performed critical administrative, investigative, supervisory, guardianship, and counselling roles, they did not directly care for children. The preferred type of care was the foster home. In many ways, the foster care system was an extension of the early emphasis on a strong volunteer contribution to child welfare, with foster parents being reimbursed only for out-of-pocket expenses rather than being paid for the care of children. This can be seen as an extension of the assumption that the care of children is a "natural" role of a mother and should be unpaid. Payment was regarded as not only unnecessary but undesirable and inimical to the natural expression of maternal love and affection.

When the University of Toronto's new Social Services Department accepted its first students into a diploma program in 1914 (all women members of Protestant churches), academic content was taught by male faculty members drawn from the departments of philosophy, psychology, and political economy. Social work practice and skills classes, however, were given by prominent women social work practitioners who served as instructors. "Investigation, co-ordination, and efficiency became the hallmarks of casework practice" in the new program (Baines, 1991: 57). Social work students were taught to deal with clients in an objective and scientific fashion so that their interventions with families could be clearly distinguished from that of earlier "friendly visitors." Collecting social evidence, in a scientific manner, enabled students to make a social diagnosis of each family and its members.

The Canadian Association of Social Workers (CASW), established in 1926, was dedicated to "upholding professional standards, encouraging proper and adequate training, and cultivating and informing public opinion regarding the professional and technical nature of social work" (Pitsula, 1979: 41). This statement of purpose was written at a time when Canadian social services were developing and social work as a profession was ill defined, but social workers were becoming aware of themselves as a distinctive group with its own skills and approaches to social problems. The first general meeting of the new CASW was held in Toronto in 1928. By this time there were 194 charter members and branches had been formed in Montreal (1927) and Toronto (1928).

The CASW goal of adequate preparation and training of social workers was hampered by the fact that in 1926 only two academic departments of social work had been established in Canada: at the University of Toronto in 1914 and at McGill University in 1918. Most early graduates were employed in Montreal or Toronto. The CASW was a participant in the establishment of new schools of social work at the University of British Columbia (1927), followed by the University of Montreal (1933), Dalhousie (1941), and Laval and Manitoba (1943). As a result of the small number of social work graduates entering the profession, there was an "experience" clause permitting association membership for individuals without social work training but who were at least twenty-five years of age, had some years of professional experience in an agency of recognized standing, and demonstrated "evidence of an educational background sufficient to warrant expectation of progress in the profession of social work" (Maines, 1959: 8).

In 1926, Charlotte Whitton became director of the Child Welfare Council, which became the Canadian Welfare Council in 1929. She deserves much credit for bringing the need for child welfare practice standards, including professionally trained staff, to the attention of Children's Aid Societies and provincial governments as a result of surveys she conducted on behalf of the CWC in the 1920s. The British Columbia experience (1927) serves as an example of her influence on child welfare in Canada in the twenties and thirties.

Concerns raised locally in Vancouver and by the Public Accounts Committee of the legislature led to the British Columbia Child Welfare Survey being undertaken. It was funded by five local service clubs and conducted by Whitton with the help of Robert E. Mills, director of the Toronto CAS. Whitton's reports at the conclusion of her surveys in other provinces, including New Brunswick, Manitoba, and later Alberta, as well as British Columbia, "were powerful indictments of institutional child care and led to a more rapid adoption of foster care practices" (Rooke and Schnell, 1987: 72). Her final report established the basis for the development of professional child welfare services in British Columbia. Its recommendations included: the need for social agencies to work together rather than as isolated units in the community; the need to make more organized efforts to keep children in their own homes rather than place them in institutions; that trained social workers be obtained to staff children's aid societies as field workers in the community helping families, rather than as institutional personnel caring for children; and that the care and maintenance of wards should be financed entirely by the municipal or provincial government. This recommendation was accepted by the province in 1930 and by the city of Vancouver in 1931.

Within two years of the report, there was a vast reduction in the number of children in institutions, primarily as a result of policy changes made at the Vancouver Children's Aid Society, which included focusing on the needs of the family rather than on the needs of children. This policy change decreased the number of children having to be placed out of their own homes. When children did have to be removed from their homes, the placement of choice became foster homes.

An amendment to the Infants' Act in 1934 made one of the duties of a Children's Aid Society "the ameliorating of family conditions that lead to the neglect of children," thus marking the first time that the preventive side of child welfare work was written into law. In 1939 the Protection of Children Act, emphasizing the more positive aspects of work with neglected children, replaced the earlier Infants' Act, and additional definitions of what constituted a neglected child were added.

In 1942, the Unemployment Relief, Mothers' Allowance, and Child Welfare branches were amalgamated under the Department of the Provincial Secretary. In early 1943, the three field staffs came together and the policy was established that every social worker should be able to give a generalized welfare service throughout the province. This meant that social workers in each office were responsible for programs of income assistance and services to clients with mental handicaps, as well as for child welfare and adoption services.

SUMMARY: THE SOCIAL CONTEXT OF CHILD WELFARE

The confident assumption of the early child welfare reformers and professionals and, indeed, the public at large was that once the welfare of children was accepted as a responsibility by government, sufficient resources would be allocated, appropriate delivery structures created, and qualified staff hired to provide services. Early policies governing child welfare were based on equally confident assumptions that the family is a stable unit, that parents possess sufficient financial resources to raise children, and that they are supported by relatives and a safe neighbourhood. These assumptions were wrenched apart when women asserted their rightful demand for employment outside the home, when families were revealed as patriarchal units that not only resulted in the economic domination of women but all too frequently in violence against women and children, and when the existence of severe conditions of poverty amid affluence became evident in the 1960s. These factors have been accompanied by the collapse of religious imperatives about appropriate behaviour and the transformation of communities from closed to open systems that have radically changed the lives and behaviour of individuals and families.

Chapter 2

The Policy and Legislative Context

Andrew Armitage

This chapter examines current policy and legislative provisions in Canada for family and child welfare. The chapter begins with a review of the foundations of family and child welfare policy. This is followed by an analysis of current policy and legislation that looks first at a narrow, residual formulation of the child welfare mandate and then at a broader institutional formulation of family and child welfare policy. The differences between the residual and institutional constructs are examined in depth through consideration of major features of policy and law, the extent of the family and child welfare system, and the approach taken to co-ordination and systems planning. A third view, social development, has not been applied in any Canadian province. Social development goes beyond residual or institutional services and demands an examination of the fundamental structures of society that lead to the need for welfare services. Chapters 5, 6, and 7 each contain some features of this view.

FOUNDATIONS

To understand the foundations of child welfare policy it is necessary to consider assumptions about family, disadvantage, culture, and the state on which policy is built.

Family

As discussed in Chapter 1, policy is based on important assumptions about the family. During the nineteenth and early twentieth centuries, when the child welfare field was in its infancy, the family was an avowedly patriarchal institution and children were seen as in need of discipline, guidance, and protection. Women had clearly defined nurturing and supporting roles but authority and responsibility was exercised by the male parent.

These foundations of child welfare were supported by the assumption that children should not and cannot look after themselves. Society was seen as a hostile and exploitative place where children were "at risk" if not protected by a father figure. In addition, there was a concern that effective discipline should be exercised over incorrigible and wayward children. The father exercised control over the labour of "his" children and in return it was his responsibility to see that they were fed and clothed – albeit in a manner in which he had a broad discretion. This discretion, however, was always subject to some limits. These existed in the provisions of the criminal law and in the historic *parens patriae* power of the English Crown to act in the best interests of children.

This nineteenth-century view of the family lingers today but is far removed from some contemporary views, which are based on the equal status of the parents and recognize relationships outside those created by descent or marriage. These relationships include those of unmarried couples, including gay couples, and of such family units as associate or foster families. From a more functional perspective, the family can be defined in terms of personal association and a common household. Families also define their own boundaries based on their sense of emotional bond; thus, one child in a foster family may be a family member for life while another is only a member for a period of temporary association.

Among family members distinctions are frequently drawn between the "nuclear" family currently sharing a common household and the "extended" family. The extended family includes all grandparents, aunts, uncles, brothers, sisters, and cousins who are active family members as evidenced by exchange of correspondence and occasional visiting. Beyond the extended family there is a third category of "distant" family members who fit the formal definition and are known to exist but who are not active members. A family is complex and finely textured, with each member being known for her or his individual personality and niche within the whole. Although the marital relationship can be dissolved, important features of the family relationship survive marriage breakdown. This leads to a special category of extended family members who have both moral and legal forms of family membership after divorce or separation.

The family is also ethnic. Each cultural and language group preserves and maintains both culture and language first and foremost at the family level. This includes distinctive patterns of association and mutual obligation between family members.

Disadvantage

Child welfare has always been associated with relative disadvantage and with middle-class views on the right way to live and raise children. The origins of child welfare relied heavily on the distinction between the "deserving" poor, who raised their children in an honest and thrifty poverty and who knew their place in society, and the "undeserving" poor, who prostituted, drank, committed criminal offences, and raised their children for a similarly "dissolute" lifestyle. The concept of saving the children and changing the children, both for their good and for the protection of society, was present in the thinking of at least some early child welfare policymakers and practitioners.

Current data on the family circumstances of children admitted to care in British Columbia show that:

Over half the apprehended children were from single parent families headed by women. . . . Eighty percent of the parents who headed families had not graduated from high school. Over half the parents either did not have occupations, were in the service sector, or in construction trades. Fifty-eight percent were on some type of income assistance program. Seventy-one percent of the families had annual incomes of less than $20,000 in 1989. (J. Campbell, 1992)

These data, and similar data from other jurisdictions, indicate that child welfare is still primarily dealing with the results of poverty and the effects of being marginalized by society. The concept of "neglect" is used to indicate child care that does not accord with middle-class standards. Yet achieving those standards may be denied by the absence of adequate housing, income, or medical care. In addition, different views about proper lifestyle and attitudes can lead to the child welfare system being used in an attempt to change the behaviour of children and parents when the real target should be a society that fails to provide adequate incomes and satisfying roles to some of its members.

Culture

From a cultural perspective Canada inherited two dominant immigrant traditions, French and English. Except in Quebec, the English tradition has been politically dominant and has been particularly important in shaping our assumptions about the relationship between cultures. The assumption of nineteenth-century imperial policy was that Britain was entrusted by God with a special civilizing and evangelical mission throughout the world. In the civil domain the role of social policy was to equip all citizens to be responsible British subjects. Immigrants from the United Kingdom needed no preparation for Canadian citizenship; indeed, a British subject had a right to vote as a landed immigrant, without having become a Canadian citizen. Immigrants from other countries could obtain the right to vote following preparation and examination before a judge of the Citizenship Court. Native people were seen as more difficult to prepare for citizenship. The Indian Act, 1876 provided for their "enfranchisement," that is, citizenship when they had either shown an ability to farm and taken ownership of land or had obtained a professional qualification.

These cultural assumptions about the relationship between peoples and races have had a major impact on the child welfare field. Within the British cultural tradition child welfare policy was a means to save children from what were seen as inadequate or unsuitable parents and to ensure that the children were brought up "correctly." This included policies through which "orphan" children from Britain were sent to Canada to be raised in healthier surroundings than Britain afforded. Parker estimates that some 85,000 unaccompanied children were sent from Britain to Canada between 1870 and 1910 alone (Parker, 1990).

For indigenous peoples, child welfare policy was one of the means used to achieve the civilizing mission of British imperial policy. This mission was behind the extensive use of residential schools for Indian children, which played a major role in the policy of assimilation until the 1970s. When the residential schools were closed assimilation continued through the expansion of the child welfare system and the placement of many Indian children in foster and adopting homes.

Immigrant minorities, particularly those of visibly different racial origins, have been treated in a similar manner. Basically, they have been told that they should follow contemporary English-Canadian child-care practices. In particular, corporal punishment and early marriage were not acceptable and in some situations were considered abuse. In addition, some religious beliefs that are not part of the mainstream inheritance have been viewed as unacceptable. Here again the child welfare system has been used to restrict their transmission, as in the case of the Doukhobors of British Columbia, or to obstruct minority health practices as in the case of Jehovah's Witnesses and Christian Scientists.

Canadian society is becoming more multicultural and tolerant of difference. We are increasingly sensitive to the imposition on Native peoples of an alien culture in a deliberate attempt to rob them of their own cultures, and there is some recognition that immigrant communities from the Third World have a right to preserve their own religion, values, family life, and culture. These different assumptions about the relationship that should exist among cultures are being slowly introduced into child welfare policy and practice.

State

The development of twentieth-century child welfare can be traced to a concern to protect children from what was seen as "inhumanity." The way for child welfare legislation was paved by the establishment of universal primary education and child labour laws, both of which provided children with specific protections outside the family. An example is truancy, a very real problem for early educational authorities, not because children did not want to be in school but because parents resisted the loss of control over the labour of the child. These concerns predated concern with child neglect and abuse but provided the framework within which neglect and abuse could be recognized and dealt with.

In the mid-twentieth century, following World War Two, the role of the state was widened in all social policy fields in an attempt to produce a better society. But by the end of the 1970s this optimistic view of the capacity and role of the state had yielded to a more cautious one that recognized limits in the accomplishments of the social services. These limits included unintended but damaging secondary effects, as when a child removed from its parents to "protect" his or her welfare is deprived of love, attention, and care because the social worker/guardian is overworked.

Three alternative approaches to social policy are residual, institutional, and social development. The early child welfare provisions and the role of the children's aid societies are characterized by a residual view of the relationship between social services and the state: "The first [residual view] holds that social welfare institutions should only come into play when the normal structures of supply, the family and the market, break down" (Wilensky and Lebeaux, 1965: 138). The residual formulation is based on the view that most families can look after themselves and that the intervention of the state can, and should, be limited to those situations where families have failed to provide for the welfare of children and the state must intervene in the family's responsibilities.

The institutional view

implies no stigma, no emergency, no abnormality. Social welfare becomes accepted as a proper, legitimate function of modern industrial society in helping individuals achieve self fulfilment. The complexity of modern life is recognized. The inability of the individual to provide fully for himself, or to meet all his needs in family and work settings is considered a normal condition; and the helping agencies receive regular institutional status. (*Ibid.*)

In the institutional approach, the family is viewed as a private institution that requires a planned and supporting environment. The state is expected to provide that environment through attention to income security, employment, day care, counselling, and other social services.

Subsequent to the writings of Wilensky and Lebeaux a third conception of social welfare, variously called the social development, structural, or radical view, has been advanced. Fundamental to this view are the examination and reform of the structures of society that have led to the prevalence of social problems. This goes beyond the service concepts present in both the residual and institutional views.

Social welfare as social development recognizes the dynamic quality of urban industrial society and the consequent need to adapt to change and to new aspirations for human fulfilment. It goes beyond the welfare state to a continuing renewal of its institutions to promote the fullest development of man. (Romanyshyn, 1971: 350)

These three views represent differences in ideology (Wharf, 1986). The residual view is an expression of conservative ideology, emphasizing the independence of individuals, the responsibility of families, and a minimal role for the state. The institutional view represents a liberal ideology, which emphasizes both the opportunities and the stresses of society and promotes collective responsibility, and an enlarged and co-ordinating role for the state. The social development view provides for more radical criticism of the society's institutions and has been advanced from a socialist perspective critical of the distribution of power and wealth, from a feminist perspective critical of the patriarchal nature of social policy, and from a First Nations and intercultural perspective critical of the assimilationist assumptions of Canadian social policy.

While these views are usually seen as competitive, they can also be seen as parts of an interrelated whole. Advocacy for a well-organized residual child welfare system that can intervene in family life to deal with abuse and neglect does not deny the need for institutional day care and parental support systems. On the other hand, the existence of good day care and parental support systems does not mean that a society does not also need to re-examine its foundations and search for new structures through which oppression by class, gender, and race does not occur.

HUMAN AND CIVIL RIGHTS AND CHILD WELFARE

During the 1980s attention to human rights issues in social policy increased. In Canada this was seen in the incorporation into Canada's constitutional documents of the Canadian Charter of Rights and Freedoms (LaForest, 1983). At the international level it was expressed in the United Nations Convention on the Rights of the Child. The concern with human rights occupied a certain amount of common ground between the conservative and radical critics of social policy. Particularly important was the way in which the Charter and the broader concern for human rights empowered challenges to the bureaucratic and paternalistic systems that had been developed.

The assumption of the early child welfare reformers was that they knew what was best for children, and that the role of government was to provide the law and resources for their views to be imposed. This assumption is contrary to an emphasis on human rights, which guards private rights jealously and requires specific reasons and due process before such rights are set aside in the name of individual or collective welfare.

To understand the current Canadian family and child welfare system it is necessary to understand both the residual system and the institutional system and the relationship between them. To understand the future of family and child welfare it is necessary to extend these formulations and consider the social development of Canadian society.

POLICY AND LAW: THE RESIDUAL FORMULATION

The residual formulation of child welfare policy is based on the need to protect a number of children from neglect and abuse. It reflects confidence in the ability of authorities to define abuse and neglect in a specific, legalistic manner, and it is based on a number of assumptions. The first assumption about the family is that normally families will not need child welfare services. Second, is that if they do need these services they will not recognize this need. Third, the problems they have should be dealt with on an individual basis under a paternalistic authority, represented by the provincial superintendent (or director) of child welfare. Each child is seen as an individual with rights to a standard of care that can be provided to him by the state should his parents fail to provide it to him directly. Furthermore, the child is seen as malleable: able, if subject to the "right" influences, to become a "mainstream Canadian." Achieving this objective requires a child welfare system with the wisdom, power, and authority to save children from harm and make wise provision for their future. This includes measures to separate children permanently from their parents and place them for adoption.

The residual formulation of family and child welfare remains the principal approach used in Canadian child welfare. The following discussion examines: (1) major features of the child welfare system; (2) interventionist and non-interventionist models; (3) the extent of the system; and (4) co-ordination with other family and child welfare agencies.

1. Major Features

Major features of child protection law in all the Canadian provinces include the following.

A. Definition of the child in need of protection. The law defines the circumstances that must exist before the state is prepared to intervene in family life. Frequently this includes the physical, sexual, or emotional abuse of the child; the withholding of essential medical care; the exploitation of the child; the child whose welfare is endangered while away from home; and the child where there is no one to act as a parent.

B. Receipt of complaints. The law contains a mechanism for reporting to a defined authority. The first step in achieving the protection of individual children is achieved by receiving

complaints, which can be anonymous, from citizens and professionals who believe child abuse or neglect has occurred.

C. Investigation. These complaints are then investigated by
social workers acting pursuant to child welfare law. The social
worker has a primary duty to assess the need of the child for
protection.

D. Action to ensure the protection of the child. Having assessed
the situation, the social worker is obliged to act to ensure the protection of the child. This can be done by a variety of measures that
differ somewhat from province to province. These take the form of:

- services to the home, such as homemaker and child-care services;
- supervisory and restrictive orders concerning both the child
  and the actions of any person who may constitute a risk to the
  child;
- agreements with the parents through which the child is admitted to care;
- the power to take custody of the child and remove him/her
  from the family to a place of safety.

E. Court supervision and decision-making. The social worker's
actions are subject to varying degrees of court supervision. In most
provinces, but not all, a warrant is needed prior to apprehension in
all but emergency situations. Following a period that varies in
length of time from province to province, and following notice to
parents and to all persons whose interest in the welfare of the child
is recognized in legislation,[1] the social worker has to appear in
court and satisfy a judge that the action taken was warranted and
that the court should make an order concerning the child. This
order may state conditions that must be observed to ensure the
protection of the child, or may make the child a ward of the
province either temporarily, pending the possibility of change in
the child's family, or permanently.

F. Guardianship. While the child is in the care of the state, either
before or after the order of a court, the law provides that the
guardianship of the child is transferred from the parents to a
provincial official who has the power of a parent to make plans for
the child. This includes the power and duty to provide care, usually
through a foster home; to consent to medical treatment; to ensure
attendance in school; to move the child to another community; to
provide an allowance; and, in the case of permanent wards, to
consent to their adoption.

G. Discharge of guardianship. Most children removed from their parents are returned and guardianship is restored to their parents. In some cases guardianship is given to a relative or to adopting parents, and in other cases guardianship is extinguished by the child reaching the age of majority.

Although these common features are found in the child welfare laws of all the provinces there are also important differences in law from province to province.

2. Interventionist and Non-interventionist Models

Richard Barnhorst (1986) makes a distinction between "non-legalistic, interventionist" and "legalistic, non-interventionist" legislation. In this discussion these are simply referred to as the interventionist and non-interventionist models. Interventionist legislation gives broad powers to child welfare authorities to intervene in families at the discretion of social workers. The non-interventionist legislation gives limited powers to child welfare authorities and requires that social workers avoid removing children from parents wherever possible. Major differences between these types of legislation are shown in Table 2.1.

Barnhorst (1986: 279) reviewed the Ontario, British Columbia, Alberta, and Yukon statutes using these criteria. His conclusions are shown in Table 2.2. Barnhorst's analysis of these key sections of child welfare legislation demonstrates that differences stem from conflicting positions on the role of the state. In 1990 the statutes in British Columbia, the Northwest Territories, Newfoundland, and Saskatchewan were of the interventionist type, while those in the other provinces tended in varying degrees toward the non-interventionist, legalistic model. Two examples of the differences between these models are provided by the approach to (a) recording policies and practices and (b) child abuse registers.

A. Recording policies and practices. Record-keeping and access to records are essential to the child welfare function. The records of the child welfare agency serve to ensure its accountability in its principal statutory functions, as well as providing the daily working tools to staff in communicating to one another. For example the agency must be able to demonstrate that it has received complaints of children in need of protection and has investigated them. As complaints can be received on a confidential basis, these records are also confidential. The records are critical to each of the major functions of the agency.

Table 2.1

Characteristics of Child Protection Legislation

Critical Areas in Child Protection Legislation	Interventionist	Non-interventionist
Principles	Broad statement of principle, e.g., "best interests of the child"	Specific statements of principle concerning parents, child, etc.
Grounds for intervention	No specific definition in law; definition through social workers and court	Clear and limited grounds stated in the statute
Initiation of proceedings	Through the apprehension of the child without warrant	Warrant or court order must be obtained
Interim custody of the child	Held by the apprehending agency pending a hearing	Hearing necessary to determine interim custody and parents' rights
Disposition	Through allocation of all the parents' powers to the state	Through specific restrictions, with an emphasis on maintaining the parents' responsibilities
Accountability mechanisms	No provision for court review	Defined requirements for return to court and review

Table 2.2
Summary of Key Child Protection Provisions

Critical Areas in Child Protection Legislation	from Interventionist —————————→ Non- to Interventionist			
Principles	B.C.	Yukon	Ontario	Alberta
Grounds for intervention	B.C. Yukon			Ontario Alberta
Initiation of proceedings	B.C.		Yukon Alberta	Ontario
Interim custody	B.C.	Alberta Yukon		Ontario
Disposition	B.C.	Yukon	Alberta	Ontario
Accountability	B.C.	Yukon	Alberta	Ontario

In the interventionist model the agency's records are held under tight confidentiality requirements that deny all access except under court order. This ensures that the agency has total control of the use of information. A child in care or a child formerly in care would at best receive summarized information from his/her record with "sensitive" information concealed. An example of sensitive information would be a placement with foster parents where abuse had occurred in the foster home.

In the non-interventionist model the policy allows client access to records and the obligation is on the agency to justify exceptions. In this system a child in care would have access to records, including the right to read her or his file and copy sections for personal use. In this model the emphasis is on protecting the rights of the individual, including protection from the errors of the state.[2]

B. *Child abuse registries.* All provinces have some mechanism for tracing cases where children are considered to be in need of protection (Vogle, 1991). However, in the interventionist model this takes the form of a master file and internal procedural requirements to check the master file system when a complaint is received. The master file is held as a confidential system for the agency's use. Agency procedures also provide for recording whether complaints are considered substantiated or not.

In the non-interventionist model it is accepted that people have a right to know of the existence of a record. Furthermore, the categories of the record are declared and the uses of the record are covered by statements in statute. The non-interventionist approach requires due process around all these transactions. The family learns of a decision to place the name of their child on the registry after a first stage of investigation. They have rights to question this decision. In addition, informing parents of the decision to place their name on the registry constitutes a first level of warning and supervision.

3. Extent of the Child Welfare System

The extent of the residual child welfare system can be seen through a review of documentary records.[3] Particularly important, because of their availability, are the records of children in care since the 1940s. In this discussion, children in care are compared to the total number of Canadian children up to the age of fifteen to reveal the extent of the residual child welfare system from one province to another and between different decades from the 1940s to the 1990s.[4]

Of importance to the development of all children's services are

Table 2.3
Proportion of Canadian Children, Aged 0-15,
by Province, 1946-86

	1946	1956	1966	1976	1986
Newfoundland	—	41	40	34	26
P.E.I.	30	35	35	28	23
Nova Scotia	30	34	34	27	21
New Brunswick	32	37	36	28	23
Quebec	32	35	34	25	21
Ontario	24	30	32	25	20
Manitoba	26	31	32	26	22
Saskatchewan	29	32	34	27	24
Alberta	29	33	35	27	24
British Columbia	23	29	31	24	20
Yukon	22	32	37	30	25
N.W.T.	27	36	42	38	33
Canada	28	32	33	26	21

the rise and decline in both absolute and proportionate terms of the number of children in the Canadian population. From 1946 to 1961 – the baby boom years – there was a 50 per cent increase in the total number of children and they increased from 28 to 34 per cent of all Canadians. By 1986 there had been a 10 per cent decline in absolute numbers and the proportion of all Canadians who were under fifteen had fallen from 34 to 21 per cent. Table 2.3 shows this changing pattern.

Table 2.4, which indicates the proportions of children in care, must be used with caution as fully comparable data do not exist. The general trends are, however, clear. In most provinces the proportion of children in care increased from 1956 to 1976 and then fell from 1976 to 1986. This table also indicates the comparative smallness of the residual child welfare system in relation to the total number of Canadian children. Except for the territories, the proportion of children in care varies provincially from 4.5/1,000 to 15.4/1,000. Nonetheless, these figures are higher than those found in most Western countries.[5] The higher Canadian figures appear to

Table 2.4
Number of Children in Care/1,000 Children, by Province, 1956-86

	1956	1966	1976	1986
Newfoundland	3.6	7.0	7.1	6.4
P.E.I.	—	—	10.4	8.1
New Brunswick	—	8.5	15.5	10.6
Nova Scotia	—	10.8	8.8	6.8
Ontario	9.4	6.9	6.7	4.5
Manitoba	—	9.9	15.1	15.4
Saskatchewan	6.8	10.2	10.5	9.1
Alberta	7.9	8.6	8.9	5.5
British Columbia	9.7	13.3	16.5	11.5
Yukon	—	—	—	23.7
N.W.T.	—	8.2	42.4	27.4

NOTE: This table is based on provincial child-in-care data as contained in ministry annual reports. There are many variations in reporting periods and record systems, with some provinces recording data on a specified date, usually March 31st, but others reporting average annual counts. In some cases no comparable data are available. For Quebec no comparable data are available.

be principally due to the disproportionate representation of Native children,[6] the reasons for which are discussed in Chapter 5. Not counting First Nations children, it is apparent that the residual child welfare system provides care to a small minority of children and has never had a major effect on children as a whole. In all but a few situations children are cared for by parents. Inevitably, the children not cared for by parents include a high proportion of the most difficult children.

A separate measure of the extent of the residual child welfare system can be developed from the number of protection investigations conducted in each year. The extent of protection investigations is a much broader measure of the impact of the child welfare system than are the child-in-care data. Unfortunately, good historical and comparative data are not available on protection investigations. In British Columbia there were 27,054 protection investigations in 1988-89, affecting 41.3/1,000 children in the province. This was five times larger than the number of children who were in care. Although there is a lack of historical data on the extent of investigations, the opinion of social workers is that there has been a dramatic increase in recent years. This has been the product of the introduction of mandatory reporting laws and the heightened public awareness of abuse.

The majority of child protection complaints are disposed of during initial inquiry. As a result, most of the work of the residual child welfare system consists of investigating complaints of neglect and abuse. The extent of these investigations suggests that as many as one in twenty Canadian children fall under some level of scrutiny and review annually. If cumulative data on scrutiny were available, the proportion of children who at some time had come to the attention of child welfare authorities would be much higher. The extent of this investigative activity has brought the child welfare system to public attention and has led to pressures for reform, particularly reforms to ensure attention to due process in child welfare investigations. These pressures have been asserted by parents' rights groups, by lawyers, and by increased media scrutiny.

4. Co-ordination

The residual child welfare system interacts with the education, health, and correctional systems. The extent of co-ordination required is substantial and has been the subject of a series of special inquiries by the provinces. Provinces vary in structure and changes are frequently made. A good example of the extent of the issues of inter-agency co-ordination and inter-organizational relationship is provided by a 1990 report on service co-ordination problems from the B.C. Ombudsman (1990a). In an illustration not intended to be comprehensive but only to show the range of programs, sixty-four child, youth, and family programs are listed under the auspices of eight separate ministries and one board.

Co-ordinating all such services is a formidable proposition. The principal approach to resolving the complexities of the relationships between social agencies has been the development of extensive protocol agreements. The function of the protocol agreement is to define the interface between the two organizations and ensure that each knows what to expect of the other. Protocol agreements have become essential to the effective conduct of child welfare and have come to constitute a new and distinct type of policy document.

POLICY AND LAW: THE INSTITUTIONAL FORMULATION

In the institutional model of family and child welfare, a fundamental assumption is that the family and children's services of the state will need to be accessed by many if not most families. A second fundamental assumption is that in most cases access will be through parents deciding to seek assistance with the task of parenting. In other cases the school system and the health system will identify situations in which the child needs assistance and will advise parents as to how best to obtain help. This view does not depend for its effectiveness on the monitoring activities of authorities but on the intelligence and knowledge of parents, teachers, and health professionals. Receiving assistance is not seen as an indicator of failure but as an indicator of a healthy ability to seek help where needed. The objective is not to save the child from the family but to strengthen the family and thereby help the child.

1. Major Features

In the institutional formulation of policy the major features are the following.

A. A positive statement of family and child welfare objectives. Quebec has a well-developed statement of this type. It begins:

> The overall objective of the Quebec Government's family policy will be to:
> – recognize the importance of the family as an institution and living environment, notably through collective support to parents, who are those members of society more directly responsible for child rearing and the family environment.
> – provide for the good of families, of individuals composing them and of society as a whole, but especially to provide adequate support to the parent-child relationship which is the nucleus common to all types of families. (Quebec, 1987)

The application of this principle is broad and embracing. It unifies all services to the family under a common philosophy and objective.

B. An epidemiological view of the occurrence of family-child parenting problems. From an epidemiological perspective some families will be under severe stress because of family and child health, development, education, and mental health difficulties. These conditions can be predicted in terms of rates of occurrence but their impact on particular families varies substantially. This situation is discussed by the Oxford philosopher John Rawls in his treatise on social justice (Rawls, 1973). In essence, Rawls argues that the existence of such conditions leads to a legitimate claim on the resources of the society to compensate the afflicted family and child. The premise for intervention is a normal rather than abnormal situation.

C. Consensual reporting. The obligation to seek assistance is seen as deriving from the parents' concern for the welfare of their own child, aided by the advice of friends and professionals who know them. However, should they decide not to seek help their decision is respected.

D. Assessment. Where help is sought the first stage is assessment, followed by advice to the parents and child concerning the resources available to them.

E. Conflict resolution. Where there are conflicts the emphasis is on resolution with the consent of all parties through mediation, but where that is not possible a court may be called on to arbitrate differences guided by the government statement of family policy. The hearing, however, is a purely civil matter without attribution of blame.

F. Guardianship. Guardianship of the child is retained by the parent or parents and is not transferred to the state.

One can find examples of these principles in the family and children's services of all provinces, but there are major differences in the way they are articulated and administered. One measure of difference is the existence in some provinces of a comprehensive legal base for all family and children's law. Different provinces vary in the extent to which they have unified their family and child law. As of 1992 the provinces of Alberta, Manitoba, Ontario, Quebec, New Brunswick, and Nova Scotia, as well as the Yukon, have brought all, or most, of their provisions for children and youth within a single statute governed by a common set of principles and policies.

Another measure of difference can be found in the extent to which official planning documents recognize the interconnectedness of services and address the distribution of power between family and child agencies. Where a single statute has been introduced, one ministry co-ordinates all family and children's services. An example is provided by Ontario, where the Ministry of Community and Social Services is clearly responsible for policy and planning for the whole complex of family and children's services. In contrast, in British Columbia, which has several separate statutes, there is no one ministry responsible for overall family and child welfare policy and co-ordination.

The establishment of a common policy and planning framework permits clarification of the different levels of the family and child service system. Different levels of intervention are recognized, with the traditional residual formulation of child welfare forming one level (the tertiary level). The result is shown in Table 2.5. In this conceptual and theoretical approach, the three levels of family and child welfare service perform complementary functions, each of the levels recognizing a different degree of family autonomy and need for professional services.

A. Primary: family independence. This first level of family policy ensures that social conditions provide a supportive milieu for families. This is what is meant by "normalization," not only for the family that cares for a mentally handicapped member but for all families. The capacity of families to fulfil this role is supported by community participation and peer support. Government can undertake many general measures to support this coping ability of families. The federal government contributes to this objective through the protection of basic human rights in the Charter of Rights and Freedoms; the recognition of the distinct First Nations, French, English, and multicultural societies; and through a universal and accessible health system. At the provincial level, employment creation and labour market policies contribute to the self-confidence of families, as do health, day-care, school, and income security services.

For both federal and provincial governments, the primary level of family policy has to be an informing theme rather than an organizing principle. However, it is a theme of sufficient importance that a minister and a ministry are identified as responsible for overseeing the total activities of government from a family perspective and ensuring that that perspective is applied to the assessment of health, education, employment, labour, and income security policies, all of which influence families but none of which are explicitly family policies. The importance of this activity has been increased by change in the social character of families and by measures to eliminate the earlier expectation that the two-parent family is the predominant form and that women are available to provide unpaid care in most homes. Most of the primary types of family service, however, are provided in and by local communities. These take the form of social development and planning, local helping networks, parent education, and day care.

Informed and committed citizens can and do contribute significantly by serving on the boards of local community agencies, but government agencies also need that contribution to maintain their

Table 2.5
Levels of Family and Child Welfare Service

Level	Primary *(family independence)*	Secondary *(family service)*	Tertiary *(family intervention)*
Role of government	Development and education	Service provision	Legal intervention
Family identity	Citizen	Consumer	Probationary
Direct contact with agency	None	Voluntary	Enforced
Typical programs	Mutual support; family life education; social planning; community development	Mental health counselling; services for handicapped; adoptions; family court services	Protection investigations; corrections; secure confinement

sensitivity to local conditions, priorities, and views. Some government agencies obtain this perspective through their own advisory bodies, for example, local health boards and family court committees. In the child welfare field a community base is provided in some provinces through the children's aid societies and in others by local planning bodies. Where these bodies do not exist, views and advice are received informally but a consistent, planned approach to receiving community comment from a family perspective is lacking. The issue of constituencies for child welfare is discussed in some depth in Chapter 4.

Local helping networks exist at many levels of formality and informality. The first level is that of the family itself, including the extended family. Beyond the family are friends and acquaintances, followed by the networks and interest groups based on common experience, for example, with problem children, mental handicap, substance abuse, etc. These community networks exist with varying degrees of formality and organization, from personal contact and support through to substantial organizations with boards, professional staff, and many volunteers. While some self-help groups are formed by the efforts of members, not all communities have the stability or capacity to provide such services to their members. Where such networks do not exist there is a need to encourage their development.

Parent education is an essential part of the primary level of family policy. An example of work at this level is the B.C. Council on the Family, which provides education and discussion groups for new parents, parent mutual support groups, parent-teen linkage activities, and information on community services and resources. The need for this activity is increased by family mobility and instability, as sources from within the extended family are less available to family members. In addition, the newer forms of family, for example, blended families, have no precedents from earlier generations to guide them.

B. Secondary: family service. The second level of family policy is the case services that families access on their own initiative. Typical situations facing families and children that can be serviced at this level are services to the parents of handicapped children; advice and guidance to parents and children in conflict; mental health services to individuals and families; support and advice to families where sexual abuse has occurred; support with adoption relationships; and advice and guidance in relation to substance abuse.

The range of services provided is very large, ranging from an office contact and a preliminary assessment that reassures a family that they have, or can obtain, the resources they need to address their own situation, through to the long-term partnership relationships that are necessary to support the family that is caring for a severely handicapped child. From the perspective of the family there are some basic requirements of services at this level. They include knowing where to go for help; competency in assessment and reliable information; service or referral on a timely basis; and a service "contract" that assures the family of the extent of help available. These basic expectations protect the independence and autonomy of families by permitting the family to remain in control. In this sense, they are empowering.

C. Tertiary: family intervention. Family intervention is the third level of engagement with families and recognizes the role of the residual form of child welfare. Disorders beyond the capacity of the home and community, and that were never recognized or addressed by self-referral, can become behaviours that are threatening to the community and/or cause protection concerns within the home. As a result, statutory intervention services are required in all jurisdictions to protect the community and to protect children from harm. However, such services are always expensive, and the powers necessary to their performance can have destructive secondary effects. Families that are the subject of protection investigations may never re-establish earlier patterns of trust and some are destroyed completely by the experience of being investigated, even where no child abuse, for example, is found to exist. Youth who have been confined associate with similar youth and an identity as a young offender can readily become a step toward becoming a criminal.

It is thus viewed as in everybody's interest to keep the use of such services to a minimum. This is expressed in comprehensive family policy statements in the principle of "least intervention."

2. Extent of the Child Welfare System

The extent of the institutional family and child welfare system is more difficult to establish than was the case with the residual system as the components of the institutional system are more broadly defined. There are two approaches to establishing the extent of the institutional system: epidemiological and service data studies and "state of the child" reports.

Epidemiological studies of family and child disorders provide an important source on the extent of the need of families for

Table 2.6
Prevalence of Disorders by Age and Sex

Age	Sex	One or more disorders	Externalizing	Internalizing	Both extern. and intern.
4-11	M	18.4	8.1	6.7	3.6
4-11	F	13.2	2.7	9.2	1.3
12-16	M	18.6	11.0	3.9	3.7
12-16	F	21.7	2.5	15.7	3.5

professional services and of the services that are used by them. Ontario has conducted a major study of childhood mental health disorders (Ministry of Community and Social Services, 1986). In the Ontario study, mental health disorders were divided into two groups, externalizing disorders, such as hyperactivity and conduct disorder, and internalizing disorders, such as neurosis and somatization (eating). Table 2.6 indicates the rates.

Similar rates of child and adolescent behavioural disturbance have been noted in U.K. studies (Peters, 1988: 7). These rates are the result of professionals applying their judgement to childhood conditions. Alternatively, when parents or school teachers are asked to identify problem behaviours they often do not agree with the survey results. In the Ontario study as few as one in four of the disorders identified in the survey was identified by parents and as few as one in three was identified by teachers. The levels of overall agreement between all sources ranged from zero to one in five.

This lack of agreement indicates that a child can be acting normally in the eyes of parents but suffering from a disorder in the eyes of the school and/or independent professionals. When the use of professional services was examined it was found that only one in six of the families was in contact with a mental health agency and only one in three received special educational programming (*ibid.*: 22). With regard to developmental handicaps there was greater agreement among professional authorities, schools, and parents. Severe retardation (IQ less than 50) was found in 3/1,000 children and mild retardation (IQ between 50 and 70) in 25/1,000. Epilepsy was found in 6/1,000 children and autism in less than 1/1,000.

The difference between professional judgement and family judgement can also be seen as an indicator of the family's ability to absorb disability and disorder and to consider "normal" what professionals consider disorder. The family's definition of health and well-being represents a very important contribution to the maintenance of health in children and one that is frequently neglected.

Many of the children who are judged in difficulty by professionals are the same children who are the subjects of protection investigations by the residual child welfare system. The extent of this overlap is not known, as the records of service systems that work with children from a protection perspective are not maintained in a form that permits ready comparison to data on children in the school and health systems. From available data it would appear that the orders of magnitude are:

- 4 in 5 children are considered to be in good emotional health by parents and professionals.
- 1 in 5 children is considered to need some level of professional assistance by professionals.
- 1 in 10 children is considered to need some level of assistance by their parents.
- 1 in 20 children becomes the subject of some type of complaint or referral to child protection agencies.
- 1 in 100 children is admitted to care.

During the 1980s there have been major studies in New Brunswick, Ontario, and Saskatchewan of the state of families and children. These studies have followed methodology developed in the United States that aims to bring all available data on family and child welfare together. Each of these reports provides a large amount of data in an accessible and comprehensive form.

3. Systems Planning

From the institutional perspective it is essential that policy and planning for children's services encompass the whole range of family and children's services in a single planning framework. The Ontario planning document *Investing in Children* (Ministry of Community and Social Services, 1988) is an example of this approach to strategic planning. In essence a single corporate planning, priority setting, and budget process is developed for the full range of family and children's services. The existence of many service overlaps and interfaces is accepted. The planning strategy at the provincial level is to develop policy directions to guide the individual planning processes of the separate agencies that implement the directions so that implementation reflects the needs of local communities. The four principal systems that are planned as a whole in the Ontario model are the child welfare service, the young offenders' service, the health developmental services, and the child treatment and intervention services.

In Ontario's *Investing in Children* developmental strategies for all family and children services include processes to ensure:

- responsiveness of service to clients and local communities;
- continuity of service to clients;
- primary prevention based on determination of "at risk" populations;
- early intervention with the youngest identifiable children;
- co-ordinated and responsive services for seriously and chronically disturbed children and youth;
- enhanced area-level planning;
- structuring a spectrum of services.

In pursuing these objectives formal linkages between agencies help to achieve a unified approach to the assessment of family difficulties. Case management protocols require that a key worker is accountable "for the total plan of care . . . with responsibility for continuity of service and ensuring that communication of case planning activity is proceeding with the child and family" (*ibid.*: 69).

The institutional approach to policy and planning encourages a careful review of the distribution of family and child welfare resources between the different levels of intervention and services. Estimates from Ontario show a total per child expenditure of $207.05 annually, of which $84.15 is spent in the residual child welfare system and $16.83 in the juvenile correction system. Thus approximately half the total expenditure is on statutory services and half on services provided on parental initiative (*ibid.*). Comparable figures from other provinces are difficult to establish, but it would appear that British Columbia expenditures on the residual child welfare system and juvenile correction systems alone total $198.12/child/year. These costs appear to approximate 75 per cent of total costs of $265.12/child/year.[7] The higher British Columbia figures can be understood partly because of the higher proportion of children in care in B.C. in 1986. However, they also indicate that there are major differences between the provinces in the balance between statutory and non-statutory services.

CONCLUSION

Although not fully implemented in any province, the common features of this institutional view of family and child welfare include:

1. A statement of government policy for the family that emphasizes a philosophy of respect, support, and least intrusion and that accords with the United Nations Convention on the Rights of the Child.
2. A single ministry of government charged with responsibility for family and children's policy and responsible for an overall corporate plan.
3. A policy and planning commitment to a continuum of services through which the province recognizes local needs and initiatives and supports and builds on them.
4. A commitment in policy, planning, and law to the principle of least intervention in family life.
5. A long-term commitment to the families of physically, developmentally, or emotionally disadvantaged children, based on service continuity and one-agency accountability for case management.
6. An assessment service in each community so that the family that recognizes a problem can obtain professional advice and a single point of entry to the services it needs.
7. A consolidation of family and children's law into a single statute providing one legal base for all statutory services.
8. A recognition of civil rights for all parties to legal proceedings based on a broad view of the family, including grandparents, foster parents, siblings, and Indian bands.
9. A clear statement of the right of families to confidentiality in their dealings with government and access to their records.
10. A recognition of the unique experience of First Nations people.

The differences in the extent to which the provisions are implemented vary, but taken together they represent the range of "orthodox" views as determined by provincial policy and legislation.

The following chapters of this book go beyond these views and challenge them by looking at developments outside the mainstream of government provision. In our view these more radical views require attention as they address underlying issues regarding the nature of our society and provide grounds for alternative visions of how to provide for the well-being of families and children.

NOTES

1. The parties other than parents with a recognized interest vary from province to province. They include Indian bands, foster parents, grandparents, and in some provinces any other person who has had custody of the child for some defined period, often two years.

2. The Manitoba Child and Family Service Act (1987) is a good example of the legalistic, non-interventionist approach while the B.C. Family and Child Service Act (1981) represents the non-legalistic, interventionist approach in its treatment of records.

3. There are problems with the child welfare database, as it has been developed by the provinces without close co-ordination of definitions. Nevertheless, the annual reports of the provincial ministries provide a record through which the scale of the system and historic changes in its approach to practice can be observed. For a full discussion of Canadian child welfare data issues, see Marilyn Callahan, *A Prototype for a National Child Welfare Data System*, project report to Welfare Grants Directorate, Health and Welfare Canada, October, 1987.

4. The age fifteen was selected because of the better availability of census data on children and youth to age fifteen. The age of eighteen is normal for discharge from care, but admission to care is not possible in some provinces after the age of sixteen. Where it is legally possible it is uncommon other than through an agreement among parents, youth, and agency.

5. The rate of children in care in the United Kingdom is 4/1,000; in Sweden it is 8/1,000.

6. The rate of Indian children in care reached 70/1,000 in the late 1970s. Although the Indian population is small, the apprehension of large numbers of Indian children affects the total figures, particularly in those areas of Canada where aboriginals are a significant proportion of the whole population. A full discussion of Indian child welfare is contained in Chapter 6.

7. The source of this estimate is an analysis of 1986-87 B.C. government ministry reports, using the same service categories as used in Ontario's *Investing in Children*.

Chapter 3

The Administrative and
Practice Context:
Perspectives from the Front Line

Marilyn Callahan

Child welfare organizations and practitioners are treated much like the children and families they serve. On one hand, they are often pilloried in the press and public forums when something goes amiss: a child under their care is abused or killed, or parents accuse workers of acting precipitously in apprehending their children. On the other hand, they are chronically neglected most of the time. The daily work of child welfare takes place without notice but often under trying conditions with very limited resources.

Much has changed in child welfare in the last four decades. From the 1940s through the 1960s child welfare organizations were characterized by their small size, reasonably flat organizational structures, and wide service mandates: family support, protection, child placement, adoptions, and foster care. Most importantly, it was a time when professional optimism prevailed; if professionals with improved training were given a relatively free hand to design and develop programs, child welfare would improve accordingly. Bessie Snider, a pioneer in child welfare in B.C., captures the flavour of the work at that time:

> ... we were providing a generalized service which we pioneered in B.C. and of which I am still very proud. ... about a third of our caseload would be mothers on Mother's allowance [$35 for a mother and child] and then about 10% of our load ... would be single people on relief. They got nine dollars a month and the next classification were those that were unemployable ... the Destitute, Poor and Sick [$20 per adult person] and ... then we did all

the families where the breadwinner or main person in the family had T.B. T.B. was still rampant then and we, though we were not nurses, had to go at certain intervals and pick up the sputum cups and get them back to head office here. . . . To be on Mother's allowance, you had to have three years residence in the province. You had to be a British citizen. You had to produce your marriage certificate and your divorce papers, if you were divorced. A single mother, an unmarried single mother, that is, would not be eligible for mother's allowance, but she probably would be eligible, if she was unable to work, for Destitute, Poor and Sick allowance. . . . And then we did all the social work histories for the provincial mental hospital and we would have to go and interview the family of the patient and get the social history. And we had a good number of unmarried parents and we visited them and helped them make the decision about whether or not they would keep their baby, or . . . have it placed for adoption, and then in Salmon Arm, I had a good number of children from foster homes. Then we had also another category of juvenile delinquents, because we would have to make the arrangements for the boys or girls (principally they were boys who'd be coming down to the Boys Industrial School in Vancouver). . . . I went out feeling that . . . I was going to cure the ills of the community. There would not be any more social problems and I made it a point to meet all the teachers, meet the principals, and of course we had to meet the policemen and . . . community people. We went and saw the municipal clerk or the reeve of the municipality of the city. We visited ministers . . . regardless of denomination because we felt that they were going to be very helpful resource people and we wanted them to know that the social worker had arrived in their community and you know and we were there to make life really better. . . . The co-operation of the community carried the day for us. (Hill, 1990: 9-11)

By the 1970s many changes had challenged previous practices: a trenchant analysis of class and race discrimination in child welfare; vociferous community and client groups that demanded participation; research casting doubts on the efficacy of professional social work interventions; an expanded funding base for services under the Canada Assistance Plan, including child welfare; and the rise of a new male managerial class in social work. The public, primarily through the media, became more watchful and less trusting of child welfare services, particularly in matters of physical and sexual abuse. All of this took place in a shifting social context that had a great impact on child welfare services: rising numbers of divorce, abortions, and single-parent families, high unemployment, and an increasingly multicultural population.

Not surprisingly, child welfare practice and organizations changed accordingly, and not always for the better. Today, most child welfare workers are employed by large, relatively homogeneous government organizations with steep hierarchies and many regulations governing the work. Commitment to professional education and practice varies widely. The work is dominated by the investigation into complaints of child neglect and abuse, with little attention paid to adoption and general family counselling. Altogether, child welfare managers and workers face considerable challenges in attracting resources and recruits to carry out their work.

At the same time, child welfare remains the crucible of social work practice. The work is fundamental and significantly affects the lives of the most vulnerable members of society: poor children, women, families from different cultures, the chronically ill, the abused and homeless. The potential for immense satisfaction for individual social workers and benefits for children and families is inherent in child welfare work. Moreover, social work has little identity or authority as a profession apart from child welfare. It is the only field of practice consistently recognized as the domain of social work. In all others, such as health, aging, corrections, and community development, other disciplines have equal or greater prominence.

The intent of this chapter is to examine the practice of child welfare workers within the context of the organizations that shape their work and to shed some new light on the conundrums that are a part of this daily life. Some of the current theoretical and practical responses to improving child welfare will be examined. For the most part, these responses are aimed at either increasing control of organizations and practice in an effort to eliminate mistakes or, alternatively, enhancing the discretion of managers and workers so that they can do the job as they see fit. At the same time, this chapter will emphasize the importance of the work and the power of front-line workers, managers, and the social work profession to shape the face of that work.

WHO ARE CHILD WELFARE WORKERS?

In Canada there are at least twelve child welfare systems, one for each province and territory, and within most provinces there are often several different organizations responsible for child welfare, such as children's aid societies in Ontario and Native child welfare organizations in many provinces. Although the federal government is responsible for funding at least 50 per cent of child welfare services under the Canada Assistance Plan (1966), it has not collected much information about these services. Thus, there are a few, spotty sources of information on child welfare in Canada and certainly no national data bank regarding the workers who carry out the job. However, it is possible to piece together information from several sources (Vinokur-Kaplan and Harman, 1986; Fryer *et al.*, 1988; Ontario Association of Children's Aid Societies, 1990a). Child welfare workers are predominately female (about 70 per cent) with a BA or BSW (about 60 per cent), and an average age of about thirty-five years old. The average length of tenure is variously estimated from eighteen months to three years (Cantrell, 1988).

Rycraft (1990) has taken a different tack on this subject and has studied workers who do in fact remain in child welfare beyond two years (an average of eleven years in her sample). She discovered four groups of workers. The "crusaders" (22 per cent) – all women with less than ten years' experience, all with social work degrees – have a strong sense of mission about their work and feel they are making a real difference in the lives of children and families. The "midway passengers" (44 per cent) have worked in child welfare for ten years or more – 80 per cent have social work degrees and 57 per cent are women – and have found a way to offset the job demands with their own expectations of themselves. While they view their jobs as important and interesting, they balance this with other aspects of their lives. The "future travellers" (26 per cent) have less than ten years' experience, 33 per cent have social work degrees, and 83 per cent are female. These workers were considered crusaders at one point but now are dissatisfied, although not bitter, and want to leave. They cite the long hours, heavy responsibilities, few rewards, and lack of advancement as reasons for their departure. The final group, the "hangers-on," represent 9 per cent of workers in her sample. All are male, half have social work degrees. They are disillusioned and emotionally worn out, but they intend to stay in the job until retirement as all are over the age of forty-five. However, they wonder if they can carry on until then.

This study is important because it underlines that it is possible to remain committed and interested in child welfare work in spite of heavy pressures and that social work education may have a bearing on worker satisfaction and longevity in the field. The challenges inherent in the work that lead to some of these responses among workers will be explored in the next section.

THE NATURE OF THE WORK

In a recent study of front-line workers in child welfare practice in British Columbia, forty respondents were asked to provide critical incidents of occasions in their recent practice when they felt powerful and powerless (Callahan and Attridge, 1990). The workers, all women, had five or more years in child welfare work, and most had a Bachelor of Social Work degree and children of their own. In other words, they comprised a highly trained and experienced group. The full texts of some of the critical incidents are provided here so that readers can sort out their own views of child welfare work and draw some of their own conclusions. Following these examples, some of the characteristics of the work will be analysed.

Powerful Incidents

I had been working with a single mother, with one child, who was an immigrant to Canada. She spoke English haltingly and had been diagnosed paranoid schizophrenic. I had an intensive, but positive experience with her two years ago when her child was taken into our care during one of her serious breakdowns.

Once again, she had a breakdown and her fifteen-year-old daughter had an ambulance come and hospitalize her. The girl had been trying to manage at home, hoping it was a temporary situation. The staff notified me that Mrs. K. would be in the hospital for a long time on this occasion. It was my job to break the news to her daughter and advise this very adult girl that she had to come into care. I knew she would be upset. The decision was either to apprehend the girl, which involved a court process, or hope that the mother was lucid enough to sign a temporary care agreement and thereby avoid court.

I phoned the nurse and psychiatrist who informed me Mrs. K. was functioning poorly on that day. I decided to visit anyway. I found her rocking and conversing with aliens in her native tongue. The hospital staff was very protective and several of them insisted on remaining with Mrs. K. during our conversation. They led her dazed into a small room were an interpreter was sitting.

When I addressed her she suddenly sat up and recognized me, smiled, and spoke my name. I carefully plodded through each section of the temporary care agreement, reading it aloud. She decided to speak in English and chose three months of care for her daughter, recognizing how fragile her mental state was at present. The hospital staff and interpreter began to intervene. Mrs. K. said:

"I know what this agreement means. I have worked with this social worker before and she stands behind her word." Mrs. K. also insisted that I take care of her daughter and tell her she loved her. Upon departure she recited almost verbatim the section of the temporary care agreement that we had just signed, stating she could terminate this agreement anytime.

Miraculously, she phoned me from home eight days later because she had been discharged. She thanked me for supporting her. I confirmed with her psychiatrist that she had done an amazing turn around after taking control and signing our agreement. Her daughter went home that day. I hadn't realized how positive my working relationship had been until then.

* * *

While on night shift, I got a call at midnight from one of our receiving resources staff, a woman, asking me to immediately remove a sixteen-year-old male child in her care because he had just assaulted her. I asked her more about the assault. She said, very quietly, that he had grabbed her breasts and punched them hard. I called the police, who met me at the receiving home.

The worker was reluctant to lay charges or act as a witness. She had several reasons: much worse had happened with other clients, she might have to work with this client again, and she worried about the Ministry's response to her if she pressed charges.

I suggested to her that this child was likely to repeat his offence with other women, that this was not the first incident, that he was old enough to know better and old enough to be responsible for the consequences of his actions. The police confirmed this but said their hands were tied if she did not press charges. The child was taken to a juvenile detention centre, not for the assault but because the police found marijuana in his room.

I spent time with this worker, listening to her deliberations and her fears. Even though she had worked for many years in this field, she had great difficulty with her decision. I tried very hard not to influence her decision even though I felt she should lay charges. I concluded by saying that it was her decision and that I would respect her regardless of what course she took.

When I left in the wee hours of the morning I felt that, for the first time in a long time, I had done an important piece of social work. I felt that I had no investment in the outcome of the decision. Instead, it was sufficient to have been there and raised some of the issues. I could feel the pain and humiliation of both her experience and her indecision.

I heard several days later that she had laid charges and gone to court. I shared in her empowerment and her pain.

* * *

I received a physical abuse complaint a few months ago. The initial complaint was of an eight-year-old boy receiving strappings. I interviewed the little boy at school and he disclosed the strappings. I went to the family home, concerned about what response my presence would elicit. Mom was very upset at first, frustrated at the system. She had told someone herself about the strappings and had been asking for help. The result she saw was a social worker at her door. We sat around the kitchen table and talked, sharing stories and concerns about parents, and gradually getting to know a little bit about each other. She talked about not liking her son and how bad that made her feel. We talked about isolation, feeling guilt over the choices your kids make, frustration for a system that can appear hostile to clients. She had prepared herself for me to apprehend her son. Because of this woman's openness and genuine caring, we were able to set up some solid survival plans which would decrease the household stress, ensure her son's protection, and address some of his mental health issues. I felt powerful because I felt I had made a difference. This family went from despair, isolation, fear, to trust, hope, options. Services were put in, and over time, I could see positive movement. For this particular family, I had the tools and time to be effective. When I left the home that first day, Mom hugged me and said, "I never thought I'd be happy to have had a social worker at my door – thank you for being here."

Powerless Incidents

My supervisor (male) and I went to investigate the possible sexual abuse of a six-year-old girl. This was the first such incident I had ever handled. The plan was that I would question the girl as we were both female. Arriving at the door, the mother was very angry, confused, scared, and unwilling to co-operate. She was also leading the girl in her remarks – hoping that we would believe them and leave. After about ten minutes on the doorstep, the mother allowed us into the foyer to talk with the daughter. The girl was scared and confused. The mother and other sister were out of sight but were in the home (which had a small entrance because it was a condominium). Needless to say the girl wouldn't talk. I felt awful about my ability to ask effective and sensitive questions. We found no information to help us either way, and afterwards the family kept the girl out of school for the final few weeks of the year. I felt powerless because I didn't feel we were in an appropriate setting to talk; the presence of the mother was discomforting; the hostility of the mother and her anger upset the girl; plus I was inexperienced and felt powerless to be a help to this girl. To top it all off, we could not approach this family again on the topic of sexual abuse. My supervisor was very helpful and skilled, but my uneasiness persisted. This took place on a Friday and I was emotionally upset about the incident all weekend and dreamed about this innocent six-year-old girl.

The next week my supervisor and I talked about the incident more, but my awful feelings didn't change. They just faded.

I felt powerless in our ability to make the little girl feel good and secure. I don't know if she had been abused but I felt unhelpful to her, regardless. I also felt powerless because the family proceeded to keep her out of school and cut the monitoring links with the teacher.

I'm sure the family was very upset and felt intruded upon. The mother remains unaware of our role and the family remains a mystery.

* * *

I was working with a thirteen-year-old girl who had been a permanent ward but who had recently returned home to live with her mother. She was originally taken into care because she had been badly burned in a house fire set by her mother's angry common-law spouse. As a result she had quite disfiguring scars on her face, chest, and abdomen.

The mother called me to her home and announced that the child was pregnant, and she wanted help in getting an abortion for her. Both the child and mother told me that she had intercourse with a classmate at school, and the child told me she did not want to give me the boy's name. I knew intuitively that this was not true and interviewed the child alone the next day. She disclosed that her uncle had raped her and had, in fact, sexually molested several of her female cousins.

Initially, I received very little support from my supervisor, the police, and no support from the family. It was as if I had opened up a can of worms, and no one knew quite how to handle it. The police had to be pressured to respond. They were not impressed with the child's disclosure and assumed that she had invited the assault as she was slow mentally and "unattractive." The family called me to a meeting one evening, which I should not have attended. The uncle told me to "get off my back or I will kill you!" For months I was very careful about having children come to my house as I feared that if he could not get me, he would attack someone in my family or friends.

After two years, this man was convicted. I think my feeling of powerlessness came from the fact that I had little or no support in the beginning. It seemed that no one wanted to hear about this abuse. I was beginning to feel neurotic about it. Gradually, as other social workers who were working with the families of the cousins became involved, I began to feel validated. I still feel badly about this child who was ostracized from her family and had to return to foster care in another province. Her mother could not protect her, and I, as her social worker, had to send her back to a place that she hated after having a horrible saline abortion. By the time we were able to get permission for the abortion, through provincial bureaucracies, she was five months' pregnant.

* * *

A three-year-old and her mother had been on my caseload for thirteen months. They were placed on my caseload after the third apprehension of the child. Shortly after the apprehension the judge had returned the child to the custody of the mother. I provided a child-care worker to work with her. Little progress was made as the mother was suffering from a personality disorder that was not amenable to change. During another of her less functional moments I took the child into care for three months. The child was again returned. Within two months another apprehension took place. At this point the father applied for custody through the Family Relations Act. Court dragged out forever. The mother had been somewhat co-operative with me and had agreed to a six-month temporary order; however, when I requested to place the child with Dad, Mom took the matter back to court and the judge returned the child to Mom. Within a week, my concerns for the child escalated and I apprehended her.

I was assisted by a male colleague and two male constables. I felt extremely impotent when the mother began to scream at me; when I watched as she lunged towards me and the male social worker stepped in front of me to protect me; when the two constables handcuffed her and led her screaming down the stairs to take her to the nearby mental health facility.

The whole year of effort flashed before me and it seemed like nothing. What had I done to help this woman? Why was nothing enough? There was a sense of betrayal that seemed to flash through her eyes and pierced my heart.

We had tried to work together. We had drawn up a contract. She was unable to keep the terms of the contract. The weekly counselling at a local family service centre had only happened once; the child-care worker often could not contact her; the Nobody's Perfect Program was only attended once; the drug and alcohol rehabilitation program was put off until tomorrow.

What could I have done differently? I experienced a strong sense of futility and helplessness.

* * *

There are some important characteristics of the work evident in these incidents. It is crucial, complex, fast-paced, risky, solitary, invisible, contradictory, and potentially divisive. Each of these will be considered.

Child welfare work is concerned with crucial life decisions that can have a profound impact on children and families.

These critical incidents clearly illustrate the importance of the work of child welfare. There are few other jobs with a mandate to enter the privacy of family life, make judgements about the behaviour of family members, and take actions that can alter significantly the membership and functioning of that family. In many ways, the powerful mandate of child welfare is an important statement about how children are valued. The sanctity of the family can be set aside if the well-being of children is threatened. At the same time, the responsibilities of child welfare workers and the organizations that employ them are awesome. If mistakes are made, children may die, parents may break down, and families may be permanently damaged.

Child welfare work is complex and takes time to do well.

The critical incidents provide examples of very challenging work. Although the incidents share many features in common, it is clear that each was unique and would require thoughtful analysis and the particular application of skills. There is little sense of routine and predictability.

Although the situations themselves are complex, the conflicting emotions emanating from them make the work even more demanding. Children are frightened or withdrawn or seriously disturbed or all of these. Parents experience a range and series of emotions: anger, hopelessness, defiance, guilt. Workers are often deeply distressed by the situation, even though they may have been involved in other similar situations in the past. It is difficult to witness the results of child neglect and abuse, and yet remain helpful to those who have apparently been responsible and optimistic about improvements. All of these emotional reactions greatly add to the complexity of the work.

Complex situations and deeply felt emotions take time to unravel and heal. Yet, workers are expected to enter new situations as strangers, ask a few choice questions, make an accurate assessment, and develop a plan. Consider the investigation of the woman with mental health problems who was having difficulty caring for her three-year-old. The worker had spent many occasions talking with the mother, interviewing the child-care worker, finding the father and determining if he was a suitable and available parent. She had to help the mother deal with her own feelings of failure about caring for her child and her anger at her spouse, all the while dealing with the mother's suspicions about the worker and the worker's own mixed emotions about her allegiances. At the same time, the worker felt pressure to act swiftly to prevent further abuse of the child. In the end, the worker has to deal with her own feelings of failure and recrimination. Given these circumstances, the importance of concentrated and regular visits would be crucial. Another time factor of the work described above is its different venues. Workers were rarely in the same place twice or in their offices. Organizing meetings outside of the office and travel to different locations add to the time-consuming nature of the work.

Child welfare work is fast-paced, emergency work.
Most of the incidents describe complicated situations where children are or could be in grave danger and where quick decisions are required. Initially, the researchers wondered if the research question – describe a situation where you felt powerful or powerless – provoked workers to recall very dramatic situations. However, at a follow-up workshop participants reviewed the incidents and stated that their work consisted mostly of protection cases in serious family situations and that the nature of the critical incidents reflected accurately their ordinary work. This observation is supported by a national study of child welfare workers in the U.S. (Vinokur-Kaplan and Hartman, 1986). These researchers found that although paperwork constituted the most time-consuming chore, working with children and families in placements and resolving emergency situations followed closely behind. The degree to which incidents such as the ones reported here make up their work is important. Over time, the complexity, intensity, and

importance of the work, coupled with its urgency, are severely taxing. It is like serving as the police officer, the ambulance driver, the doctor, the nurse, the clergy, and the secretary for each traffic accident, day after day.

Some workers commented frankly on the excitement of the work. No two investigations were alike. No one could be sure what would happen when the worker knocked on the door. For some, the lack of predictability, combined with a conviction of the importance of the work, provided an immense sense of satisfaction and interest. For others it greatly increased their feelings of risk and vulnerability.

Child welfare work is risky.

Most of the persons in the critical incidents felt unsafe. As noted above, young children are frequently at risk, either because of direct physical or sexual abuse, or because of the unpredictable nature of the care they received. Parents are unsafe. Fathers may be at risk of criminal proceedings and mothers may fear losing their marriages and their children, and they may feel vulnerable for their own personal safety.

In many instances, workers remarked on their own feelings of vulnerability. They are in unfamiliar surroundings away from their office, alone or with one or two others, and they are often dealing with people who feel very threatened. Although some clients react passively, albeit unco-operatively, others actively threaten the safety of the worker and her colleagues. This sense of risk is not an idle one, as indicated in the above instances, where a child-care worker was assaulted and several social workers were threatened. Ironically, the worker's presence may increase the feelings of vulnerability for family members. What had been a private concern within the family becomes a public one, with the presence of public officials. Family members may then realize that the family unit itself is at risk. While they may have felt unsafe within the family, it is at least a familiar battleground. As a result, the worker may have no allies in the family, not even those members who will seemingly benefit from her actions.

The organization itself has a great potential to enhance or exacerbate the worker's feelings of security. The fact that individual cases of such complexity and importance are assigned to individual workers means that the support of their immediate supervisors is crucial to their feelings of safety. The existence of an inspections and standards unit in most child welfare organizations, while laudable from some points of view, increases feelings of vulnerability and makes the support of other colleagues, particularly supervisors, even more important.

Although the work is fraught with lack of safety, many of the rewards occur when feelings of safety are improved or restored. Clients emerge feeling that their security is assured and can move on to other aspects of their development. Workers gain confidence and optimism about their own development when they feel that their organization is behind them, both in their professional actions and personal feelings.

Child welfare work is oriented to individuals.

As mentioned above, individual workers are assigned individual cases, much like the professional work of doctors and lawyers and unlike the work of other women's professions. Nurses usually share cases with a ward team and patients in the hospital are able to communicate with one another, offering support and companionship. Teachers are assigned groups of pupils who are in regular contact with one another. Teachers also share duties with other colleagues and most often are not responsible for teaching all subjects with one class. In many social agencies, social workers work in teams, sharing joint responsibility for cases and/or working with groups of clients. However, in child welfare work, not only are workers assigned individual caseloads but their clients most likely have no contact with other clients. Even within one family, members may have different interests and concerns and thus may not be able to gain support from one another.

In the critical incidents described above, it was difficult for workers to share responsibility with colleagues. Although informal consultation is theoretically possible and certainly occurred, workers rarely see each other in action and have to make time to consult, usually after the fact. Colleagues most knowledgeable about their work may be police officers, public health nurses, child-care workers, and teachers who are employed by different organizations. Formal responsibility for the actions of workers rested with the supervisor. Just as workers dealt individually with clients, supervisors dealt individually with workers. Some initiated team consultations, but these had an informal status within the organization.

It was evident from a few critical incidents described in the research that supervisors work in a similarly independent fashion and are held responsible for the work of individual workers and their caseload. Whether supervisors hold case conferences and meet together informally was not evident from these incidents.

The individual orientation was complicated by another variable: no one had much choice about who they reported to. Clients are assigned workers for the most part, just as workers are assigned to supervisors who, in turn, are assigned to area managers and so forth. Supervisors may be able to choose new workers but they inherit incumbents when they take their position.

It is not surprising that the work is organized in such a fashion, given the views of the society about the private nature of child care within families and given the professional ethics of social work, which enshrine confidentiality. Nonetheless, there were some costs evident in the critical incidents. Clients are very much alone in the situations. They cannot commiserate with or support others, or even take group action as patients and pupils can. Workers must rely on themselves a great deal and often cannot benefit from the immediate support and advice of colleagues. Supervisors have to count on the judgement of workers without similar advice and support – so it goes up the bureaucracy. And all clients, workers, and supervisors must hope they are assigned persons with the necessary skills, knowledge, and good will to do the job. If not, the risks to themselves increase further.

Probably the most significant outcome of this approach to work is that it encourages a sense of individual responsibility and obscures the impact of social conditions. It is clear in the critical incidents that circumstances well beyond the control of the worker may actually determine the outcome of any investigation. Workers are expected to carry out their jobs in the face of inadequate resources, and clients often live in inadequate housing in chronically depressed neighbourhoods and suffer constant poverty. These circumstances cannot be used to excuse worker performance. Nor will they be the focus of any client investigation the worker makes. Social conditions are the background for the work. Individual behaviour and coping are the foreground.

Important aspects of child welfare work are not visible and not valued.

Comforting and counselling family members are not easily observed activities, particularly when they take place in a client's home or in a private office without others present. Moreover, they are not necessarily activities that can be described fully, nor do we often have language to do justice to the complexity of this work.

Consider again the social worker who responded to the teacher's concerns about one of her pupils who was receiving strappings at home. The worker first "interviews the little boy at school and he discloses the strappings." This activity is a highly skilled one. The worker must make sensitive arrangements with the teacher for a time and place for the interview. She then must help the teacher prepare the child for the interview and spend time herself getting to know the child and providing assurance. The disclosures must be carefully noted and recorded afterwards. Finally, the child must be helped to deal with feelings that may have arisen from his "telling a family secret." There are several tasks within each step and each must be accomplished successfully or the disclosure may not occur or the child may suffer embarrassment and pain in the process. However, although the teacher may witness some of the work, the bulk of it occurs between the child and the worker in private.

The worker then went to the home of the mother and found her very upset. It was clear that the worker explained her role and the prospects of help sufficiently well for the mother to agree to sit at the table and talk further. And this was what they then did – talk, about raising kids, about anger, about guilt and the lack of control parents can feel. The worker carefully shared stories with the mother and helped her feel that she was not alone. The worker also listened without making judgements and helped the mother consider possible options for help. All of this was very demanding work. Had the worker threatened the mother from the outset or not been able to direct the conversation toward getting help, the outcome would have been very different. At the worst, the mother may have continued to beat her son and apprehension may have occurred.

Even if there were witnesses to this work, they may not have viewed the above action as work. Instead, they may have observed two women sitting at the kitchen table talking about raising children. Caring for children is not viewed as highly skilled or important work overall but as something that women ought to be able to do naturally. Thus, the crucial aspect of child welfare work – helping parents, particularly mothers, with child care – is similarly devalued.

Although not apparent in the critical incident, it is unlikely that this work became a significant part of the organizational record. It may have been recorded in one or two lines in a file. It was probably not discussed at length with either the supervisor or other workers. The worker was probably not praised for her efforts and, over time, she herself may not regard it as a highly skilled piece of work.

The work that was more noticeable, measurable, and recorded took place when efforts like the above were unsuccessful. Then, children were removed from their homes, an action that required highly conspicuous tasks: policemen and workers taking children, parents yelling, placement in foster homes, court appearances, court reports, forms, memos, consultations. Even within this more public forum, much of the difficult work remained in the background: helping children deal with the move, attempting to continue links with the parents, giving solace to harried foster mothers, and so forth. Yet, this essential work, albeit invisible, often meant the difference between successful and unsuccessful placements.

The fact that essential parts of the work remain concealed at the case level and within the individual district office means that the higher levels of the organization and the general public are also unaware of many aspects of the work. And, in a similar way, managers and politicians are not rewarded for preventing child abuse or for assisting families to care for their children. However, they are accountable for the perceivable aspects of the work when they go wrong, just as workers are.

There are some profound implications resulting from the invisibility of important work. First, because it is not visible and not rewarded, it can become devalued by workers and the organization. Over time, it may be viewed as not requiring a high degree of skill or meriting a high priority. Second, it places the worker and the supervisor in more vulnerable positions vis-à-vis one another. The supervisor must trust that the worker's account of what transpired with the client is a full and accurate one and that the worker-client interchanges have been done well. There may be very little other evidence. Even if the supervisor questions the worker thoroughly about whether certain issues were raised or specific information obtained, the worker's recollection must be trusted. Moreover, too much questioning can lead to feelings of distrust. And, as noted above, supervisors may well be dealing with workers not of their choosing and with situations of critical importance. Their vulnerability is clear. In the last analysis, should things go very wrong, the organization will be examining whether the largely visible work was done well: were the policies followed, the forms completed, the recording done? The actual quality of the interchanges will be hard to measure and may become further devalued by workers, supervisors, and eventually the organization as a whole.

The finding that important work is invisible and not valued is a curious one. Such work is well described in the social work practice literature and is taught in schools of social work. In some agencies and certainly in private practice it is the essence of the enterprise.

What has occurred in public child welfare practice to create this situation? As noted above, it may be that the balance between helping and policing has been upset. The contradictory nature of these tasks is also a factor.

There is a final irony regarding the invisibility of work: workers have the mandate to investigate mothers for their inability to "parent," work that is also largely invisible. Parents, usually mothers, are judged largely on the visible aspects of their work: the children's health, clothing, behaviour, etc. The quality of the transactions between mothers and children are largely invisible and can be similarly devalued. Workers are expected to record evidence of poor "parenting." Successful efforts are not necessarily identified or recorded.

Child welfare work frequently demands that the worker take on contradictory roles within the family.
In the critical incidents involving the protection of children, workers were expected to carry out two crucial investigations. First, along with the police, they had to determine if an offence had occurred under the Criminal Code or child protection legislation or both. Second, they had to assess whether the children could live safely in their own homes. In actual fact, the first task often meant investigating the father or other male figure and the second involved assessing the mother's capabilities to be a protecting parent. Usually these investigations proceeded in tandem and without much time for deliberations. At once, the worker was the prosecutor of the offender, defender of the children, and judge of the parents.

The difficulty in managing these expectations and preserving at the same time the good will of all parties was evident in the critical incidents. Knowing the worker's role in the police investigation, it was often difficult for other family members to relate to the worker. By doing so, they were being disloyal to a family member upon whom they may be totally dependent. Moreover, they had a larger context in which to consider this person's behaviour. All of this made it very difficult for the worker to gain the trust of other family members and carry out the second investigation. However, as mothers know, without some co-operation with the worker they risked losing the children. Unless the relationship with the male person was at the stage where this crisis was viewed as an opportunity for the mother to sever the relationship, then both she and the worker were placed in a difficult situation.

In terms of the protection of children, it was crucial to foster this relationship with the mother. Moreover, the worker's skills and professional orientation may be better adapted to developing collaborative working relationships than gathering evidence. The fact that workers are women and that many offending parents are men who have difficulties relating to women adds to the complications.

Some outcomes of this contradictory set of tasks were evident in the critical incidents. Workers were placed in very difficult situations and were often abused verbally and threatened by offenders with or without the police presence. Their power to do much about this was limited. Second, workers were often alienated from their potential allies in the situation, the non-offending parents. This made it more difficult to assess whether the non-offending parent, usually the mother, could protect the children. Although not evident from the critical incidents, the question is then raised about whether workers are thus more likely to judge apprehension as the safest course of action in many such situations. Further, given the other qualities of the work – its urgency, its isolation, and its invisibility – apprehension may be even more appropriate.

Child welfare work involves three kinds of authority, and the potential for conflict among them is always present.

Child welfare workers are required to assume several different and conflicting roles that emanate from different sources of authority. First, child welfare workers operate under the authority of child protection legislation in their investigations of child neglect and abuse. This legislation permits them to enter homes, make inquiries, bring charges, and remove children from their homes. This authority is not granted to them as individual social work professionals but as employees of a bureaucracy with its own set of governing principles and policies. Second, many child welfare workers are professional social workers and members of a professional association with its own code of ethics and expectations. Finally, parents have authority. Except in unusual circumstances, as set out in the legislation, parents are assumed to have authority to care for their children as they see fit.

The job can be done best when there is agreement between these three kinds of authority: the family situation is one that the legislation dictates should be investigated, and the bureaucracy, usually the supervisor, supports such intervention. In addition, the professional mandate of the Code of Ethics for social workers similarly agrees that intervention is required and it is possible to do so in ways that also respect professional ethics. The family or at least some family members agree to participate in the investigation and subsequent helping process. In these cases the social worker is able to practise in ways that support her professional obligations, training, and good sense. Some of the powerful incidents are examples of this alignment of authority.

However, most critical incidents did not reveal this degree of harmony. Sometimes the legal/bureaucratic and professional authority is at odds with the parental authority. In these situations, if the legal/bureaucratic authorities remain firm the worker is nonetheless able to carry out the investigation. Yet, it is extremely difficult to investigate people who do not co-operate and to gain the trust of people who feel threatened by the worker's authority. Moreover, this kind of investigation sometimes leads to conflict with professional obligations. For example, treating the client with respect and maximizing self-determination of the client are two professional obligations that are sometimes difficult to implement.

If the legal/bureaucratic authority falters in the face of parental resistance or is too weak or unclear to provide authority for intervention, as occurred in several of the powerless incidents, conflict sometimes arises between professional authority and the other two. Workers feel the obligation to proceed from a professional point of view but have support from neither their organization nor the families to do so.

There is some evidence in the critical incidents that the lack of harmony between the legal/bureaucratic and professional on one side and parental on the other was an expected part of the job and could be managed. Part of professional skill was learning how to do so. Where there was substantial disharmony between legal/bureaucratic and professional, however, workers felt most powerless and disaffected. In the face of a lack of support from the law, their organization, and the family, they had no authority to intervene. Yet what remained was professional guilt for their inaction.

Child welfare work divides women from within and from each other.

Caring for children has traditionally been assigned to women and, in the process of carrying out this work, women have worked together to support and advise one another. In the critical incidents, the picture was very different. The individual mother was alone and was seemingly failing in her task of protecting and caring for her children. She had to deal with these feelings of failure. At the same time, accepting help from another woman, the worker, had the potential to create further internal conflicts. Women workers were similarly torn. They had to witness the seeming lack of care of another woman for her children, and their offers of support, understanding, and assistance were often refused. As noted earlier, women workers were often separated from one another because of the individual assignment of their work and its location.

Mothers and workers were further divided from one another by differences in race and class. One-quarter of the critical incidents involved Native children and their families while all of the workers in our research group were non-Native. Although not explicit in some incidents, it was clear in many others and in research studies that families served by the child welfare system are poor (National Council of Welfare, 1975; Swift, 1991; Novick and Volpe, 1989). Social work wages, while not handsome, exceed poverty levels. Although these barriers to understanding can be surmounted, they provide yet another division among women in child welfare.

The position of women vis-à-vis men was more traditional. The mothers often felt accountable to their male partners or fathers. Similarly, women workers were accountable to their supervisors, many of whom were men. In many ways, the situations presented the worst of the traditional patriarchal system. The control was vested in the men and the women were divided from one another. Women's traditionally invisible work connects rather than divides (Rose, 1978; Waerness, 1984; Cebotarev, 1986). The fact that women did not have equal control in their families or in the organization set up to help these families may be a crucial factor in the way the work has developed.

In summary, it is difficult to compare the job of a child welfare worker to other positions. In some ways it is similar to police work, yet the clarity of authority and partnership are missing. In other ways it resembles the job of public health nurses, who often work alone in homes and the community administering caring services. Yet these nurses do not have the same degree of authority and much of what they do – inoculations, well-baby clinics, prenatal classes – is more visible and less stigmatizing. Some of the work is similar to that of municipal tax assessors who may arrive unannounced to re-evaluate property, but assessors' work is less personal to the family and rarely brings them shame. There are also some elements of the work of the psychiatrist who analyses and of friends who support and help with the day-to-day work. Ultimately, child welfare work has the potential to make profound differences in the lives of children and their families.

DIFFERENT LENSES FOR ANALYSING AND IMPROVING CHILD WELFARE WORK

Many different perspectives provide explanations for the above challenges in child welfare work. Each of these explanations brings with it a particular theoretical and ideological lens and offers particular remedies to improve practice.

1. Role strain: contradictions, ambiguity, overload

It is evident from the above critical incidents and discussion that child welfare work is fraught with profound strains. The contradictions are clear: save the child from harm but keep families together; police family performance yet support family strengths; satisfy personal and professional obligations for good practice yet deliver service within the mandate of the employing organization; work collaboratively yet bear the responsibility of that work individually. Much has been written in child welfare literature about theses contradictions and their impact on worker satisfaction, worker health, burnout, and turnover (Littner, 1957; Wasserman, 1970; Daley, 1979).

Harrison (1980) has demonstrated that role conflict and role ambiguity together are crucial components of job dissatisfaction for child welfare workers and that job dissatisfaction is markedly higher among child welfare workers than other occupations. Harrison surveyed workers in highly regarded child welfare agencies in Minnesota where salaries compared very favourably with other occupations. He concludes that the essence of role conflict is trying to manage the roles of both helper and investigator, which, while theoretically compatible in the social work literature, is extremely difficult to manage in practice. This is particularly true with the rapid increase of complaints to be investigated, the litigious nature of much of the work, and the increasing expectations for paperwork and accountability. These tasks take precedence over opportunities for helping people, yet the professional and personal obligations to help remain with the workers. The conflict is created not just between what workers have to do but between what they do and what they believe they ought to do. This finding is supported by a national study of child welfare workers in the U.S., which concluded that there are large gaps between how workers actually spend their time (paperwork, emergencies, routine case management) and how they would like to spend their time (working with children and families in their own homes, developing resources for clients, and developing their own professional skills) (Vinokur-Kaplan and Hartman, 1986).

Harrison also concludes that role ambiguity, the inability to know what is expected and what constitutes success, is more important than role conflict. The potential for ambiguity is evident from the critical incidents at the beginning of this chapter. Much of the work is invisible, and workers, managers, and clients have different expectations of what ought to be done. Ambiguity robs workers of a sense of competence.

Role overload results from simply too many different duties (counsellor, manager, organizer, clerical worker, investigator), as well as from the sheer volume of the work in any one area. Several studies have documented the increasing amount of work and its impact on workers (Falconer and Hornick, 1983; Daley, 1979). One of the most ironic outcomes of overload is that workers often avoid contact with clients because they know that clients will be angry at them for not returning their phone calls and for other seeming slights. Avoiding contact leads to more disgruntled clients and more dissatisfied workers. It also leads to distraction. Workers may not pay attention to the clients they are serving because they are thinking about the cases they are not attending to (Fryer *et al.*, 1988).

The literature on role strain has been useful in sorting out some of the difficulties in child welfare work. It raises questions about child welfare policies and the conflicting ideologies that jostle for position in developing those policies (Karger, 1981; Walker, 1986). Are child welfare workers to be investigators of the few, as residualists might argue; supporters of the vulnerable, as those with an institutional perspective might suggest; or innovators and developers, as radical proponents might recommend? Because there is no agreement on this ideological debate, child welfare workers are expected to sort out the conflicts on a daily basis in their work with clients and in their internal dialogues with themselves. An analysis of role strain also helps workers realize that their experiences on the job are shared by others and are inherent in the nature of the work rather than in their individual performance. This draws a direct line between role strain, worker stress, and worker performance (Maslach, 1982; Daley, 1979; Harrison, 1980; Jayaratne, Chess, and Kunkel, 1986). Some workers can then take comfort in the knowledge that their performance is a natural reaction to stress rather than a result of their own incompetence. They can also identify more directly with the feelings and behaviour of many of their clients.

Role strain can also lead to an examination of which workers manage best in child welfare in spite of the inherent stresses and strains, and can point to organizational features that help workers to cope (Falconer and Hornick, 1983). Rycraft (1990), in her study of workers who remain in child welfare, found that those workers who had a strong sense of mission about the purpose of child welfare work, those who were able to move among child welfare jobs to find one that matched their skills and preferences, those who had supportive supervisors, and those who have made an investment in the organization in terms of years of service, friendships, and professional commitments tend to remain in the field. The implications for child welfare organizations are clear from this study.

The role strain approach is also limited. In spite of a broader analysis of the causes of role strain and its impact, many of the suggestions for tackling the issues begin and end with individual workers and their improvement. Thus, some studies suggest that workers should focus on their own self-care and develop ways to manage the seemingly inevitable stress of the work. Others emphasize training, particularly for new workers. Given the weakness of the analysis, it is not surprising that remedies are modest. The emphasis on an analysis of roles also casts a particularly bureaucratic light on the nature of the work and implies that roles are somehow discrete from one another. In fact, in many of the critical incidents cited above, the worker engaged in many roles at once. Role analysis also emphasizes what the workers do for and to others: counsel, advocate, investigate. Instead, as the critical incidents illustrate, the pressure and satisfactions of child welfare work often emerged from workers' interaction with the clients in an ongoing way, exchanges not captured in an analysis of roles.

However, there is a more significant drawback to a focus on role strain. It results in the inevitable implication that workers, managers, and policy-makers should strive for ideological coherence and administrative consistency. If there could be agreement on a mission for child welfare, if the contradictions could be removed, if the unpredictable work could be made more predictable, if the invisible work could be more visible and measured, then the job could be improved and the satisfactions increased. In fact, these remedies have not proved curative, as the next section indicates.

2. Corporate management

This approach identifies the problems in child welfare work as emanating from inadequacies in the management of child welfare organizations. It provides an alternative to the long history of a humanistic approach to management in child welfare by managers, usually social workers who rose from the ranks of workers to become the administrators in child welfare organizations without training and without an ethos of management. Instead, corporate management is founded on the beliefs of scientific management, which emphasizes definable outputs, clear lines of responsibility, and efficient use of resources. The application of corporate management to child welfare work results in a reformulation of the mission of child welfare, from one that defines outcomes for clients, improving child care, and family functioning to one that defines outcomes for the organization, providing efficient and effective service within a legal mandate and organizational resources. Decision-making moves upward because knowledgeable people are redefined as those who know about the organization rather than the problems of the clients and front-line service delivery. The task of management is to develop units of workers with outcome goals (clients served, cases transferred) and to meet these goals while limiting expenditures. Managers develop careful information systems to track these activities. There is a strong conviction that, with better management and more specific policies and procedures, the work can be engineered and the consequences of role strain can be minimized and controlled.

The influence of a corporate management approach to child welfare has increased markedly in recent years. Three particular and related examples are illustrative. First, in many jurisdictions in Canada, there has been a shift in the way that child welfare services are provided and funded. Previously, much of the work was done by government child welfare workers or by workers in non-profit agencies funded by block grants from government. Increasingly, government now uses service contracts to accomplish the same work (Ismael and Vaillancourt, 1988). Thus, instead of providing general support to an agency for its family support work, for example, government may offer the same agency specific contracts to deliver particular services to a selected group of clients. In the process of contracting, the work is transformed. It is made much more specific and there is a focus on process rather than results. Many contracts include what service will be provided, to whom, and by whom in what period of time, but they are not nearly as specific in terms of outcomes. Agencies that previously may have had a hand in developing the services are now limited to their delivery. Neither they nor government have a particular stake in the outcomes, unless things go terribly wrong (Reckart, in press).

Since the advent of contracting, many government workers have a sense that some of the enjoyable work – adoptions, developing resources, working with children in specialized resources – has disappeared and they are left with the not so satisfying task of monitoring tough protection cases and supervising agencies that deliver the rest of the work. For those in voluntary agencies there is a similar sense that the exciting work of developing resources on the basis of community need is replaced by carrying out work designed by government.

A second example of the corporate management approach in child welfare is the development of standards of practice. Each task of child welfare work is carefully delineated so that workers will have guidelines for their work and managers will have the capacity to monitor whether the work was carried out according to the specifications. For instance, instead of "visiting foster homes to review the situations of children in government care," workers may have a checklist of questions to pose to foster parents and children, guidelines for conducting the interviews, and a timeline governing the frequency and length of visits. After each visit, workers complete forms indicating that they have performed the duties as required. In many ways, this approach to practice is similar to the contracting of services between government and voluntary agencies. The emphasis is on developing clear tasks and a specific process for carrying out these tasks rather than the actual outcome. These is a hope that services will be standardized and that clients will receive the same service no matter where they live or who is their worker. Many workers have found that this prescriptive approach to practice, while eliminating management ambiguities, fails to address the ambiguities in their work. They live in a fast-paced world of unique circumstances that often do not fit the rules, yet they ignore these rules at their peril.

A third example of corporate management practice is found in the development of case weighting systems to deal with chronic workload problems. Case weighting, not unlike contracting and standard setting, involves a process of examining the complexity of different kinds of cases, measuring the work required, and assigning personnel and dollar figures to each case type. Campbell (1991) reports on one such project undertaken by management and union at the Metro Toronto Children's Aid Society. As the project unfolded it was clear that workers and managers had different expectations: workers hoped a case weighting system would make visible their work overload and the stresses inherent in the job; management hoped that the system could provide them with an examination of worker efficiency and possible ways to predict and cut costs. Workers discovered that it was extremely difficult to quantify the tasks in each case and assign stress levels, in spite of careful efforts to do so with the assistance of research personnel. In the end, the project was self-defeating for them. As the depth of the work was lost in the objective reporting system, their argument for more workers was similarly doomed. Moreover, through the process of quantifying their work, they began to adopt a more managerial stance toward it and lost their own sense of the uniqueness of clients and their problems.

In many cases, workers, unions, and managers in child welfare have supported a corporate management ethos and style. For managers, it allows them the opportunity to practise management as they would in any other bureaucracy and to become expert at their craft. It means increasing mobility and stature as they leave behind the amateur approach to management, which many believe is a characteristic of social service organizations. As many of these managers are men in a "women's profession," they may be particularly keen to put distance between themselves and this legacy of social services.

For workers, corporate management offers protection from the many strains evident in their work. Their work will be defined and regulated and they will have some protection from the seemingly unlimited demands of child welfare work. It is easy to understand why a more rational approach to measuring the work and matching it with resources would appeal to this worker:

> This fall I have had a sense that I was unable to manage the work within the time allotted. I found myself torn between cutting into my private time at the beginning and end of the work day. In an office that was designed to have eight experienced social workers and a district supervisor there were days when there were four people at our morning meeting, with only one or two with powers to apprehend. The others were auxiliary workers and very new. The previous day I had priorized and re-priorized to see that the day's critical investigations got done, that some phone calls got made and, at least, messages left if I couldn't speak to someone. I had documents, evidence and photos to get from the police station to organize for court and a caseload of five family service files and four child-in-care files that I had to carry because after the apprehension I hadn't time to write the recordings and send them to the family service team. I had given the supervisor a memo of twelve cases that fell into the category

of delayed investigations (over five days old) that had been too far down the priority list to be seen yet.

I found myself beginning to doubt my competency even though intellectually I could understand that there was far too much work for the workers available or the hours we had. I worked through coffee, working through lunch, still at my desk at 7:45. I found that I was being critical of myself if I couldn't continue my file recording or documents on one case while I was dealing with another case on the phone or conferring with an inexperienced colleague who had dropped in for another case conference. I got less patient with these "drop-ins" even though they had been given no training before being assigned to an intake office and despite the fact they were performing wonderfully considering the circumstances and the lack of positive feedback. But then, I was having trouble remembering to give myself positive feedback!

The clients I saw probably got the best I could give – but even when I was listening to them I was jumping in my head to plan treatment and outcomes rather than just being "in the moment" and listening. And I worried about the people I didn't see – the ones on the delayed list. Were the children in danger and was I failing to protect them? Would the family have to go into crisis one more unnecessary time before they would get seen?

The ones I saw listened dispiritedly when I told them about the three- to six-month waits for intensive counselling and only brightened a little when I told them homemakers would be in to provide them with respite. I referred them to self-help groups but recognized that most were too isolated, too "guilty" to risk exposing themselves and their problems to strangers without a friendly aide to keep them company the first time or two. (Callahan and Attridge, 1990)

Although possible benefits of corporate management to the problems of child welfare are easily identified, experience suggests that it promises more than it can deliver. Most importantly, it blurs the mission, a commitment to improving the lot of children and families, that has sustained many child welfare workers in the face of difficult working conditions. As noted at the beginning of this chapter, child welfare work is complex and not easily reduced to quantifiable pieces. Yet corporate managers, with their mission of reducing expenditures, require itemized tasks. The feeling and caring aspects of the job, the real invisible work that often spells the difference between success and failure, have not been identified in standards of practice and case weighting efforts and are further discredited by these systems. As workers record work that does not really matter and don't chronicle work that does matter, the chasms between their actual work life and their reported work life become wider.

The codifying of the work and the transfer of case decision-making from worker to manager have other disadvantages. As noted above, child welfare work is characterized by its complexity and fast pace. It is difficult to convey the totality of the experience to superiors, to have access to them when required, and to carry out their decisions if they contradict professional and personal judgement. Workers may be encouraged to practise subversively. For instance, the worker who helped her colleague deal with a sexual assault may or may not wish to give many details about her actual work. She may not wish to report that she had spent several hours (overtime) with a colleague who had been sexually assaulted and had advised her equally on the prospects of ignoring the assault or reporting it. She may then have to justify her actions and may have been chastised for not acting decisively or for responding at all. In response, managers may be inclined to write more and more policies for tracking workers. But as Considine (1987: 2) states: "The elegant logic of the handbook is quickly subjected to a thousand compromises." Moreover, the process of surveillance diminishes trust among all levels of the organization. The development of strict lines of authority increases the individual nature of the work, one of the features of child welfare practice that workers find alienating already.

3. Making policy through practice: the street-level bureaucrat

This approach begins from very different assumptions than the framework of corporate management and has less currency in the present child welfare system. Rather than trying to create coherence and order through rationalizing the system, proponents of this approach suggest it is more useful to examine how front-line workers actually carry out policy in their day-to-day work. From this experience, broader-level policies can be developed – a bottom-up rather than top-down approach to policy-making. Lipsky (1980) in his classic text, *Street Level Bureaucracy*, examined the work of several different professionals – police, teachers, nurses, social workers, and others – and identified three particular features of the work: conflicting goals, inadequate resources, and elastic demand (as services improve, demands for them increase).

These features form the context for the activities of workers and managers within the bureaucracy. Although managers try to control work, street-level bureaucrats are impossible to govern through traditional managerial methods because of their superior knowledge of the actual work and the solitary nature of the job. Instead, since they must ration resources and their own energy, they make decisions about who should receive what kind and how much service on a daily basis often as a result of their own values and assessment of what will work rather than on official agency policy.

Moore (1987) has extended the analysis of the street-level bureaucracy to include an examination of the transactions that occur between the bureaucrat and client, the essential technology of the human services. Rather than operating from a reductionist frame of reference only, how to limit work and maximize resources, Moore suggests that street-level bureaucrats operate in a highly interactive and social fashion; as the worker acts to solve problems, the client responds and the worker modifies and responds again. Over time, workers, like politicians, learn by experience and reflection to react to certain situations, to select appropriate means for response, and to aim for some kind of outcome. Ambiguity, conflict, and overload are dealt with daily in this mediating process where both workers and clients are active participants. The excitement and challenge of the work often arise from the complexity of this interplay.

> The "technique of managing" the subtle and ramifying encounters expected from such logical outlines defies the ordinary language of bureaucratic process. It is a delicate drama involving the staging and presence of actors who typically have not previously met, based on the interplay of tacit threats and promises. It is a civil wrestling match to establish the purpose and boundaries of the encounter and the respective rights and obligations of the two (or more) principals. Ambiguity is experienced by these politicians [workers] as a set of quandaries, possibilities, and choices skilfully discerned. (Moore, 1987: 84)

The critical incidents presented earlier provide evidence of the complexity, ambiguity, and unpredictability of the circumstances of each case. When workers were able to weave their way through the maze of interactions and, through skill and wits, bring some sort of satisfactory outcome for clients, they felt powerful. Where the circumstances were so confounding or beyond their power to influence, or both, workers felt powerless. Replacing workers' practice wisdom with a set of rules is a fruitless pursuit.

The analysis of street-level bureaucracy leads to some definite recommendations about how human service organizations and work should be structured and managed. Traditional bureaucratic structures and authority patterns are deemed inappropriate. Instead, the notion of bottom-heavy organizations recognizes that much of the responsibility for decision-making is already in the hands of the workers. This inverted organizational pattern views managers as resources for workers with the task of mediating workers' needs with politicians and the public. In the process, it is hoped that clients will be able to present their needs openly and that workers will be able to respond without having to wrap these needs in appropriate bureaucratic packages.

The case for changing child welfare organizations according to the experience of street-level bureaucrats has gained momentum in recent research that examines what makes organizations and people work (Peters and Waterman, 1982; Kramer and Schmalenberg, 1988). A recent study by the Auditor General of Canada (1988: 107-10) confirms that findings from the corporate and health care sectors apply to government departments as well. Four important characteristics of successful government departments are identified:

1. *Emphasis on people*: . . . People are challenged, encouraged, and developed. They are given power to act and to use their judgement. There is a caring attitude in these organizations, based on the belief that, in the long run, high performance is a product of people who care rather than of systems that constrain.

2. *Participative leadership*: . . . The leaders envision an ideal organization, define purpose and goals, then articulate these and foster commitment in their people. . . . Staff feel comfortable consulting their peers as well as those above and below them. Although formal levels exist for administrative purposes, there are no boundaries that inhibit collaboration in achieving organizational goals.

3. *Innovative work styles*: Staff . . . reflect on their performance, on the environment. . . . They learn from experience. . . . They maintain strong monitoring, feedback and control systems, but only as useful tools. The . . . organization seeks to be self-reliant and to control itself rather than relying on control from outside.

4. *Strong client orientation*: People . . . focus strongly on the needs and preferences of their clients. They derive satisfaction from serving the client rather than the bureaucracy. . . .

Interaction is strong within the organization, but it is perhaps even stronger between the organization and its clients.... There is a strong alignment of values with their central agency.... Organization members are able to talk in concrete terms about intangible things such as mission and values.

Reasons for not implementing these approaches in child welfare are often couched in corporate management terms. Staff are limited and often cannot be spared for development. The political nature of the work discourages managers from giving staff a free hand in making decisions. The geographical and psychological distance between staff and management discourages easy discourse and give and take in daily decisions. It is often not clear who the client is in any one situation: the child, the parents, the community, the government. However, if the National Parole Board and sections of the RCMP are singled out for distinction in the Auditor General's report because of the presence of such characteristics, it must be possible for many child welfare organizations to transform similarly.

Current arguments about improving child welfare have divided along the demarcations represented by the corporate management and implementation perspectives. One says there should be less discretion for workers, one more; one says policy-making should emanate from the top down, the other from the bottom up; one says government should define those children and families requiring service, the other that families and children should define their own needs. However, two other approaches to changing child welfare practice and organizations do not really fit into this dialogue. Instead, these approaches tackle the fundamental purposes of child welfare and recommend significant changes that in turn present new models for social work practice and organizations.

4. Social control and social weathervane

This approach to child welfare essentially states that child welfare organizations have very little to do with the protection of children or the support of families, no matter how they are structured or mandated. Instead, proponents argue that child welfare serves two primary functions, and the problems inherent in the work can best be understood in relation to these functions. First, child welfare organizations exist primarily to ensure that the poor do not abandon the responsibility for their children and that poor families rear their children to be functioning members of the community, equipped and willing to take on necessary, perhaps undesirable, jobs or at least to fend for themselves. Child welfare punishes those parents who do not fulfil these duties. First Nations people have presented the most cogent evidence to support this argument. They have indicated that the child welfare system has been used first to assimilate and then to annihilate their people. Chapter 5 provides an examination of this argument.

Second, proponents of this view suggest that child welfare, particularly as it is portrayed in the media, serves the purpose of shoring up the family not just on an individual basis but overall. Parton and Parton (1989) have written the best explanation of this latter point of view. They trace the rise of child abuse as a phenomenon in Britain that occurred at the same time as the rise in divorce rate, the seeming abandonment of family values, an increase in abortion, and so forth. Child abuse was something of a bellwether, a phenomenon that could be used to focus concern on the family rather than on the social conditions confronting families. In the process, political action on behalf of traditional family values could be mustered.

This approach leads to a different analysis of child welfare organizations and the problems facing workers. Workers in child welfare, it is argued, suffer from a crisis of authenticity. Although they are trained to help others and expect to do so, they know that their work, while individually helpful at times, in fact covers up the larger problems of poverty, racism, and gender inequality. By practising within a framework based on maintaining these inequalities, workers sustain the continued endurance of these conditions. Supporters maintain that, in the short term, workers should use their position inside the organization to collect evidence of the social conditions of families and to broadcast this research. Workers should also respond to individual needs and use these interactions to educate clients about the kinds of structural changes that are required to deal with their situation. In this way, clients can become empowered, just as workers are, when they understand the larger context of their plight. Workers can also use their position to educate other professionals, community members, managers, and politicians.

According to this perspective child welfare organizations as they are presently constituted should be disbanded over the long haul. Instead, the aim of child welfare should be to redress power imbalances in society that contribute to the neglect and abuse of children. Child welfare can be best carried out by a balance of different organizational forms that provide opportunities for powerless groups to gain control. One such organization is the child welfare service developed by the client groups: Native child welfare organizations, women's child welfare services, child welfare organizations based on ethnic and geographical origins. Self-help and advocacy groups provide another avenue of service and strength to client groups. Professional services should be devoted to transforming educational, judicial, and governmental attitudes and responses and to supporting the voices of the disempowered.

5. Feminist approaches to caring and to analysing bureaucracies

This explanation states that the problems in child welfare are the result of devaluing the care of children, which in turn is related to the devaluing of work that women do and the separation of women's work into the private sphere of the family where it is further buried. Because of this history, little is understood about the complexity of caring and the circumstances under which it is best performed. Feminist perspectives challenge a corporate management approach to child welfare on the basis that corporate management begins from an assumption that caring work is an unspoken, at times unnecessary part of child welfare work and, when it does occur, it is to be viewed as work like any other. Corporate management further obscures the holistic nature of caring by breaking down tasks and counting them. In the process, it further divides women from their long-standing way of working together in the care of children and further discounts their wisdom.

Feminist perspectives also force an analysis of child welfare problems grounded in the long-standing discrimination against women. Economic disadvantage and violence against women and children are deeply embedded in all social institutions. Child welfare obscures these realities by identifying a select group of the most vulnerable women and children and implying that they are different somehow from the rest.

Feminist remedies to problems in child welfare are somewhat different from those with a social control perspective. Rather than disbanding child welfare organizations, feminists argue that child welfare should be expanded to include the care of all children. Crimes against women and children should be dealt with by the courts. Feminist suggestions for structuring organizations fit in part with the street-level bureaucracy approach, with the proviso that women should have responsibility for child care in public commensurate with their private responsibilities. However, feminists also argue that public organizations should have fluid boundaries and collective management approaches and should break down the artificial boundaries between the private and public worlds of workers. Feminists underline the fact that these are pie-in-the-sky remedies if the notions of women's work and violence against women are not similarly addressed by society at large. In Chapter 6, feminist perspectives are analysed in depth.

CONCLUSION

The task of sorting out directions for change in child welfare is not an easy one. Chapters 6 and 7 in particular will develop the themes identified in the above analysis more fully. However, some broad directions are clear. There are really two major debates: one about structure and style between the corporate style of management and the street-level approach, the other between those who argue for reforms in structure and style and those who argue for a radically changed mission for child welfare that focuses on disadvantage and inequality.

It seems easier to debate structure and management style than it is to tackle the mission of child welfare. Structures are within the grasp of most of us to tinker with, even within our own departments or units. To tackle the meaning of child welfare and galvanize support for major rethinking is a formidable task. Yet, this is what many child welfare workers do, day after day. They have their own mission and they find opportunities to put it into practice in spite of constraints. The powerful incidents cited at the beginning of this chapter provide examples of these efforts. To these workers, being powerful meant working in concert with people so that they could define their own problems and successfully tackle some of them. In the process, clients or other workers acknowledged the efforts of the worker. Pioneers in child welfare did not necessarily agree with one another but they did share a common commitment to improving the lot of children, a commitment that bound them together and sustained them through many hazards. Attention to client self-determination, respect for workers, and commitment to a cause must be fundamental components of any new mission for child welfare.

Chapter 4

The Constituency/Community Context

Brian Wharf

> On the basis of my 24 years of effort I can tell you that our failures can be traced to a single fact: we have never in this country been able to put together a broad based truly effective advocacy or lobbying group whose central goals are a better life for children and families. (Zigler, 1986)

This quotation from a leading child welfare authority in the United States can be applied with equal force to Canada. While there are many national, provincial, and local agencies and associations that in some fashion or another are concerned with the welfare of children, they function for the most part in isolation from one another and from the provincial ministries that provide child welfare services. The purpose of this chapter is to provide an overview of the work of some of the major constituencies in child welfare and from this review build a case for the development of policy communities and community governance in child welfare. The case is strengthened by the discussion in Chapters 5 and 6 and completed in Chapter 7. Constituencies are viewed here as support groups for child welfare and they range from national organizations with a broad social policy mandate to community agencies with delegated authority to provide child welfare services.

As noted in previous chapters, the responsibility for providing child welfare services is vested in provincial governments. Not only do these governments establish child welfare legislation and policy, but for the most part provincial ministries deliver services to children and families. A significant consequence of these structural arrangements is that citizens in nine provinces and the territories have only a limited capacity to influence child welfare policy and practice. A personal example will illustrate the point. When living in Burlington, Ontario, I was elected to the board of the Hamilton/Wentworth Children's Aid Society. During my term of office board members influenced the work of the Society by introducing ultimately successful motions to limit the length of time board members could serve and by requiring that consumers and foster parents be represented on the board. A further contribution was the initiation of a research study on the role of foster parents. When I moved to Victoria, B.C., there was and remains no opportunity to participate in the activities of the regional and local offices of the provincial ministry. Influence is limited to participating in reviews of legislation and to voting in provincial elections.

The discussion in this chapter is organized by distinguishing among four different types of constituencies: advisory councils, voluntary child and family service agencies, advocacy organizations, and community-based agencies that govern child welfare. All of these organizations are viewed as constituencies for child welfare since they have the capacity or at least the potential to influence policy and practice. Attention is disproportionately placed on advocacy and community governance structures since these not only are the most numerous on the Canadian child welfare scene, but also have the most potential to influence policy and practice.

ADVISORY COUNCILS

The governmental landscape is littered with advisory councils. At the municipal level city and village councils have a long tradition of enlisting citizens to provide advice on the complex issues that beset municipal governments. A similar listing of advisory councils can be found at the provincial level. Thus provincial governments have established councils for the family, for seniors, for persons with disabilities, and for women and a host of structures to provide advice on the environment, forestry, fishing, and labour/management issues. However, despite the popularity of this structure, no provincial government has formed a council with the specific purpose of advising its ministry on child welfare. It can be argued that child welfare policy and practice should be included as an integral component of the mandate of councils of the family. Yet this has not occurred, and mandates for these organizations typically exclude the statutory child welfare services.

Other countries, such as Australia, have established advisory councils for child welfare. For example, the state of Victoria formed the Victorian Family and Children's Services Council. The Council has undertaken a number of reviews of protective services and substitute care arrangements. Its reviews provide an ongoing source of advice for the minister and in some instances its opinion differs from that provided by senior officials and professionals within the bureaucracy. Thus the Council argued for the separation of protective and preventive services, while senior officials took an opposing view. Such clashes of opinion can provoke healthy policy debates within the department and indeed at higher levels in government (Victorian Family and Children's Services Council, 1990).

The best-known advisory council in the social policy field in Canada is the National Council of Welfare. The Council has not only analysed existing and proposed federal policies in income security, housing, and health care, but has insisted on the right to publish its frequently critical reports. Thus, rather than providing confidential advice to the minister, the Council has from its inception adopted an advocacy stance usually found in social movements and client rights organizations.

The crucial issue for all advisory councils is whether their advice is heeded. Attempts to track the influence of councils on government policy are few and far between. One review was undertaken by Doris Shackleton, who established two criteria to assess impact: "the council is consulted by government while policy and particularly legislation is in the planning stage, and it has to its credit at least a couple of occasions when the government altered some decision because of its intervention" (Shackleton, 1977: 100). On the basis of these criteria Shackleton flunked all of the national advisory councils!

Shackleton's criteria deserve careful scrutiny. While reasonable at first glance, they do not recognize the context facing advisory councils. If they are to influence policy their advice must fit with the priorities and ideologies of the government. If such a fit occurs the essential contribution of the advisory council is one of support, and while in some instances support can be valuable, the question can be raised – Why bother with an advisory council that simply confirms existing or proposed directions? On the other hand, if the council proffers advice that challenges firmly established views, it is likely to be dismissed. Thus, a succession of federal governments have consistently rejected the advice of the National Council of Welfare to continue and improve universal income security programs, to establish a progressive system of taxation, and to eliminate loopholes in income tax for the corporate sector and upper-income classes. The salience of this observation is supported by Sandra Burt's study of the influence of women's groups on social policy.

> Policy success did vary significantly according to the nature of the claim. About one half of the social service and other claims were met, compared with about one third of the role equity or role change. . . . The gender related demands of women's groups challenge deeply rooted perceptions of women's and men's appropriate responsibilities. In the short term women's groups have difficulty affecting changes which lie outside the range of what is considered to be normal or acceptable. (Burt, 1990: 24-26)

However, challenging the normal and acceptable is the *raison d'être* of social reform and advocacy groups. Lessing talks about challenges as "screwball ideas":

> What one can observe happening over and over again is that some minority view which is regarded as totally crazy, ten years later is a mainstream view. . . . I'm always interested in looking around and seeing what totally screwball ideas are out on the edge and which of them are likely to be in the centre quite soon. The forces that support them are the fact that they are needed, that they correspond in some way to reality. . . . (Lessing, 1991)

It is our contention that the "screwball ideas" advanced in this book can be connected to the reality of child welfare. They represent the ideas and concerns of practitioners and consumers that have not been incorporated into policy but have the potential to reform child welfare. The final chapter considers some "screwball ideas" and ways of bringing them into the centre.

Advisory councils have considerable potential as a constituency for child welfare. They provide a window into the world of child welfare through which citizens who would not ordinarily have an opportunity can learn about the public issues and private troubles that surround and confound child welfare. Advisory councils can review policy and practice, and if they are sufficiently courageous to follow the example of the National Council of Welfare, their reviews will contain innovative proposals for change. Such reviews should be placed in the public domain in order to inform the public and provide information for advocacy groups. Advisory councils must have a broadly based membership including consumers, professionals, and citizens.

VOLUNTARY CHILD AND FAMILY SERVICE AGENCIES

A rough classification of voluntary child and family service agencies yields one group that has come into being as a consequence of the philosophy of privatization and a second group established, mostly by women, to supplement and extend the services provided by child welfare departments. The first group represents an extension of government since they provide services to meet needs identified by staff of the ministry. Frequently the services are highly specialized and are provided to individuals and families on a contract basis for specified periods of time. Alternatively, contracts are awarded for services such as day care or homemaker in a particular geographic area on an ongoing basis. In both instances, however, the nature of the service to be provided, the dollar value of these services, and the extent of the time period are determined by the ministry. These agencies, then, depend on government for their existence. Their ability to influence the type of service to be funded and the amounts to be paid are further weakened by the competitive nature of the contracting approach. Agencies must compete for contracts, a strategy that diminishes their capacity to present a united front in arguing for change. Hence, while these agencies provide useful services and may have important insights and contributions, they are peripheral to child welfare policy.

The second group of agencies supplements and enriches the services provided by the ministry. These differ from those described above in that they were established as a consequence of voluntary efforts. The tasks of identifying needs and developing programs to meet the needs were carried out by clients, citizens, and professionals independently of the formal child welfare system. A partial listing of the agencies established in this fashion includes family service agencies, transition houses, family places, sexual assault centres, rape relief centres, and parents in crisis. Many of these agencies are supported at least in part by government funds, but they cherish and value their independence. Chapter 6 provides more detailed information on agencies based on feminist principles, and hence no further elaboration is provided here. It is, however, necessary to add that despite the contributions they have made both by the services provided and in the innovative approaches to governance, these agencies have also had little impact on the formal child welfare system. The time and attention of staff and board members have been devoted to developing services and administrative structures and to fund-raising. Some have also expressed concern that advocacy efforts will jeopardize funding from federal and provincial governments.

ADVOCACY ORGANIZATIONS

Again, two kinds of advocacy organizations exist. The first consists of national and provincial agencies that rely on research and the preparation of briefs to influence policy. The second and emerging group is made up of client rights associations.

Advocacy groups face the same dilemma as advisory councils in attempting to influence social policy. Thus, efforts directed toward such significant social policy concerns as the elimination of child poverty and the development of universal day care have been consistently rejected by neo-conservative governments that have been in power federally and in many provinces for the past decade. The task facing advocacy groups is therefore formidable. Typically, they lack access to the corridors of power in the national and provincial capitals and they possess extremely limited resources to conduct research and mount campaigns.

In addition, the powerful social movements – labour, women, and First Nations – have neglected child welfare. While many band and tribal councils have sought to gain control of child welfare, it has only recently become a priority in the First Nations movement, and neither labour nor the women's movement has embraced child welfare in their campaigns for equality for workers and women. In a very real sense children are the orphans of the major social movements in Canada.

A partial list of the most prominent national and provincial advocacy organizations includes the following:

The Canadian Council on Social Development
The Vanier Institute for the Family
The Child Poverty Action Group
The Laidlaw Foundation
The Canadian Council on Children and Youth*
The Canadian Child Welfare Association*

---

*In January of 1992 cccy and ccwa amalgamated to form Children * Enfants * Jeunesse * Youth, but a scant six months later the new organization disbanded because of lack of funds. Comments on the work of these two founding organizations are included in following discussion.

The Ontario Association of Children's Aid Societies
Society for Children and Youth of B.C.

These organizations share a number of common characteristics.
They are dedicated to improving the well-being of children, their
reforms call for the elimination of child poverty and the introduction of universal day care, and their principal strategies include
research, the submission of briefs to governments, and public
education.

The Canadian Council on Social Development

Since it was founded in 1920 as the Canadian Council on Child
Welfare, CCSD has undertaken a variety of activities to advance the
cause of children. These activities include the organization of
conferences like the first and second Canadian conferences on day
care held in 1971 and 1982 respectively. They also included the
preparation of a number of books and reports ranging from a
series of fact books on poverty in Canada to *Organizing for the
Homeless, Foster Care and Adoption in Canada,* and *Native Children and the Child Welfare System.*

> Our major new initiative with respect to children is the estab-
> lishment of the Centre for International Statistics on Economic
> and Social Welfare for Families and Children. The Centre will
> better enable researchers in Canada to assess the state of chil-
> dren and families in Canada by increasing access to domestic
> data bases. It will also enable us to compare Canada's record
> with that of other industrialized countries by providing access to
> international data bases like the Luxembourg Income Study.
> (Johnston, 1991)

Of the Council's many contributions to child welfare its inquiry
into *Native Children and the Child Welfare System* is of particular
interest for this book (Johnston, 1983). This represented the first
national research study of the responses of provincial child welfare
departments to child neglect and abuse among First Nation families. It documented the failure of provincial programs to respect
First Nation traditions and culture, and to address environmental
issues that contributed in a significant way to the capacity of First
Nation families to care for their children. The importance of this
inquiry is that it exposed a national tragedy and provided a documentary base for reform. We return to this inquiry and the importance of its discoveries in Chapter 5.

The Vanier Institute of the Family

The Vanier Institute came into being as a consequence of the interest of the late Governor General of Canada, Georges P. Vanier, and Madame Pauline Vanier. Since its inception in 1965 the Institute has funded research, published briefs, monographs, and a quarterly magazine, *Transitions*, and made numerous presentations to Senate and House of Commons committees with the objective of influencing social policy on behalf of families.

An important theme of the work of the Institute has been a critique of the piecemeal, haphazard approach to social policy. Thus, the Institute has proposed a comprehensive child-care policy for Canada that includes:

1. Family policies which enable parents to provide full-time child care to their young children if they so choose and if they are able.
2. Workplace policies which enable employee parents to assume a greater proportion of their child-care responsibilities if they so choose.
3. A system of non-compulsory child-care arrangements including in-home care, centre care, for-profit care, non-profit centre, workplace and co-operative care, providing real choice to meet the needs of parents and children. (Vanier Institute of the Family, 1986)

The Child Poverty Action Group

"CPAG is a public interest advocacy and research group working to end poverty for families with children" (Popham, 1992). It was established in 1985 by a group of academics and community practitioners and has received financial, staff, and organizational support from a number of agencies, including the Laidlaw Foundation, the Social Planning Council and the Metropolitan Children's Aid Society Foundation, all of Metropolitan Toronto.

During its first five years CPAG issued a series of reports outlining the dimensions and impact of child poverty and proposing strategies for change. The reports include: *A Fair Chance for All Children* (1986), *Poor People Are Not the Problem, Poverty Is* (1990), *A Choice of Futures: Canada's Commitment to its Children* (1988, in collaboration with a number of national agencies) and *Unequal Futures* (1991). These reports have been presented to the provincial government in Ontario and to the federal government and have been discussed at countless community forums.

Since 1991 we have broadened the focus for our public education and advocacy efforts to include the need for universal day care, the provision of adequate, affordable housing as well as an educational system that is responsive to poor children and public support for appropriate health and social services. Much of our current work centres on Campaign 2000, a national initiative to end child poverty by the year 2000. (Popham, 1992)

Campaign 2000 is dedicated to convincing the federal government that it must live up to its commitment to end child poverty by the year 2000. The commitment is expressed in the form of a resolution passed unanimously in the House of Commons on November 24, 1989, that "This House . . . seeks to achieve the goal of eliminating poverty among Canadian children by the year 2000" (House of Commons, 1989). CPAG is supported in this campaign by several national agencies, including the Canadian Council on Social Development, the Vanier Institute of the Family, Family Service Canada, and the Canadian Institute of Child Health, by the Laidlaw Foundation and other foundations, and by a network of community partners consisting for the most part of social planning councils and anti-poverty groups.

It should be added that the formidable challenge of a campaign dedicated to the elimination of child poverty in Canada is being supported by a core budget of $40,000, a staff member loaned by the Family Service Agency of Metropolitan Toronto, and funds for specific projects, such as the research for and writing of *Unequal Futures*, supplied by foundations and the Social Planning Council of Metropolitan Toronto.

The Laidlaw Foundation

After a two-year period of extensive consultation and planning, the Foundation created the Children at Risk Programme. . . . The ultimate goal of the Children at Risk Programme is to improve the well being of Canadian children. The Programme attempts to achieve this ambitious goal in a variety of ways: first, by contributing to an increased understanding of the factors that promote or limit a child's quality of life and life chances; second by advocating changes in policies and professional practices to better reflect that increased understanding and last, by promoting the development of greater leadership capacities among individuals within specific at-risk communities. (Laidlaw Foundation, n.d.)

Marvyn Novick, the program director for the Children At Risk Unit, has elaborated on its mission by noting that it has

> defined historical domination as one of the three primary conditions of social risk for children with particular reference to the black and aboriginal experiences in Canada. CAR work emphasized the link of economic and social dimensions of child welfare and is working on a community systems approach for the mutual empowerment of practitioners and residents in the organization of social support for children and families. (Novick, 1992)

In addition to its pioneering initiatives in the Children At Risk program and its financial support of the Child Poverty Action Group, the Foundation has funded the advocacy work of a number of community organizations, including the Social Planning Council of Ottawa, the End Legislated Poverty Group in B.C., and the St Louis de Parc community in Montreal. Indeed, the Foundation is emerging as one of the leading social policy agencies in the country.

The Canadian Council on Children and Youth

CCCY was founded in 1956 and concentrated its early efforts in sponsoring conferences to bring together child-serving professionals. It later launched several inquiries into the effects of poverty on the health and well-being of children (*Poor Now, Poor Later,* 1987; *Wasting our Future: The Effects of Poverty on Child Development,* 1988) and on the case for a national child-care strategy (*Caring For Our Children,* 1988; *Eight Years Later,* 1988). In the eighties the CCCY continued its work on child poverty in collaboration with other national organizations and gave particular attention to the problem of child sexual abuse, which culminated in its response to the federal government's inquiry, *Reaching For Solutions* (1990). In turn, one of the outcomes of this response and one of the legacies of the Council is Caring Communities, a research project designed to identify effective community programs to prevent the sexual abuse of children. A second legacy of the Council is the Canadian Coalition for the Rights of Children, which has prepared materials for youth workers, teachers, and others to educate young people about their rights and responsibilities and the UN Convention on the Rights of the Child.

The Canadian Child Welfare Association

The CCWA was founded in 1983 with the following objectives:

- to further and advance an understanding of welfare affecting children and families by facilitating the exchange of ideas and information;
- to increase knowledge in child welfare matters by conducting and promoting research, providing consultation to interested organizations, providing information to legislative bodies to further the passage of sound legislation;
- to promote public awareness of the special needs of those children and their families who receive or require child welfare services;
- to develop and promulgate high standards and methods for a high quality of service to be performed by all organizations and individuals working with or caring for children and their families;
- to encourage programs of staff training in the delivery of child welfare services and family support services. (Canadian Child Welfare Association, 1986)

The CCWA was formed in an effort to give leadership to the child welfare enterprise represented for the most part by provincial ministries and children's aid societies. In effect, it sought to become the national counterpart of the Ontario Association of Children's Aid Societies, but after it received some start-up funds from Health and Welfare Canada no permanent funding was available from either federal or provincial sources to support this ambitious objective.

The principal legacy of CCWA is the Youth in Care Network. Recognizing that children and youth had little say in the substitute care arrangements developed for them by child welfare agencies, the CCWA brought together "graduates" of substitute care at a national conference, and with financial assistance from Health and Welfare Canada, the graduates and the CCWA launched the Youth in Care Network. Some evidence of the need for this network comes from the fact that children and youth are now seldom excluded from child welfare conferences or meetings.

The Effectiveness of Advocacy Organizations

If the Shackleton criteria of altering national social policies are taken as the test of effectiveness, the work of the organizations discussed above cannot be considered successful. They have consistently advocated that universal programs such as family allowances should be strengthened as the principal strategies to eliminate child poverty. By contrast, the Mulroney government has just as consistently favoured reducing the role of the federal government in social policy and has pushed ahead with selective as opposed to universal programs. Thus in January, 1993, a new and targeted child tax benefit replaced the family allowance program. We return to a discussion of the role of the federal government in the final chapter.

However, an alternate view of the effectiveness of these organizations can be posited. In the first place they have kept child poverty on the social policy agenda by issuing reports, holding conferences, and meeting with the Ministers of Finance and Health and Welfare. In the second place they have documented the impact of poverty on the lives of children in a detailed and graphic fashion and have articulated the case for universal programs. An example of the strenuous arguments for universality comes from *Unequal Futures: The Legacies of Child Poverty in Canada*:

> Universality ensures that benefits and services are made available to everybody on equal terms rather than being confined to the poor. Parents, regardless of their level of income, can proudly accept their Family Allowance cheque because they receive it in recognition of the extra costs involved in child raising and not because they are living in poverty or are labelled "needy". Experience has shown that services and benefits directed at the poor alone soon become poor programs as middle class people see themselves no longer having a stake in defending and improving them. (Child Poverty Action Group and Social Planning Council of Metropolitan Toronto, 1991: 37)

The level of debate around child poverty and other child welfare issues has been enriched by the work of these advocacy organizations. That they have not succeeded in persuading the Progressive Conservative government, in power since 1984, to take a social development approach to social policy should not be taken as evidence of failure. Indeed, given the divergence in ideologies and priorities between the government and these organizations, agreement on fundamental social policies is simply not possible.

It would be inappropriate to conclude this review without even a passing mention of provincial advocacy groups. Two very different provincial organizations are the Society for Children and Youth of B.C., which is in many ways a provincial counterpart of the national organizations discussed above, and the Ontario Association of Children's Aid Societies, the provincial voice of the children's aid societies in that province.

Society for Children and Youth of B.C.

The goals of the SCY are:

1. To identify unmet needs of children and youth and to promote services to meet these needs.
2. To educate the community regarding the needs of children and youth.
3. To influence social policies relating to the well-being of children and youth.
4. To provide a forum for interdisciplinary exchange and action in relation to issues affecting children.
5. To cooperate and collaborate with other organizations with compatible objectives. (Society for Children and Youth of B.C., 1991)

The SCY has gone through three distinct phases. In its early years, from 1974 to 1977, it focused on community education. In the second phase, lasting to approximately 1982, the SCY concentrated on research and on developing demonstration projects. Among some significant accomplishments during this phase was the development of the "Feeling Yes, Feeling No" Child Abuse Prevention Program, which has been implemented in school districts throughout Canada. The third phase has seen an emphasis on advocacy, particularly in child abuse, on the needs of adolescents, and in the field of recreation. "SCY's leadership culminating in heavy lobbying for the acceptance of Bill C-15 (amendments to the Evidence Act and Criminal Code in relation to child sexual abuse) and the acceptance of prevention programs as part of elementary school curricula demonstrated the organization's advocacy effectiveness" (Society for Children and Youth of B.C., n.d.).

Like the Child Poverty Action Group and, indeed, the vast majority of advocacy organizations, SCY's resources are extremely limited. Its core budget is $65,000 and the expansion of the executive director's work week to four days is relatively recent.

The Ontario Association of Children's Aid Societies

The OACAS is the umbrella organization of children's aid societies in Ontario. Founded in 1912, "OACAS, in support of its members, is the voice of child welfare in Ontario, dedicated to providing leadership for the achievement of excellence in the protection of children and in the promotion of their well-being within their families and communities" (Ontario Association of Children's Aid Societies, 1990a: 4-1). The OACAS represents fifty children's aid societies, each of which appoints a board member to the OACAS board. Given the extent of its membership, a budget of $1.8 million, and a staff of twelve, the OACAS is a force to be reckoned with in child welfare in Ontario.

The OACAS Advocacy Inventory (1991) lists twenty-two ongoing activities during that year. The activities range from specific projects involving, for example, obtaining funds for education and training programs for the staff and foster parents of member agencies, to broader social policy efforts such as increasing provincial funding for child welfare and protesting the decision of the federal government to cap the Canada Assistance Plan.

Parent Rights Organizations

A new phenomenon on the child welfare scene is the emergence of groups of parents who have been inappropriately charged with child abuse. The context for the emergence of these groups is set by two factors: the explosion in the reporting of child abuse coupled with a determination on the part of many jurisdictions to confine child welfare programs to investigating these complaints. In B.C., for example, the number of investigations jumped from 262 in 1975 to 791 in 1979, to 31,429 in 1990-91. However, the number of staff failed to keep pace with the increase in complaints. Indeed, in 1983, at the height of a recession and the beginning of the increase in the number of complaints of both abuse and neglect, the provincial government terminated a family support program that had earlier been hailed as an effective preventive program. (For further discussion, see, among others, Callahan, 1985; Cruickshank, 1985; Wharf, 1985.)

The consequences of a dramatic rise in the number of complaints and an inability to provide support services to families are predictable. Obliged by legislation to ensure that children are protected and lacking options other than apprehension, child welfare workers apprehend. Again, it is patently apparent that under these circumstances some investigations will be hurried and some apprehensions unwarranted. In turn, it is not difficult to understand the reaction of parents who have been falsely accused of child abuse.

One response to such accusation has been the formation of local chapters of the U.S.-based Victims of Child Abuse Laws. At the time of writing a Victoria man accused but never charged with sexually abusing his daughters is attempting to organize a chapter in Victoria. However, according to Lesley Wimberley, the national president of VOCAL in the U.S., "A lot of accused people are very afraid to come to a public meeting. They feel they will be ostracized if anyone finds out they have been accused of such a heinous deed" (Dedyna, 1992). This reluctance to become involved has hampered the organizing efforts of VOCAL, and at least in Canada, VOCAL chapters have been slow to emerge. In view of the antagonistic relationship between parent rights groups and the child welfare system, there has been no opportunity to work together in reform actions that would benefit children and parents.

COMMUNITY GOVERNANCE

The fourth example of a constituency for child welfare is community governance. In this model, control of child welfare services is delegated to an organization governed by a board of directors consisting of locally elected citizens. Perhaps the best-known examples of this arrangement in the human services are the boards of education that exist in most provinces. These school boards are composed of citizens who run for election at the same time as candidates for municipal government. With resources provided by and within a legislative context set by provincial governments, they are responsible for elementary and high school education in defined geographic areas. (The funding arrangements for school boards vary across the country. In some jurisdictions the province funds the costs of elementary and secondary education; in other provinces funding is shared between the provincial and municipal governments.) Other examples of community governance are the Children's Aid Society structure and the local health and social service centres in Quebec. The case for community governance is summarized by Cassidy:

Community organizations have more access to local information: they frequently have the advantage of a long memory and of the collective family histories of those most deeply involved in various activities.

Commitment to and the chance of success are greatly strengthened when those who have to live with the outcomes of governmental activities are involved in decisive ways in such activities.

The need for transactions between external and local parties is reduced and as a result programs and service tend to be more appropriate, efficient and effective.

More integration between government strategies, programs and services takes place as citizens rather than bureaucracies assert their needs.

Involved publics are more aware of community problems and the resources which might be available to address them. (Cassidy, 1991: 18)

Various approaches to and understandings of community governance have been developed. For example, Rein identifies three variations of local governance: political decentralization, where policy-making authority is devolved to local units; geographic decentralization, which requires locating service units in a community or neighbourhood; and administrative decentralization, which grants a degree of autonomy to the staff of local offices (Rein, 1972).

Our approach is derived from but extends the above framework. Community governance requires three components: decentralized services, delegated control, and a community work approach to practice. Hence, rather than distinguishing among these dimensions, as in the Rein framework, they are seen as mutually reinforcing aspects of community governance.

The discussion here is concerned with statutory child welfare services. However, some useful organizational precedents can be found in the voluntary sector. Agencies like transition houses and sexual assault centres are governed by women rather than by residents of a particular geographic area. The concept of community governance, thus, can embrace rule by a constituency (a community of interest) as well as control by residents. It is quite possible and indeed desirable, therefore, that transition houses and First Nation band councils take on the responsibility of governing child welfare services. Chapter 7 elaborates on this notion in some detail.

Decentralized Services

The uniform pattern of services in child welfare, whereby services are provided either by offices of provincial ministries or children's aid societies, does not allow comparisons of the outcomes of different structures. However, one opportunity occurred when the provincial government in Manitoba embarked on a large-scale reform of child welfare in Metropolitan Winnipeg. The Children's Aid Society was disbanded and six community-based agencies were established.

Regionalization, as the policy change was known, involved a high degree of territorial decentralization, substantial administrative decentralization and partial political decentralization. Powers related to legislation and policy formation, the provision of financial resources and accountability for service standards were retained by the province and these limited the extent to which agencies were in fact politically and administratively decentralized.

However, accountability to the community was strengthened by the adoption of a governance structure which included an elected board from the agency's geographic region. . . . By the summer of 1985 child and family services were being offered from more than twenty sites throughout Winnipeg. (McKenzie, 1991: 59)

This decentralized service structure was accompanied by the adoption of a community work approach whereby the staff of neighbourhood offices involved consumers and residents in developing programs to support families, and by a "user-friendly" approach to service. The consequence of increased accessibility in both geographic and service terms became evident in a relatively short period of time.

During the first three years of the decentralized service system the numbers of families served by homemakers more than doubled (112 percent) and this was substantially higher than the increase reported outside Winnipeg (62.9 per cent).

Interview results indicated that there was a substantial increase in voluntary counselling services provided to families in the first two years of the community-based system.

There was an increase in the use of voluntary agreements between parents and child welfare authorities in the provision of substitute care and greater use of short-term placements. There were also fewer contested hearings and more co-operative relationships between social workers and agency clients. (*ibid.*: 61)

Indeed, the creation of community or neighbourhood offices with a low level of bureaucratization is eminently sensible for child welfare services. Both staff and consumers prefer small, informal agencies in which they feel welcome and can exercise some influence over day-to-day operations.

Delegated Control

Five experiences with delegated control of child welfare services are outlined below: the Children's Aid Society structure in Ontario; First Nation control; the integrated service structure in Quebec; and the relatively brief experiences in B.C and Manitoba.

As noted in Chapter 1, children's aid societies have provided child welfare services in Ontario since 1893 and constitute a well-established and integral component in the provincial pattern of services. Certainly none of the task forces and commissions established to inquire into the age-old issue of co-ordination of services and the appropriateness of dividing the responsibility for health and social services among the province, county, and municipal governments and voluntary agencies has called for the elimination of children's aid societies. And the list of inquiries is a long one. In relatively recent memory it includes a succession of discussion papers prepared by the Ministry of Community and Social Services in the 1970s, and the reports of the Provincial/Municipal Social Services Review (1990) and the Advisory Committee on Children's Services (1990). The latter report recommended a strengthening of community responsibility:

> The Ontario government must establish locally elected children's authorities that have responsibility for planning, systems management and resource allocation for social, educational, health and recreational services for children within their areas of jurisdiction. These authorities must be accountable to the provincial children's authority and to their communities. (Advisory Committee on Children's Services, 1990: 121)

One of the few attempts to articulate the advantages of the CAS structure is contained in a brief compiled by the Ontario Association of Children's Aid Societies to a task force assembled in 1973 to review social services in Ontario. The brief pointed to the innovative projects developed by CASs, to the number of volunteers serving as board members (1,000) and in a direct service capacity (4,000), and to the capacity of CASs to assume an advocacy role on behalf of children. The brief concluded by stating:

Ontario, with its 50 children's aid societies, leads all other provinces in innovative programming in the field of child welfare. This province has a smaller number of children in care per capita than any other in Canada. (Ontario Association of Children's Aid Societies, 1973)

During the next decade all provinces succeeded in lowering the number of children in care, but, as noted in Chapter 2, by 1986 Ontario still had the fewest children in care with 4.5 per 1,000.

It is regrettable that the OACAS has not been able to prepare reports similar to the one noted above on a regular basis. Given that Ontario is the only province with a long history of delegated control in child welfare, information on projects developed for and with communities and on the advocacy efforts of CASs would be invaluable for the continuing development of child welfare services. Nevertheless, Ontario has the most progressive child welfare legislation in the country, has always had the lowest percentage of children in care, and has led the way in innovative approaches to practice. It is no coincidence that this record of achievement has been accomplished in a province characterized by community governance and a strong advocacy organization at the provincial level.

Chapter 5 presents a detailed account of First Nation experiences in governing child welfare services, and it is unnecessary to foreshadow that discussion here. Suffice it to say that in their relatively brief experience with control of child welfare services First Nations have demonstrated a capacity to care for neglected and abused children in their own communities. One review noted that First Nation communities have transformed the hitherto sacrosanct notion of permanent planning by developing "a flowing pattern whereby a succession of substitute care homes are used, all with the objective of keeping the child in the community he/she knows and calls home" (Armitage et al., 1988). Nevertheless, First Nations have experienced some troubles in governing child welfare, and these are noted in a later section of the chapter.

The Quebec arrangement of regional and local health and social service centres has been in place since the mid-seventies. Although widely and deservedly credited with bringing health and social services out of the Dark Ages into the twentieth century, the promise of achieving local control through elected boards has been realized only in a very incomplete and partial fashion.

The local Community Service Centres were confronted with a technocratic impatience to centralize, which could not tolerate diversity for very long, or with the heterogeneity of health and social practices developed through interaction with different clienteles. . . . The history of the Regional Health and Social Service Councils is a prime example. These councils remained an extension of the Ministry and in no way represented regional interest. (Lesemann, 1987: 167)

The Community Resource Board legislation in B.C. was in place for a scant four years before being repealed. It sought to establish a pattern of integrated and decentralized services governed by boards of locally elected citizens, but was implemented in a fully formed fashion only in Vancouver and in four communities where out-patient health and social services were brought together. One review of the experience commented that:

Regardless of the eventual legacy of the Community Resource Boards it is indisputable that they were an unqualified success in arousing energy and generating excitement about the human services where little had existed before and little remains today. The reforms provoked professionals to think about new ways of delivering services and provided an opportunity for large numbers of citizens to learn about and contribute to the human services. (Clague *et al.*, 1984: 288)

The earlier discussion of the Manitoba reforms indicated that the regional approach resulted in accessible and well-utilized services and in the development of family support and other preventive programs.

The demonstrated benefits of decentralized, community-based child and family services included increased community participation and improved service responsiveness. . . . Despite many limitations, regionalization was associated with more positive relationships with parents, increased use of family-based methods of substitute care, a reduction in the long-term separation of children from their parents and an increase in the utilization of local community resources where placement was required.
The influence of community-based boards and other interest groups can have an important effect on whether services advance principles of equity and justice. In this case community boards were instrumental in influencing service innovation and in pressing for the necessary resources to meet new service demands. (McKenzie, 1991: 64)

Indeed, regionalization may well have been too successful. In 1991 the Progressive Conservative government that inherited regionalization from its NDP predecessor collapsed the six regional child and family centres into one metropolitan structure. In a telephone interview with the author, a senior official in the Ministry of Community Services acknowledged that the new minister wished to deal with one rather than six agencies all clamouring for increased resources. The regional structure was seen as too messy and too vigorous in its demands for improved services. The official announcement indicated only that the new structure would be more efficient and gave few details. Since the decision occurred without warning and in the month of August, when many board members were away from the city on vacation, this ambitious regionalization reform ended without protest.

THE COMMUNITY WORK APPROACH

Relatively little of the practice literature in child welfare addresses either community work or organizational innovation by line staff.... For the Child Welfare worker in particular, community work, including efforts to introduce organizational and institutional innovations and to influence public policy on behalf of children and their parents, must become a central concern of practice. (Germain, 1985: 122)

Previous chapters have described the extent to which environments shape behaviour and the difficulties facing child welfare agencies that try to change environments. These difficulties include staff whose educational preparation has led them to frame problems in individual terms. An example will illustrate the point.

A woman came to the agency asking that her three children be taken into care temporarily. Her former husband had returned the children without advance notice, thus breaking their agreement that he would look after the children for a specified period while she was getting her life together. She was living in one room, had a low-paying job, and had neither the space nor the money to provide for her children.

When the student social worker discussed this woman's request for temporary care with the agency supervisor, a humane and progressive man, she was asked to appraise the client's "real motivation" to look after her children. The supervisor felt that if [she] . . . really wanted to be a mother, she would find suitable housing and child care – this in a city where housing for low-income people was very scarce. . . .

Later, when the oldest child had to be taken into care . . . the student was advised not to record housing as the reason. . . . The agency, it was explained, did not take children into care . . . because of housing. . . . The woman's depression, her disorganization in crisis, and the stress she was under were suggested as the real reasons for temporary foster placement. (Gilroy, 1990: 63-64)

A more apt illustration of the conversion of a public issue (the lack of affordable housing) into a private trouble (the depressed state of the client) would be difficult to find.

The predisposition to frame problems in individual terms is reinforced by the crisis-oriented nature of child welfare practice. It is difficult to give attention to environmental issues when a succession of crises occupies the time and attention of staff. In turn, both of these influences are shaped by the prevailing residual approach to policy that restricts child welfare agencies to the behaviour of individuals while neglecting the need for environmental changes.

The community work approach outlined here is anchored in a perspective that reframes both the mandate and the traditional relationship between staff and clients. It is acknowledged that implementing this reframing will encounter resistance. The enlargement of mandates will be opposed by many policy-makers, particularly those of a residual cast. The revision of the relationship may be difficult for professionals who, because of their own oppressed state, have neither the time nor the inclination to treat clients as partners in a common enterprise (see Lipsky, 1980; Callahan and Attridge, 1990). Nevertheless, the consumer is viewed here as an important contributor who possesses the most complete information about her situation and whose active involvement in the process of change will play an important part in determining success or failure.

Community work has been conceptualized in a variety of ways. The first attempts relied on the work of community organization theorists such as Murray Ross and Ben Lappin of the School of Social Work at the University of Toronto (Ross and Lappin, 1967). Their approach was based in a largely benevolent view of power and its distribution in society. It emphasized the importance of a developmental process whereby residents would take charge of their neighbourhood and be able to bring about significant changes in their environment. The Ross and Lappin approach was implemented in only a few child welfare agencies, with some notable examples occuring in children's aid societies in Ontario (Barr, 1979; McEachern and Harris, 1973).

This approach to community work has been described by Rothman as "locality development." Together with similar conceptualizations such as ecological theory, locality development represents an attempt to place private troubles within the context of public issues. But such a placement is at best partial, and, as will become evident in forthcoming chapters, these conceptualizations fail to address the issues of class, race, and gender and are nested within a largely benevolent view of power. Thus, if individuals and communities are empowered to take charge and if accurate research reports documenting the impact of poverty on children are brought to the attention of policy-makers, changes will occur.

A second and very different conceptualization of community work came from Saul Alinsky and related most directly to urban neighbourhoods in the United States (Alinsky, 1969, 1971). Alinsky's social action approach was rooted in an analysis of power that argued that the conditions of poverty and poor housing resulted from a deliberate oppression of the poor by the elite. Hence, the primary change strategy advocated by Alinsky was to wrest concessions from municipal officials and corporations by organizing strikes and demonstrations and by slowing down, if not immobilizing, the work of oppressive organizations such as banks, industries, and public bureaucracies. In Canada social action strategies were practised primarily by welfare rights organizations and other protest-oriented groups and have not featured prominently as an approach to community work practice in child welfare. Such strategies are entirely appropriate for social movements and for parents' rights groups such as VOCAL. While they are beyond the pale for the professional child welfare worker in her role as a staff member of a child welfare agency, workers can use these strategies to protest the inadequacy of resources and poor working conditions as members of a feminist organization or a union.

In sum, locality development is an appropriate and useful strategy for child welfare agencies. It can be and has been used to ground staff in the realities of the day-to-day living of their clients (Barr, 1979), to create safe neighbourhoods (Wilson and Kelling, 1989), and to develop social support networks (Whittaker, 1983). It is, in short, an extremely useful strategy for dealing with the "ordinary issues of social policy," but it is wholly unable to come to grips with the "grand issues" (Lindblom, 1979). Locality development is necessary because it is one very useful way of binding staff and consumers together and because it can bring about some changes in local environments. But it is insufficient because it abides by and fails to challenge the conventional wisdom in child welfare. Some of the strongest challenges have come from feminists and First Nations people, as will be discussed in later chapters.

The Effectiveness of Community Governance

Given the limited experience with community governance in Canada it is not possible to arrive at an unequivocal assessment of effectiveness. The evidence is scanty but is nevertheless sufficient to persuade us that community governance is preferable to the existing structures of provincial control. The first plank in the argument is built by Cassidy's enumeration of the advantages of community governance. The second plank is derived from the contention that the existing structures are completely unsatisfactory and must be reformed. The evidence for this assertion was assembled in previous chapters and is confirmed by a review conducted by the Laidlaw Foundation. The review concluded that "There is an inertia in the mainstream institutions on how to reorient protective services and programs. . . . Protective programs within mainstream agencies were rarely cited as best practice models" (Laidlaw Foundation, 1990: 32-35).

Child welfare, however, should not be completely controlled by communities. We agree with the recommendations of many reviews of the present arrangements for delivering social services that provincial governments must be responsible for establishing legislation and overall policy, setting budgets and allocating funds to community agencies, establishing and monitoring standards of services, and operating specialized services (see Clague et al., 1984). But the responsibility for providing services and for contributing to policy and legislation on the basis of the knowledge and experience gained by delivering services should be delegated to agencies located in and governed by communities.

Such partnerships are unevenly balanced because the control of funds and legislation is vested in the province, and the arrangement is frequently characterized by squabbles about the allocation of resources and the appropriateness of existing policies. In particular, a continuing and frequently divisive controversy revolves around whether the responsibility of the province to monitor standards constitutes a necessary exercise or an unwelcome intrusion into local affairs. While difficult to manage, the standard-setting and monitoring function constitutes a substantial guarantee against the emergence of the condition of acute localitis (Montgomery, 1979). Acute localitis refers to the possibility that if left to their own devices, communities might become so isolated and insulated that their standards vis-à-vis the care of children or health conditions would violate national and provincial standards. Examples that spring to mind are communities of Jehovah's Witnesses, which forbid blood transfusions, and isolated communities that have allowed incest and the sexual abuse of children to become a normal condition of life (Beltrane, 1985; Wood, 1986). Despite the management problems that the partnership structure inevitably creates it contains the very distinct advantage that two structures, a community agency and a provincial ministry, are both intimately concerned about and committed to the cause of child welfare.

However, the partnership arrangements outlined above cannot be applied to First Nations. While some of our earlier writings may have indicated agreement with the arrangement whereby provinces delegate authority to First Nations, we are now persuaded that the First Nation right to self-government, including child welfare, is inherent and cannot, therefore, be delegated or transferred from other governments (Armitage *et al.*, 1988; Wharf, 1989).

Yet it is clear that First Nation communities are not immune to the condition of acute localitis. An investigation carried out by Justice Brian Giesbrecht in Manitoba revealed many instances of child abuse in communities where child welfare services were governed by band councils (Giesbrecht, 1992). Similar stories of children being abused by men and in some instances by chiefs or others in positions of authority were told in a series of investigative reports by the Victoria *Times Colonist* in July, 1992. And in September a hereditary chief in Port Alberni was jailed for three years after pleading guilty to charges of repeated sexual assault of a young child between 1983 and 1985. In this case the family and child service agency of the Nuu-chah-nulth tribal council did bring charges against the chief.

"People are angry we are sending people to jail. But there has to be consequences to their actions," said Debby Foxcroft, a member of the band and social worker with the Nuu-chah-nulth tribal council.... "We have incidents of five generations of abuse in a single family. But my vision is that the next generation will be healthy, happy and free from abuse." (Nathan, 1992)

While the condition of acute localitis does obtain in First Nation communities, it is inappropriate to attempt to overcome this condition by imposing the standards of "white" provincial ministries. Rather, as Hudson and Taylor-Henley suggest,

> there should be some kind of mechanism which enables those trapped in a conspiracy of silence in their communities access to some body external to the community and the service agency. This body would need investigative and decision-making powers and be independent of the First Nations and aboriginal political structures. (Hudson and Taylor-Henley, 1992)

THE INFLUENCE OF THE MEDIA

While not an organized constituency in the same sense as advisory councils, advocacy organizations, and community governance structures, a discussion of forces affecting child welfare would not be complete without mentioning the media. Indeed, while their attention to and reports of child welfare have all too often been characterized by sensationalism, the media have performed an important function in holding up child welfare practice to public scrutiny.

The interest of the media has been sparked by the changes in child welfare over the past two decades. From a field of service characterized by the adoption of the children of unmarried mothers and the supervision of wards in long-term foster care, interrupted only rarely by the occasional report of child neglect and abuse, child welfare is now dominated by serious allegations of neglect and abuse. When parents dispute allegations made against them, when adults disclose that they were sexually abused as children by natural or foster parents or by caretakers in charge of residential schools, and when allegations take the form of criminal complaints, their actions shift the formerly private world of child welfare into the public domain and in turn arouse the interest of the media.

Some indication of the turbulent world of child welfare and the determination of one newspaper not to let the turbulence go unrecorded can be found in the coverage of child welfare by the Vancouver *Province* in 1985. Between January and May the *Province* gave extensive coverage to nine serious cases of physical and sexual abuse. Many of these reports were featured on the front page with banner headlines such as "The Ministry of Human Resources bungles again." The minister and her deputy became so incensed at this "media persecution" that they met with the publisher to demand the paper cease its unrelenting attacks on the ministry – a not atypical attack on the messenger! (For reviews of child welfare in B.C., including media coverage, see Armitage, 1989; Callahan, 1985, 1989; Cruikshank, 1985; Wharf, 1985.)

The interest of the media in child welfare has been displayed in a variety of forms: newspaper coverage of abuse cases, magazine stories and documentaries devoted to street kids and young prostitutes, and books such as *Ritual Abuse* (Marron, 1988), *Unholy Orders: The Mt. Cashel Story* (Harris, 1990), and *Nobody's Children* (Kendrick, 1990).

Space does not permit a detailed portrayal of media coverage of child welfare. Rather, it is our contention that the media have made a distinct contribution by taking child welfare into the public domain. In the absence of appeal mechanisms in child welfare (except, of course, through the court system) and of strong advocacy organizations, the media often serve as a forum of last appeal. Thus newspaper reporters and editors frequently receive calls from distraught parents whose children have been removed and who have been accused of neglecting their children and investigated by staff of the local child welfare agency. While some complaints are based on serious instances of abuse or neglect, others, from estranged spouses or hostile neighbours, are launched from motives of revenge.

After taking such calls newspaper reporters try to elicit information from child welfare staff to separate fact from fiction. However, child welfare staff are prohibited by legislation from providing any information about a client or an investigation. The policy of confidentiality that protects both complainants and clients is not without foundation. It ensures that complainants need not fear reprisal from those they accuse of neglect and abuse and that the private world of family relationships does not become a matter for public gossip.

There is a remarkable and hitherto unnoticed parallel between the discretion exercised by child welfare workers and by journalists. In some instances child welfare workers have to decide whether to remove a child on the basis of information obtained from a complainant and impressions from a first visit. Similarly, after hearing only one side of the story, journalists must decide whether to take a parent's story seriously and display it on the front page. To a large extent both are hampered by the policy of confidentiality. The child welfare worker cannot disclose the identity of the complainant and hence is unable to gain the client's views with regard to the motivation underlying the complaint. In addition, she cannot release information to the journalist, and as a consequence media coverage lacks complete and accurate information.

The point is forcefully illustrated by a set of stories that appeared in *British Columbia Report* about the Balfour family in Coquitlam, B.C. The ten-year-old daughter of the Balfours was removed from their home because of a report that Mr. Balfour had sexually abused his daughter. "Who made this complaint, asked the flabbergasted couple. The social worker could not say. It was anonymous, she explained" (Burnham, 1990a: 12). Later, when the reporter sought an explanation, "A Social Services spokesman [*sic*] had no comment. The matter, she explained, is before the courts" (Burnham, 1990b: 23).

While professionals have often criticized the sensational nature of media reports of child welfare, they of all people should recognize that reporters are as encumbered by ideologies and personal belief systems in developing an approach to child welfare as are policy-makers and professional staff. Some journals, such as *British Columbia Report*, have taken a residual position and view child welfare policy as an unnecessary intrusion into family affairs. Thus, typical headlines in this journal include "Fighting government child grabbers" and "Socreds back the family, whack landlords and social workers." Other journals and newspapers have adopted a reformist role by investigating such contentious and complicated matters as the plight of street kids. Still others take seriously the responsibility to report the difficulties experienced by parents faced with unwarranted and unsubstantiated allegations of neglect.

We suggest that child welfare policy and practice should not be characterized by complete and slavish adherence to the principle of confidentiality. In the first place, confidentiality prohibits the possibility of social learning; the public is unaware of the reasons for apprehension and knows little about the difficulties facing child welfare workers, such as those described in Chapter 3. One consequence of the lack of information is that child welfare staff and agencies are blamed both for premature and unwarranted apprehension and for not intervening in situations that result in further injury or death. In turn, this lack of understanding results in hostility toward workers and agencies and a consequent refusal to support reforms and to award additional resources for prevention and protection services.

It is possible that community-governed agencies would allow press coverage of board meetings in the same way that the press now attends meetings of municipal councils and boards of education. But the most drastic change in confidentiality will occur if the reforms outlined in the following chapters are adopted. If, as we suggest in the following chapters, neglect is eliminated from the statutes and abuse is dealt with by the criminal justice system, the relationships between clients and staff will be fundamentally changed. Child welfare services will focus on supporting rather than investigating parents. In addition, the press will be able to cover the criminal proceedings of child abuse since these will be placed in the public domain of the courts.

To conclude, it is clear from the foregoing discussion that child welfare is too important to remain closeted within provincial ministries. We have become all too aware in recent times of the deviant behaviour that can occur in closed structures, despite the very best of intentions. While residential schools were "total institutions" (Goffman, 1961) that were effectively closed from the view of the public, provincial ministries have conducted and continue to conduct the business of child welfare in secrecy. Indeed, only the courts and the media have presented opportunities for the public to learn about child welfare, and neither is entirely satisfactory.

The agencies and associations discussed in this chapter have a very positive contribution to make in opening up child welfare. Their contributions are different and it should not be assumed that one structure will suffice. Advisory councils can promote the cause of child welfare by enlarging the scope of participation, by extending the range of information, and by suggesting reforms. Advocacy groups can conduct research and, on the basis of their findings, conduct campaigns for change. The most powerful structure, community governance, possesses the capacity to tune services to local needs and on the basis of their experience contribute to the development of provincial legislation and policy.

Yet the quotation at the beginning of the chapter remains as a telling observation on the health of policy communities in child welfare. To be sure, organizations such as the Vanier Institute, the Laidlaw Foundation, the Canadian Council on Social Development, and the Child Poverty Action Group have made valiant efforts to improve the lot of children in Canada. But their efforts are hampered by meagre funding, and the collapse of the Canadian Child Welfare Association and the Canadian Council on Children and Youth attests to the absence of public-sector commitment to policy communities in this country. Unfortunately, the likelihood of firmly funded policy communities being established in the near future is dim. We return to this discussion in the final chapter.

Part II

New Directions for Child Welfare

Chapter 5

Family and Child Welfare in First Nation Communities

Andrew Armitage

From the passage of the Indian Act in 1876 until the 1960s child welfare for First Nations people in Canada was dominated by the policy of assimilation, which used educational methods to change the culture and character of their children. Church-operated residential schools were the central institution used in this strategy. When the policy of assimilation was replaced by the policy of integration, the residential schools were replaced by the child welfare strategy in a second attempt to ensure that the next generation of Indian children was different from their parents. Children separated from parents considered by child welfare authorities to be negligent or abusive were raised in foster care or adopted. In the current period of movement toward self-government many First Nations communities are taking control of their own child welfare programs to ensure that the next generation of Indian children is raised in their own communities and culture. This chapter examines the principal phases of this history with a particular focus on the reasons for past and present policy and the extent of the impact of these policies on First Nations people.

CHILD WELFARE JURISDICTION AND FIRST NATIONS PEOPLE

The Canadian constitution established family and child welfare as a provincial jurisdiction. However, responsibility for First Nations people, and specifically for status Indians, is federal. As federal law and constitutional obligations take precedence over provincial ones, the federal government has the primary responsibility for establishing family and child welfare policy and programs for status Indians.

Until the 1960s federal authority was directly exercised, but since the early 1960s the federal authority for family and child welfare policy for status Indians has been delegated to the provinces. Nevertheless, the consistency with which the Department of Indian Affairs has acted has resulted in similar developments in Indian child and family services throughout Canada. The differences that exist are a combination of differences between Indian people's culture, history, and closeness to non-Native settlement and differences in provincial child welfare policies. To discuss provincial and territorial variations fully would entail separate discussion of each of the ten provinces and two territories. Therefore the provinces of British Columbia and Manitoba and the Yukon Territory have been chosen to illustrate the variations in policy and practice.[1]

In Manitoba, status Indians comprise 8 per cent of the population, and at least another 8 per cent are Métis or non-status Indians. Manitoba is a prairie province in which Indian land was ceded to the Crown by treaty. In the early 1980s Manitoba Indians developed a series of child welfare agreements with the province and the federal government. These were the first of their type and offer one comprehensive model for providing First Nations with authority for child welfare.

British Columbia has a smaller proportion of First Nations people, 4.6 per cent, and few Métis. In British Columbia, Indian land was annexed by the British Parliament, without treaty or discussion with most of the First Nations people who were living in the province (McEachern, 1990). Although child welfare agreements have been developed in the late 1980s with some of the Native peoples of British Columbia, the approach is much more varied than in Manitoba, comprehensiveness is lacking, and Native support for the delegation of provincial child welfare authority is not universal.

The Yukon provides an example of a remote area where status Indians form 21 per cent of the population and where, until the Second World War, many First Nations people were left relatively untouched by the Canadian government. A child welfare agreement exists with one of the Yukon Indian bands. In addition, the Yukon illustrates some of the difficulties that remote and small communities have in assuming authority for child welfare.

In the 1960s provincial authority was extended to Indian people living on reserve land through the operation of Section 88 of the Indian Act. This section has the effect of incorporating into the Indian Act all provincial law not contrary or alternative to federal law. Section 88 does not, however, have the effect of transferring any fiscal obligation to the provinces from the federal government. As a result the federal government remains responsible for the cost of all services to status Indians. As the provinces rarely fund services to Indians from their own revenue, family and child welfare programming for status Indians is determined by the services the federal government is prepared to fund.

In addition to status Indians living on reserve, the Canadian constitution recognizes that the Inuit, Métis, and non-status Indians also have rights that predate Confederation. There are at least as many Inuit, Métis, and non-status First Nation peoples who receive service as provincial residents. In recent times they, too, have increasingly sought distinct institutions sensitive to their culture and heritage.[2] However, this chapter deals principally with family and child welfare measures for status Indians, who have been the subject of separate law, separate programs, and separate institutions.

As all status Indians are registered there are separate records on their rights, location, band membership, and children and on services provided to them. The records were initially developed as a record of band members and of the obligations of the Crown pursuant to treaties with Indian peoples. When the objective of assimilation was being pursued the records were used to show the progress that Indian people were making toward this goal. In the latest period the records reflect the financial obligations of the federal government to reimburse the provinces for service to status Indians.

From 1867 to the 1960s family and child welfare policy toward status Indians was an integral part of the general Canadian social policy of assimilation. In the 1960s this was gradually replaced by a policy of integrating services to status Indians with services to non-Natives. More recently, in the 1980s policy changed again to favour some degree of community and administrative self-government under the terms of tripartite (federal-provincial-band/tribal council) agreements (Cassidy and Bish, 1989).

These three principal stages of Indian family and child welfare policy are each characterized by differences in policy, law, and administration. The stages provide the framework for this chapter. Discussion of regional and provincial variations among British Columbia, Manitoba, and the Yukon principally deal with the latest period, during which First Nation peoples have had a more active role in initiating changes.

POLICY AND PRACTICE IN THE ASSIMILATION PERIOD: 1867-1960

The foundation for family and child welfare policy toward Natives in the assimilation period was provided by early Christian missionary endeavours. These had been endorsed by the Bagot Commission, which was established in 1842 to provide guidance to colonial Indian policy in the period leading up to Confederation. The Commission concluded that day schools were inadequate to the task of assimilating the Indian children. Canadian historian J.R. Miller summarizes the Commission's argument, which recognized a problem with earlier Indian schooling policies in which the children had remained under

> . . . the influence that parents exerted when the young scholars returned from class. It recommended the establishment of boarding schools with farms in which children could be taught agriculture or a trade, assimilated in the absence of a parent's influence, equipped to forgo annual presents, and readied to take up individual plots of land under freehold tenure. (Miller, 1989: 106)

This early conclusion was confirmed by the Davin Report of 1879. Residential school historian Jean Barman indicates the Report's effect:

> The Davin Report approved American practice with the proviso that schools be operated so far as possible by missionaries, who had already demonstrated their commitment to "civilising" Canada's Indians. The Department of Indian Affairs accepted the proposal. Preference was given to the creation of large industrial residential schools located away from reserves, and, a few years later, to boarding schools nearer reserves for younger children. There, attendance would be ensured, and all aspects of life, from dress to use of English language to behavior, would be carefully regulated. (Barman, 1986)

While day schools were used they were considered to be less satisfactory because of the greater influence of parents and the problems of maintaining attendance.

Initially the Indian response to educational opportunity for their children was positive, but this did not extend to the deliberate attempt being made to reshape the lives of their children (Miller, 1989: 107). Nor were the early results as fruitful as expected. Duncan Campbell Scott, a leading Indian Affairs official, noted in 1913 that the "most promising pupils are found to have retrograded and to have become leaders in the pagan life of the reserves" (Scott, 1913: 615).

The response of the Indian Affairs Branch was to decide that the early policy, with its assumption of assimilation and civilization within one generation, was too optimistic. The Department of Indian Affairs Annual Report (1897) notes that

> only the certainty of some practical result can justify the large expense entailed upon the country by the maintenance of these schools. To educate children above the possibilities of their station, and to create a distaste for what is certain to be their environment in life would be not only a waste of time but doing an injury instead of confirming a benefit on them.

In 1904 the Minister of Indian Affairs, Clifford Sifton, was equally forthright when he said in Parliament:

> I have no hesitation in saying – we may as well be frank – that the Indian can not go out from school, making his own way and competing with the white man. . . . He has not the physical, mental or moral get-up to enable him to compete. He cannot do it. (Hall, 1971)

These concerns were reflected in a new, more frugal policy introduced in 1910. Barman uses excerpts from Duncan Campbell Scott to document the change to a policy intended

> to fit the Indian for civilised life in his own environment. . . . To this end the curriculum in residential schools has been simplified, and the practical instruction given is such as may be immediately of use to the pupil when he returns to the reserve after leaving the school. . . . Local Indian agents should carefully select the most favourable location for ex-pupils [with] most careful thought given to the future of female pupils . . . protected in so far as possible from the temptations to which they are often exposed. . . . (Barman, 1986: 120)

The temptations were seen as coming from white men of "the lowest type" to whom the girls were exposed because the previous curriculum of the residential schools had made "the girls . . . too smart for the Indian villages."

Chief Assu of the Cape Mudge band in British Columbia recalls the result of this attitude in his own experience.

> We got our start on education through the church school on the reserve and in the [residential] schools run by the churches in Port Alberni, Chilliwack and Alert Bay. The trouble was that Indians were only allowed to go to grade nine, and then had to get out. . . . I wanted my boys to go to high school so I went to see the Indian agent, M.S. Todd, and told him so. He said to me, "Nothing doing!" I asked him, "Isn't it for everybody?" and he answered me, "Not for you people." (Assu and Inglis, 1989: 95-96)

Indian education was provided by the churches, which received operating grants from the federal government. The approach to Indian education expressed by the Indian agent and by Sifton and Scott was not unwelcome to the churches. The churches' objective was the establishment of their own form of "Christian citizenship" (Grant, 1984: 185). Paganism had first to be defeated, but beyond that there was the opportunity to build a more perfect world, insulated to some extent from the mainstream of Canadian society. Assimilation to a society in which white people were too often greedy, drunk, and immoral was not the objective of the enterprise. The Roman Catholics combined this objective with the additional objective of keeping Indian people apart from the influence of the Protestant majority in English Canada.

Collaboration between church and state was close. The government payment for education served to support an organized church authority that was much stronger and larger than would have been possible on missionary donations. In addition, church officials often assumed roles as magistrates, school inspectors, and Indian Affairs officials, serving to extend their power. Bishop George Thonloe of Algoma noted "the very fact of the civil power being behind would, in the main, suffice to make clerical supervision more efficient" (*ibid.*).

On the west coast of British Columbia this partnership was brought into effect in an attempt to destroy the system of arranged marriages and "potlatch" feasts, which were central to coastal Indian culture. Halliday, the Indian agent in Alert Bay, wrote:

> No boy who has been trained at the Industrial School can get a wife by wooing her and following the ideas he has learned at school but must go back to the potlatch to buy one. One lad in

speaking on this point said to me that one might as well be a eunuch as keep out of the potlatch. (Cole and Chaikin, 1990: 50)

The assault on the potlatch and on coastal Indian culture culminated in Alert Bay in 1922 with a series of trials of Indian people on charges of potlatching. Those convicted were imprisoned and the regalia, dancing gear, and copper plates (a traditional symbol of wealth used in the feast) were all confiscated. Shortly afterwards, in 1924, a new two-storey brick residential school was opened and all the school-age children were confined to the school and its immediate fenced grounds.[3]

After World War Two the concept of a separate set of segregated social institutions for Indian people was called into question. The Special Joint Committee of the Senate and House of Commons, which reviewed the Indian Act (1946-48), was urged to abolish separate Indian schools and the revised Indian Act of 1951 committed the federal government to the integration of Indian people into Canadian society. The new Act provided authority for the federal government to negotiate agreements with the provinces for services to Indians, including education.

Nevertheless, the role of the residential school in the suppression of Indian culture and in the preparation of Indian children for Christian civilization continued into the 1960s. Table 5.1 shows the extent of the residential school system that operated from the 1890s to the 1960s.

Table 5.1 indicates several important features of the overall pattern of Indian education during the residential school period.
(1) In any one year a substantial number of Indian children between the ages of six and fifteen were not in either residential or day school systems. While a minority of these would have been attending regular provincial schools, many were not in school at all. (2) The low attendance figures for day schools were an important reason why the residential schools were considered superior institutions. (3) At the peak approximately one-third of all Indian children between the ages of six and fifteen were in residential school. Since many children did not stay in residential school beyond the age of twelve the impact of the residential school was felt by at least 50 per cent of Indian children. In some communities this meant that all the children were being removed, while in others the removal was selective.

Residential schools were not evenly distributed throughout Canada. Table 5.2 shows the provincial pattern of distribution and the percentage of Indian children in residential schools in each

Table 5.1

Indian Children in School, 1901-61

Year	Resid. Enrolled	Resid. Average Attend.	Day School Enrolled	Day School Average Attend.	Indian Children 6-15	No./1,000 in Res. Schools
1901	1,698	1,517	7,878	4,600	14,362	118
1906	3,697	3,309	6,391	2,983	14,794	255
1911	3,842	3,382	7,348	3,381	15,590	247
1916	4,661	4,029	8,138	4,051	16,547	282
1921	4,783	4,143	7,775	3,931	17,028	281
1926	6,327	5,658	8,455	4,940	20,969*	301
1931	7,831	6,917	8,584	5,314	22,347*	350
1936	8,906	8,061	9,127	5,788	23,689*	375
1941	8,774	8,243	8,651	6,110	26,854*	330
1946	9,149	8,264	9,656	6,779	28,639*	319
1951	9,357	8,779	15,514	13,526	31,052*	301
1956	10,501	9,378	17,947	16,254	38,565*	272
1961	8,391		20,896		50,292*	166

*Numbers of Indian children estimated from counts taken in non-census years.

SOURCE: *Canada Yearbook.*

Table 5.2
Residential and Day Schools by Province, 1936

Province	Resid. School Enrolment	Day School Enrolment	Total School Enrolment	% Res. School of Total Enrolment
B.C.	2,163	1,633	3,796	57
Alberta	1,917	37	1,954	98
Sask.	1,735	521	2,256	77
Manitoba	1,009	1,416	2,425	42
Ontario	1,618	2,890	4,508	36
Quebec	55	1,590	1,645	3
N.S.	148	281	429	19*
N.B.	0	330	330	—
P.E.I.	0	20	20	—
N.W.T.	193	66	259	75
Yukon	68	123	192	35

* Percentage of children in residential school in the Altantic region of Indian Affairs is based on enrolment in all three provinces.
SOURCE: Department of Indian Affairs, *Annual Report 1936.*

province. The concentration of residential schools was greatest in the prairie provinces and in British Columbia, while day schools were more common in Ontario and in eastern Canada.

In the North and in the Yukon the philosophy was different. Here the civilizing mission of the churches found little support in the Indian Affairs Branch. Yukon historian Ken Coates characterizes government policy in the territories in the period up until World War Two as "best left as Indians," and writes:

> The federal government's objective for the Yukon Indians departed in several significant respects from declared national objectives in the period before 1945. Several of the elements contained in the Indian Act, including encouraging self sufficiency, protection of natives from white society and support for their Christianization, found their way into Yukon practice although seldom as a result of deliberate administrative decisions. There was, by contrast, no commitment to assimilation. The authorities, even though aware of their power to force change, remained convinced that the Yukon Indians should be left as Indians. (Coates, 1988: 248)

In practice this meant that many Indian children in the territories did not attend school at all. The 259 children reported enrolled in the Northwest Territories in 1936 were drawn from a known school-age population of 847, an enrolment rate of 30 per cent, not including those children who were not enumerated. With the construction of the Alaska Highway as a strategic road during the war, the Yukon and the North became much more accessible. This was also a period in which universal access to services was emphasized. As a result the emphasis in Indian policy in the North became one of enforcing education and settlement.

The Role of the Residential School

The residential school was the central institution of child welfare policy during the assimilation period. The internal operation of the schools followed a similar pattern across Canada. Writing in the 1960s, Native scholar Richard King provides a detailed account of how the typical residential school was run, in his book *The School at Mopass.*[4]

The school at Mopass was the Anglican-operated residential school at Carcross in the Yukon, built in 1946 to hold 150 students between the ages of five and fifteen. The school was the successor to a much smaller residential school that had operated in the Yukon since the gold rush of the 1890s. In 1962-63, when King was a teacher in the school, there were 116 children, only two of whom were older than twelve. The school offered five years of schooling and children left when this was completed. The assignment of children to the school was the complete responsibility of the local Indian agent, who used criteria of family need and responsibility as well as educational grounds.

> Sometimes children are removed from their homes and placed in residential school because of the neglect on the part of their parents who are told that the children will be allowed to stay at home if the parents "straighten up". At other times reluctant parents have been forced to keep their children at home because the agency thought that the sense of responsibility for the children's welfare would have a stabilising effect upon a disintegrating family situation. (King, 1967: 54)

Basil Johnston, who was a pupil in a residential school in northern Ontario in a village named "Spanish," provides a personal account of the effect of these policies on his mother, a single parent, in *Indian School Days*.

The mothers and grandmothers cried and wept, as mine did, in helplessness and heartache. There was nothing, absolutely nothing, that they could do, as women and as Indians, to reverse the decision of "the Department". Already they had suffered the anguish of separating from husbands; now they had to suffer the anguish of being dispossessed of their children; later, they would have to suffer the alienation from the children who were sent away to Spanish. It is no wonder then that when my mother, during a visit to the hospital at Owen Sound, saw the Cape Croker agent who was convalescing there, she expressed the sentiment that she wouldn't give two hoots if he never got better. (Johnston, 1988: 8)

Children went to residential school for ten months of the year. They had to travel long distances, so return was next to impossible once they were there. Children came from all over the Yukon to the Carcross School. The Indian agent collected them in September and returned them in late June. Parents could pay for them to go home at Christmas or Easter, but few did. For a few children the school was their only home because the Indian agent did not approve of their parents.

Within the schools only English could be used as a language and even the Indian names of students were suppressed. At the Carcross school the names recorded were often duplicated when only one English name was available – "Joe" Joseph, "Tommy" Thomas, "Jimmy" James – and always, for ultimate government identification and assurance of payment, the government registration number was used. Internally, the schools were rigidly segregated between areas where children could go and areas that were out of bounds. This included a similar designation of areas in the grounds of the school. Boys were segregated from girls and weekly and daily timetables were tightly regulated. The supervisory staff, usually young priests in training, indicated the end of one activity and the start of another by using a whistle outside and a bell inside.

The curriculum of the school at Carcross was established by adopting the British Columbia "Programme of Studies for Elementary Schools," which contained not one word of Indian content. Although variations were possible, it took an unusual teacher or principal to assemble alternative or additional teaching materials and then persist through the lengthy process of obtaining approval for their use. As a result the curriculum lacked any local content or Indian culture.

Visitors to the school were not encouraged. Richard King noted that

The staff knows that many children are welfare cases and has heard lurid tales of drunkenness , sexual promiscuity and family neglect about various parents. No records are available to show which families are in such categories and which have children in the school simply because the family home is remote. The staff therefore tends to assume that the visitor is in the dissolute category. . . . The visitor is seated on a bench in the open hall-way outside the chapel, and the child or children to be visited are brought to stand before the visitor during the interaction. . . . The visitor hugs the child, repeats its name several times, then sits and talks intermittently until the cumulative discomfort becomes intolerable and the visit ends with another hug, a few pats, and admonitions to be good and to write letters. (King, 1967: 52)

In King's view the school served to reinforce barriers between Indians and the non-Indian community, inducing in the Indians a passive institutionalized behaviour in which their true selves were carefully concealed and the outside world from which they came was romanticized. Basil Johnston confirms this impression with his account of how the boys he knew lived from month to month and year to year with the hope of early release from the schools.[5]

The residential school program was also a failure as an educational preparation, even for those limited roles for which it aimed to prepare children. Basil Johnston writes that one of the school principals at Spanish, Father Oliver, undertook a study in 1945 of the school records from the establishment of the school in 1825. "He found no record of a graduate of the school who had established himself in a business related to his interests [while in the school] or training, be it shoemaking, tailoring, swineherding, shepherding, milling, blacksmithing, chicken raising, dairy farming, canning, barbering, carpentry, plumbing or janitoring." Jean Barman also draws attention to the inequality of the education received by Indians as compared to that of non-Native students (Barman, 1986: 126).

In the end, the residential schools were no preparation for life in any type of community – not for the Indian community from which the children's parents came; not for the urbanized white communities to which some tried to go; not for the idealized Christian community that was in the minds of the missionaries. In a documentary program made by Yukon Indians for the Canadian

Broadcasting Corporation's northern television network, the producers suggest that the residential school best prepared its graduates for other institutional communities, particularly jails and mental hospitals, to which a disproportionate number of the former students, their friends, and peers appeared to have gone.

There is also the difficult subject of the abuse of Indian children within the residential school system. Richard King drew attention to the stories of dishonesty, cruelty, sexual deviance, and promiscuity that circulated in the school at Carcross. Basil Johnston heard similar stories of other schools during his period in the school at Spanish in Ontario. More recently there have been a series of prosecutions based on adults' memories of abuse, principally sexual abuse, as children. The following account from the *Vancouver Sun* concerning the Williams Lake residential school in British Columbia is representative.

> Sellars spent almost nine years at this Catholic run school, where he was not only sexually abused by a priest, but cut off from his family, constantly hungry, frequently strapped, and put down along with his friends as a "dirty little Siwash", a cruel nickname he still does not understand. . . . An Oblate priest and brother have been convicted of sexually abusing more than 15 young natives at St. Joseph's in the 60s, and a third, Prince George Bishop Hubert O'Connor, also an Oblate, stands charged with molesting five young females while he was a supervisor. . . . There was also old fashioned discipline which rarely let up. Girls were strapped if they were caught looking at boys across the segregated playground. Kids were punished by having their hair chopped off. Boys who wet their beds had to wear the urine-stained sheets over their heads. (Todd, 1991)

Finally, the death toll in the residential schools in the earlier years of the century was significant, principally due to tuberculosis, pneumonia, and other epidemic infectious disease to which the children were exposed in the dormitories of the schools. Jean Barman cites one estimate from Scott, in 1902, "that fifty per cent of the children who passed through the schools did not live to benefit from the education they received therein" (Barman, 1986: 8).

POLICY AND PRACTICE DURING THE CHILD WELFARE PERIOD, 1960-80

The transition from the residential school to the child welfare system had begun in the 1950s through a change in the use of residential schools from educational to alternative parenting institutions. The residential school was used as a general welfare resource for the care of children who, in the view of local Indian agents, were not being competently cared for by their parents. (This is perhaps, in part, a commentary on the effects of the residential schools, as these parents were now the second or third generation of former pupils of the schools.)

The separate nature of welfare institutions for status Indians attracted attention during the 1946-48 hearings of the Special Joint Committee of the Senate and House of Commons. In a joint presentation to the Committee by the Canadian Welfare Council and the Canadian Association of Social Workers, the argument was developed that Indian people should enjoy the same services available to other Canadians (Canadian Welfare Council and Canadian Association of Social Workers, 1947). This included the family and child welfare services provided by the provinces. Patrick Johnston summarized the argument of the brief:

> the brief said that "the practice of adopting Indian children is loosely conceived and executed and is usually devoid of the careful legal and social protections available to white children", and as wards of the federal government, "Indian children who are neglected lack the protection afforded under social legislation available to white children in the community". The practice of placing children in residential schools was also condemned.
>
> The brief concluded that the best way to improve the situation was to extend the services of the provincial departments of health, welfare and education to the residents of reserves. (Johnston, 1983: 3)

The argument presented in the submission was accepted by the Joint Committee and led to changes in the Indian Act. The Act, as amended in 1951, provided for provincial health, welfare, and educational services on reserves under the terms of agreements to be negotiated with the provinces.

There were problems with the approach proposed by the Canadian Welfare Council and Canadian Association of Social Workers. In the 1940s family and child welfare services were provided mainly in urban centres. The objective of these services was the best interests of the individual child, which was operationalized through three principal activities:

1. a family service program of counselling and support to families where children were not being well cared for;

2. a placement program for neglected or abused children (principally using foster homes) for whom the Children's Aid Society obtained guardianship by application to a court;
3. a program of adoption for children needing permanent alternative parents.

Implementing this approach in rural and remote communities was replete with difficulties. The family service program called for professional counselling skills and strong support services; the placement program required foster homes and other more specialized resources; and the adoption service was primarily designed to serve unmarried mothers who voluntarily relinquished infants to be placed with childless adopting couples. None of these expectations worked well outside the urban areas where they had been developed, and for the Indian communities there was the additional problem that the services had no cultural connection to the communities. Nevertheless, as residential schools were closed and the students were integrated into provincial education systems, the Department of Indian Affairs negotiated agreements with the provinces to transfer responsibility for attending to the children's general welfare from the department to provincial child welfare agencies.

These discussions did not result in a single pattern of services across Canada. The stance of each province toward extending services to Indian families and children differed. All provinces recognized that serving Indian people could prove to be expensive and sought terms that would be to the province's financial advantage. The result was described as

an incredible disparity in the quantity and quality of child welfare programs available to status Indians from one province to another. In some instances there are disparities within a province. This myriad of differing policy approaches results in unequal treatment of Indian children across Canada. (Johnston, 1983: 20)

In the federal government's Hawthorn Inquiry (1964-66) into services to status Indians there was substantial discussion of Indian child welfare and of the move to provide services through the provinces. Approval of a provincial role was expressed provided that service was requested by Indians. Recommendation 56 states: "All possible efforts should be made to induce Indians to demand and to accept provincial welfare services." Recommendation 65 states: "When Children's Aid Societies extend their services to

Table 5.3
Status Indian Children in Care, 1966/67–1988/89

Year	Children in Care	Children 16 and under	CIC/1,000
1966-67	3,201	93,101	34.3
1970-71	5,156	95,048	54.2
1975-76	6,078	96,493	62.9
1980-81	5,716	94,916	60.2
1985-86	4,000	99,213	40.3
1988-89	3,989	102,529	38.9

SOURCE: Indian and Northern Affairs, Basic Departmental Data, 1989, Table 18.
The total number of children in care is the total of days of care paid by Indian
Affairs divided by 365, not including any preventive or alternative services.

Indian reserves, the appointment of Indians to the Boards of
Directors should be sought, and consultations between the
societies and the Band Councils should be encouraged." These
recommendations, with their concern for Indian initiation and
participation, were not followed when the transfer of authority
took place between the federal government and each province.

At the working level the transfer of responsibility led to provincial social workers receiving a series of allegations from Indian
agents, rural school teachers, local police, and priests regarding
child neglect or abuse in the Indian community. The response of
the provincial child welfare authorities, often working at a great
distance from people with whom communication was difficult and
without local support services, was to remove the children from
their parents and place them in non-Native foster homes.

In the 1950s the number of status Indian children per 1,000 in
the care of provincial child welfare agencies had been so low that
statistics were not kept, but by the mid-1960s the number was
already substantial and increases continued until the mid-1970s.
Table 5.3 shows the extent of this growth. These numbers should
be seen as minimum figures because informal, unbilled, and adoption placements are not included.

The impact of the adoption program on Indian families and
children was substantial. Adoption operated principally without
the voluntary consents usually found in the non-Native community. Typically, young children would be removed from their parents as children in care and then application would be made by the
provincial child welfare agency to the court to waive adoption

Table 5.4
Adoption of Status Indian Children, 1965/66–1985/86

Year	By Indians	By Non-Natives	Total	Births	Adoptions/ 1,000 births
1965-66	43	122	165	8,942	18.4
1970-71	36	205	241	8,756	27.5
1975-76	95	446	541	8,127	66.5
1980-81	127	441	686	8,459	81.1
1985-86	191	344	535	11,158	47.9

SOURCE: Indian and Inuit Affairs, Resource Centre, Ottawa.

consent. Placements were then made with non-Native families. Table 5.4 shows the extent of this program. In 1978-79 in British Columbia, 26.3 per cent of all adoptions were of Native children and in Manitoba that figure was 48.7 per cent. Children obtained from the Indian community were not necessarily placed in Canada. As late as 1980 a majority of the Indian children from Manitoba were placed in the United States. This proved to be a disastrous practice, dislocating children from their roots and making them vulnerable to abuse in poorly screened placements.

The total impact of this well-intentioned but fundamentally flawed approach to First Nations children was that in the later 1970s and early 1980s one in seven status Indian children was not in the care of his/her parents at any one time. As many as one in four status Indian children was spending at least some part of childhood away from the parental home.

There were also marked provincial and regional variations in the percentage of Indian children in care as fractions of all children in care. Patrick Johnston, working with partial data in the early 1980s, was able to outline the main features of this pattern, as shown in Table 5.5.

It is also possible to compare the rate per 1,000 children in care between the status Indian and non-Native population for those provinces with a significant Native population. Table 5.6 provides this comparison.

These data had not been available prior to Patrick Johnston's research in the late 1970s. The data showed that the provincial child welfare systems were removing Indian children from their parents and communities at an alarming and unprecedented rate. In the North and in western Canada the extent of the removal of children was 40 per cent or more of all children served, yet this fact

Table 5.5
Indian Children in Care by Province

Province	Year	Status C.I.C.	Non-Status C.I.C.	Total Native C.I.C.	Total All C.I.C.	% Native of all C.I.C.
B.C.	1978-79	1,692	1,208	2,900	7,369	39.2
Alberta	1978-79	1,498	1,085	2,583	6,844	37.7
Sask.	1978-79	1,390	500	1,890	2,909	65.0
Manitoba	1979-80	1,134	n/a	1,134	3,788	29.9
Ontario	1978-79	n/a	n/a	1,097	14,008	7.9
Quebec	1978-79	590	12	602	28,870	2.1
N.B.	1978-79	n/a	n/a	80	2,270	3.5
N.S.	1978-79	n/a	n/a	81	1,959	4.1
P.E.I.	1981	14	11	25	233	10.7
Nfld.	1978-79	n/a	n/a	108	1,221	8.8
N.W.T.	1980	71	104	175	368	47.5
Yukon	1978-79	n/a	n/a	109	194	56.2

NOTE: "Non-status" includes Métis and persons of recognizable Indian descent as judged by departmental social workers for statistical purposes.

SOURCE: Johnston, 1983, using available provincial data.

Table 5.6

Status Indian and Non-Native Children in Care, 1978-79

Province	Status C.I.C.	Status Children	Status C.I.C./1,000	Other C.I.C.	Other Children (000's)	Other C.I.C./ 1,000
B.C.	1,692	21,241	79.6	4,469	545	8.2
Alberta	1,498	23,505	63.7	4,261	463	9.2
Sask.	1,390	20,830	66.7	1,519	230	6.6
Manitoba	1,134	19,518	58.1	2,654	245	10.8*
Ontario	1,097	22,561	48.6	12,911	2,051	6.3
N.W.T.	71	3,049	23.2	193	13.4	14.4
Yukon	109	996	109.4	85	5.4	12.0

NOTE: Status children in care for 1978-79 are as given by Patrick Johnston. All status children are as provided by special tables available from the Department of Indian Affairs resource centre, Ottawa, for 1978-79. "Other" children in care indicate non-Native children in care as calculated by deducting both status and non-status children in care, as provided by Patrick Johnston, from all children as of March 31, 1979, as provided in the annual reports of the respective provincial departments of welfare. All other children are from the 1976 census, less status Indian children and an allowance for non-status and Métis children when these have been deducted from the "other" children in care. In the case of Manitoba where there was no estimate available for non-status and Métis children in care, so they are included in the "other" categories.

SOURCES: Johnston, 1983; Department of Indian Affairs resource centre; provincial child welfare statistics, Census of Canada.

was not acknowledged by attention to community, historical, or cultural differences.

Brad McKenzie and Peter Hudson from the University of Manitoba summarized the available explanations of this overrepresentation of Indian children (McKenzie and Hudson, 1985). The principal explanations were:

1. The psycho-social argument, which interpreted child neglect and abuse in terms of individual deviance. This was the dominant argument recognized in the child welfare system.
2. The cultural change argument, that Native peoples were undergoing rapid social change and that this was resulting in high rates of family dysfunction.
3. The economic deprivation argument, that Native people were poor and deprived of adequate housing and social services and that this resulted in increased use of the residual child welfare system.
4. The historical argument, that Native people had been deprived of their land and had been systematically institutionalized, losing the coping capacities of their own culture but never obtaining an alternative.
5. The racial argument, that Native peoples were being systematically rejected and stigmatized by the non-Native majority.
6. The colonial argument, that the child welfare system was part of a deliberate assault on Native society designed to make changes in Native people.

McKenzie and Hudson found this last argument to be the most persuasive.

By the 1970s the child welfare system had become the successor to the residential school system as an alternative care system for Indian children. It was most active in those regions of Canada where the residential schools were most often used. It was introduced to accomplish some of the same purposes as the residential schools and it has been subject to some of the same types of internal child abuse problems as the residential schools.

There were many signs of a continuing record of abuse of Indian children while in the care of child welfare authorities, a record that had continued in some cases following their adoption. In Manitoba the Kimmelman Inquiry drew attention to the abuse of Indian children placed for adoption in the United States (Kimmelman, 1985). In Alberta, Harold Cardinal shared his own experience in his book *The Unjust Society* (Cardinal, 1969), and in British

Columbia Chief Wayne Christian was deeply influenced by the suicide of his brother, which followed being a child in care (Wharf, 1989). These well-known instances precipitated many memories of abuse from former children in care. Today, in the early 1990s, the situation is in many ways similar to that described by Richard King in his description of rumours of abuse in the residential school. Most children in care know of abuse but many do not wish to revisit the circumstances of their abuse. In addition, formal studies of the abuse of Indian children while they were children in care are lacking.

There are also some important differences between the residential school period and the child welfare period. The child welfare system had not been planned to change the culture of Indian people. The system was designed for non-Native people living in urban areas and was then exported to rural and Indian communities to provide equality of service. This export of services had overlooked significant differences between the society where the system originated and the one on which it was imposed.

Children were removed from their parents without regard to differences of history, culture, or race because the assumption was made that these factors were much less important than physical health, diet, housing, absence of alcoholism in the home, and the other standards through which social workers judged the absence or presence of neglect or abuse. It was assumed that children were pliable. Once a child was admitted to care or placed for adoption, the child welfare system assumed that childhood was primarily a period of physical and emotional development in which prior heritage and culture were relatively unimportant. It was assumed that the heritage and culture of adopting parents or foster parents could be acquired by any child. Racial origin was not seen as a serious problem because, although the child was unmistakably different from his/her non-adopted siblings, it was assumed that some basic education in the history and culture of Native people would provide the child with a sufficient understanding of his or her own origins. Finally, it was assumed that the loving, caring values of adopting and foster parents would ultimately be effective in protecting the child physically and emotionally from the (rare) instances of racial prejudice to which they might be exposed.

The Native children were, in many ways, more vulnerable to the pressure to assimilate in the child welfare system than they had been in the residential school. In the residential school there was the companionship of their peers, the annual return to home community and parents, the daily presence of many other Indian people, and the knowledge that this was an experience that their parents had been through. In addition, the children knew they were there because they were Indians from a specific First Nation people.

None of these sources of support was available in the child welfare system. The children were isolated from each other, usually losing contact even with their immediate brothers and sisters. They were there, not because they were Indian, but because their parents were judged by social workers and a court to have treated them in an abusive or negligent manner. There was no promise of return to their home community and people. All the pressures were to put all those things that made them Indian behind and to become non-Natives. No wonder the records of Indian children in foster homes and adoption homes contain repeated stories of the attempts of the children to scrub the brown colour off their skins. It was the colour that made them different and, in a way they could not understand, unacceptable.

The nineteenth-century Indian Act and the Indian Affairs administration it produced had the colonial and racial objective of shaping the next generation of Indian people for a Christian civilization, of assimilation into mainstream society. In the mid-twentieth century child welfare policy-makers, social workers, foster parents, and adopting parents made the assumption that the Canadian world they knew was the only world worth pursuing. Most wanted only the best for the Indian children. But the result of their actions was to assert pressure on Indian children to reject their own origins and acquire others. The pressure was exacerbated by the underlying racial attitude toward people of visibly Native descent that prevented many from being accepted in non-Native society.

CURRENT POLICY AND PRACTICE CHANGES, 1980-PRESENT

The latest and last stage of family and child welfare policy toward the Indian people is a response to the concerns with the child welfare system identified in the 1970s. Although the provincial child welfare systems remain in control of legislation, a distinctive feature of this stage of development is the initiative that Indian people have taken in developing proposals and negotiating agreements. As this occurs First Nation communities are developing service models of their own that reflect the experience of their communities, culture, and history. Although a general pattern to these developments can be seen throughout Canada, there are also substantial variations between different First Nations peoples and provinces. As a result, after some general observations on Canadian developments as a whole, this section includes a more detailed discussion of the specific changes occurring in Manitoba, British Columbia, and the Yukon.

Concern that the child welfare system might be inappropriate for First Nations peoples had existed before the detailed work of Johnston in the late 1970s. The Hawthorn Report (1966) referred to the advantages of agreements with Indian bands and tribal councils. But this idea had not been incorporated into policy in a systematic way. The earliest agreement that involved a band as a direct signatory was completed in 1973 between the Blackfoot band, the Alberta Ministry of Social Development, and the Department of Indian Affairs. In 1976 the tenth report of the Royal Commission on Family and Child Welfare Law (Justice Berger, chairman) dealt extensively with Native families in British Columbia. Among its recommendations were procedures to ensure that Indian bands were notified of all protection and adoption hearings affecting the children of band members (Royal Commission on Family Law, 1976). There were also proposals to provide Indian families with adoption subsidies so that Indian children could be placed in the Indian community. At Spallumcheen, in British Columbia, the Indian band passed a by-law in 1980 giving the band the authority to operate its own child welfare service (McDonald, 1985). The by-law could have been disallowed by the Minister of Indian Affairs, but instead it was allowed to stand, indicating a willingness to look at new ways of providing service to families and children.

In 1978 a year-long review of social services to Indian communities in Ontario was undertaken on a tripartite basis, recognizing the interests of the federal and provincial governments and the Native people. The review included a field study of services in Native communities, using local Native interviewers. The findings of the study included summary comments from Indian communities, indicating their view that:

- It is unfair to place Indian children in white homes.
- Fostering should not be encouraged off reserves.
- Children's Aid does not keep in touch; they just come in an emergency.
- A Native family service worker is needed on the reserve.
- The foster allowance should be increased to enable Indian

people to foster Indian children. (Technical Assistance and Family Planning Associates, 1979: 5-7)

In Manitoba a tripartite committee prepared a report on Indian child welfare (Manitoba Tripartite Committee, 1980) in June, 1980, and this was speedily followed by a comprehensive proposal from the Four Nations Confederacy encompassing all bands in the province. The proposal was directed to the Department of Indian Affairs and dealt with three stages for the assumption of responsibility for child welfare: orientation, development, and operation.

From these beginnings in the late 1970s and early 1980s there was a rapid development of child welfare agreements with Indian bands in the five years between 1982-83 and 1986-87. The scale of development can be seen in Tables 5.7, 5.8, and 5.9.

The child welfare agreements were made on an individual basis with bands or tribal councils. The services provided under the agreements vary. Some cover only preventive and support services, leaving all statutory authority with the province; others provide for the band or tribal council to exercise statutory authority, pursuant to an agreement between the Native jurisdiction and the province. The signatories to agreements also varied. Where the agreement covers support funding the agreement was usually between the Department of Indian Affairs and the band or tribal council. Where the agreement was for the exercise of statutory authority there is sometimes a tripartite, band-province-department agreement and sometimes two separate agreements, a band-province agreement providing for the exercise of statutory authority and a band-department agreement providing for program funding to the band. The exercise of statutory authority by bands and tribal councils has usually required change in provincial legislation. Alberta, Manitoba, Ontario, and the Yukon have added major new sections to their child welfare legislation to provide a clear legal framework for the agreements, and similar changes are under consideration in the other provinces. Agreements have usually provided control over child welfare for Indian families living on reserve lands, but there are a number of interesting provisions for services to families and children when away from the reserve. These and other detailed variations that meet the individual needs of bands and provinces require study at the provincial level.

In the latest period, from 1987-88 to 1990-91, there have been few new agreements as the Department of Indian Affairs began a moratorium on new negotiations and funding arrangements in 1986, pending a review of policy. The policy review was released in

Table 5.7
Agencies (Bands) Administering Child Welfare Programs

Year	B.C.	Alta.	Man.	Ont.	Que.	Atlantic Region	Yukon
1981-82	1 (1)	1 (1)	2 (9)				
1982-83	1 (1)	1 (1)	5 (34)				
1983-84	1 (1)	2 (10)	6 (59)		1 (1)	3 (3)	
1984-85	1 (1)	2 (10)	6 (59)		3 (5)	6 (6)	
1985-86	1 (1)	2 (10)	6 (59)		5 (7)	9 (21)	
1986-87	2 (14)	3 (15)	6 (59)	1 (14)	5 (13)	11 (23)	1 (1)
1987-88	2 (14)	3 (15)	6 (59)	4 (56)	7 (15)	11 (23)	1 (1)
1990-91	2 (19)	3 (15)	7 (60)	7 (84)	7 (15)	11 (20)	1 (1)

SOURCE: Department of Indian Affairs, press release, 6 April 1988; 1990-91 data from direct inquiry of department.

Table 5.8
Staff Employed by Indian Child Welfare Agencies

Year	Agencies (Bands)	Staff
1981-82	4 (11)	46
1982-83	7 (36)	105
1983-84	13 (74)	219
1984-85	18 (81)	275
1985-86	23 (98)	321
1986-87	29 (140)	415
1987-88	34 (184)	

NOTE: An additional twenty tribal councils, representing 118 bands in British Columbia, Alberta, and Saskatchewan, were in the process of negotiating agreements in 1988.

SOURCE: Department of Indian Affairs, press release, 6 April 1988.

Table 5.9
Federal Expenditures on Indian Child Welfare

Year	Expenditure	% Increase
1981-82	$34.7m	
1982-83	$37.6m	8.2
1983-84	$43.7m	16.2
1984-85	$50.8m	16.2
1985-86	$63.9m	25.8
1986-87	$70.6m	10.5
1987-88	$77.9m	10.3

SOURCE: Department of Indian Affairs, press release, 6 April 1988.

1989 as a discussion document, *Indian Child and Family Services Management Regime: Discussion Paper* (Department of Indian and Northern Affairs, 1989). This was a response to the tripling of child welfare costs and what is referred to as "unplanned and ad hoc growth." As a result, the paper established limits on the types of agreement that could be considered. A minimum of a thousand children must be covered, child-care services were excluded, and provincial legislation and standards must be followed. The discussion paper also indicated that new agreements will only be possible "as resources become available." Although the document was referred to as a discussion paper, it has been used as policy in the years following its release.

The implementation of policy at the provincial level shows many variations.

Manitoba

Manitoba provides the best example of a comprehensive approach to First Nation child welfare using tripartite agreements as the principal mechanism. The first comprehensive agreement for all child welfare services other than adoption was reached with the Dakota Ojibway in July, 1981. This was followed by additional agreements in the next three years until all rural and reserve areas of the province were covered. In addition, in 1984 the Ma Mawi Wi Chi Itata Centre (We All Work Together to Help Each Other) was opened to provide non-statutory services to Indian, Métis, and non-status Indians in Winnipeg.

The child welfare agreements followed a joint report from the Manitoba Indian Brotherhood and the federal and provincial governments that had been issued in 1980. The guiding principles of the agreements were:

1. Indians have special status as defined in treaties, and through provisions of the Indian Act.
2. The family is the first resource for the nurturance and protection of children, but families do need support for their parenting role and children, for a variety of reasons, may need substitute care.
3. All children need care, nurture, and protection.
4. As a result of culture, geography, and past experience, Indian people have special needs.
5. Preservation of Indian cultural identity is of importance in terms of both language and customs, within the framework of tribes, bands, extended families, and individuals.
6. The provision of services must involve Indian people, recognize their priority needs and the current variety of service modes. (Goreau, 1986)

The Manitoba Child and Family Services Act was revised in 1986 to provide an explicit legal base for recognizing Indian communities and for transferring to them authority to act as agents of the province. The service expansion is shown in Table 5.10.

Evaluations of the Manitoba child welfare agreements have been undertaken by staff of the School of Social Work at the University of Manitoba and by the management consultants Coopers and Lybrand (see, e.g., Hudson and McKenzie, 1987; Hudson and Taylor-Henley, 1987). Although each of the assessments recognizes that the Indian-managed agencies have substantial achievements, concerns are also expressed. These include:

Table 5.10

Manitoba: Status Indian Children in Care, Agreements, 1981-89

Year	Dakota Ojibway	AWASIS*	Anishinabe	West Region	Southeast Region
1981	68	–	–	–	–
1982	85	–	–	–	–
1983	108	116	37	35	30
1984	150	315	85	81	43
1985	174	286	134	106	81
1986	207	307	199	137	127
1987	212	373	n/a	105	160
1988	244	384	n/a	149	153
1989	258	382	n/a	179	n/a

*AWASIS is the Indian agency responsible for child welfare services to communities in northern Manitoba.

SOURCE: Manitoba, Department of Family and Child Services, 1981-89.

- the high proportion of children in care by court order;
- the underuse of homemaker and family day-care services;
- the accountability and responsibility for follow-up case services (Hudson and Taylor-Henley, 1987);
- the difficulties due to multiple accountability to First Nations, to the Manitoba government, and to the funding conditions of the federal government;
- the problem of attracting and retaining staff with accreditation in social work. (Coopers and Lybrand, 1990)

A central problem identified in both reports is the contradiction between "respecting the reemergence of Indian self government insofar as Indian family and child services is concerned, while at the same time [maintaining provincial] ultimate responsibility for the protection of Indian children and service standards" (Hudson and Taylor-Henley, 1987: iii).

This problem has been even more difficult to resolve in urban areas where there is a mixing of status and non-status Indians, Métis, and non-Native peoples. In Winnipeg, with 650,000 people, the Native peoples number approximately 50,000. The Indian social agency Ma Mawi Wi Chi Itata (Ma Mawi) was established in 1984 to serve this complex urban Native community. Ma Mawi does not have any statutory authority. The responsibility for initiating court action and maintaining formal guardianship remains with provincial agencies. Instead of exercising control authority,

Ma Mawi derives its authority from a philosophy of mutual support and empowerment based on a common recognition of oppression (Hill, 1987).

The first annual report of Ma Mawi expressed this philosophy in the following manner.

> We understand the child welfare system as a system which has evolved, in the dominant culture, to deal with the problems of industrial society. Within the Native community, the child welfare system is a system that deals with the symptoms of larger social problems – racism, poverty, underdevelopment, unemployment, etc. The theoretical base of Ma Mawi Wi Chi Itata Centre is grounded in the understanding of child welfare problems as the result of the colonial nature of relations between the aboriginal people and the Euro-Canadian majority. . . . We understand our practice, which flows from this theory, as a process of decolonization. We see this as a conscious process through which we regain control over our lives and resources. (Ma Mawi Wi Chi Itata, 1985)

Ma Mawi has an annual budget of over $2 million and serves more than 500 families each year. The approach to services is holistic and is based on the supports provided to Native families through their extended family networks. The philosophy of decolonization and empowerment is expressed in the administration and staffing of Ma Mawi. All board members and staff of the agency are Natives. At Ma Mawi the agency computer system is used to provide extended family tracing. This ensures that connections to appropriate relatives are made wherever possible and that where this is not possible, service is provided by a person who fills the role a relative would have filled.

The practice philosophy at Ma Mawi recognizes that "Empowerment confers upon a collective the opportunity to decide what is of value within its indigenous traditions, and what is of value from external sources" (Laidlaw Foundation, 1991). Mainstream values and practices (for example, the social work Code of Ethics) have a prominent place in the work of Ma Mawi, but they are used alongside declarations of Native family teaching. Ma Mawi aims to have positive relationships with all Winnipeg and Manitoba agencies and engages actively in advocacy, exchange, and collaboration. The strength to undertake this work comes from a clear understanding of Native values, which provides the agency with a recognized independent identity. Ma Mawi is not the only Native Manitoba agency to articulate these values, but as the largest

Native urban agency in Canada it serves as a good example of Native understanding, policy-making, and practice.

British Columbia

British Columbia provides an example of a province where the First Nations role in child welfare has been developed in an *ad hoc* manner. Despite the lack of a comprehensive approach in the 1980s, First Nations people throughout the province are much more active in the child welfare field than they were in the 1970s. In the 1990s the level of activity continues to increase.

A review of child welfare developments in British Columbia refers to most of this approach as "muddling through" (Wharf, 1989: 16). The principal characteristic of "muddling through" is negotiation between the local provincial ministry child welfare office and the Indian band. As First Nations people have become more aware of the effects of the child welfare system on their families and communities they have asserted greater control over their relationship with the local offices of the Ministry of Social Services and Housing.

The Native community in British Columbia is aware of the historic fact that they were dispossessed of their land without treaty or compensation. Increasingly, they have found that militant actions such as road blockades, forestry obstruction, and unauthorized fishing are effective in making the non-Native community deal with land claim issues. This approach to dealing with the non-Native community has also been applied to the child welfare field.

The child welfare by-law passed in 1980 by the Spallumcheen band illustrates this forceful approach to asserting authority and policy-making. The band by-law authorized the band to conduct its own child welfare program. Chief Wayne Christian was himself a former child in care and his experiences with the child welfare system are described in the following quotation.

Much of Chief Christian's concern with child welfare practices were a result of his own experiences as a child in the care of Human Resources from age 12 until 18. He was removed from his mother's care along with his nine brothers and sisters and was profoundly influenced by the dissolution of his family. Chief Christian went through several foster homes, separated from his siblings, and finally settled in one for a number of years.

Chief Christian stated that his mother was almost destroyed

by being without her children, and as a result ... turned to alcohol as a release. Chief Christian was able to make the change back to living on the reserve when he was 18 years old. One of his brothers was not as successful and committed suicide after being unable to cope with the transition from foster home to reserve life. (Wharf, 1989: 10)

Following the passage of the band by-law Chief Christian organized a protest on the front lawn of the home of the provincial Minister of Social Services in Vancouver, refusing to move until the right of the band to operate its own child welfare program was recognized. In 1980 public sympathy was with the band and the minister conceded.

In the 1960s and 1970s social workers were prepared to "invade" local Indian communities, assisted where necessary by the police, and remove children, but in the 1980s there was little support from the non-Native community for such actions, nor were social workers confident that such direct intervention was appropriate. As a result, the day-to-day activities of social workers were dependent on community collaboration in providing information, keeping appointments, providing access to children, and using alternative child-care resources. Achieving such co-operation required that respect be shown to the local Indian band chief and to community elders. Interviews were arranged through the band office and advice was sought before action was taken. The initiative for the social worker to visit the reserve shifted from the workers to the invitation of the bands. In the course of time these local arrangements were formalized in local protocol agreements.

In 1991 in British Columbia there are formal agreements with two tribal councils and two independent bands,[6] covering approximately 10 per cent of status Indians living on reserve. Most arrangements continue to be made at an informal and local level. Neither the agreements nor the local arrangements are recognized in the British Columbia Family and Child Service Act beyond a provision requiring that bands be notified of court hearings affecting children who are band members. However, the Indian bands and tribal councils are, *de facto*, in control of child welfare on most provincial reserves. An increasing number of band social service staff are obtaining professional qualifications in social work and related disciplines and in some cases are better qualified than the social work staff in local ministry offices. This has been recognized by some local justices, who now look to band social workers for professional advice in disposing of child welfare cases rather than to the provincial ministry. Thus in British Columbia practice has changed before policy.

In urban areas change has been slower. There is no agency in British Columbia comparable to Ma Mawi in Manitoba. The Indian friendship centres that can be found in most urban communities provide, among other functions, some support services to Indians living off reserve, but they lack the professional sophistication of Ma Mawi. Partly to compensate for the lack of autonomous urban Native social service organizations the provincial ministry has established a special unit in Vancouver for First Nations child welfare. The unit has been staffed, insofar as possible, by Native staff members.

Yukon Territory

The Yukon illustrates some of the problems of remoteness and small community size that characterize northern Canadian communities. The total population of the Yukon is 25,000 people, of whom 5,000 are Indian. These 5,000 people live in widely separated communities and in 1952 were divided for administrative purposes by the Department of Indian Affairs into thirteen bands. The Champagne/Aishihik band, which is recognized as one of the strongest bands in the Yukon, has 500 members, 300 of whom live in the Yukon capital, Whitehorse, and 200 at the band's principal community, Haines Junction (there are no Indian reserves in the Yukon). Of the 500 members, 200 are children or youth.

In the 1970s the proportion of Indian children in care in the Yukon exceeded one in ten, and additional children were placed for adoption outside the Yukon. In the 1980s this proportion declined, and the Yukon government supported the principle of Indian bands providing their own child welfare services. The Yukon Children's Act was revised in 1984 and provides for the delegation of the Director of Child Welfare's powers to a society serving as the child welfare authority for an Indian band.

One such agreement, with the Champagne/Aishihik, has been established. The band appointed a child welfare committee and employed a Native social worker to provide services to Native families. Working in a small community where all members know one another leads to substantial differences of practice from those found in mainstream child welfare systems (Armitage *et al.*, 1988). Examples of such differences include the following.

(1) *Protection complaints.* There is no such thing as an anonymous protection complaint. Instead, there is a daily monitoring of

those families who are known to have problems providing care to their children in accord with community standards.

(2) *Intervention*. Intervention in the affairs of a family is a matter for the extended family, since it carries responsibility for its members, including children and youth. Foster homes could only be found when plans were made with family members for a specific child and a home could be found through knowledge of the obligations of extended family members to the child.

(3) *Court action*. The court is never used. The community either settles the matter internally or lives with the problem.

(4) *Decisions*. The mainstream Yukon child welfare system gave a great deal of attention to making the best decisions and plans for the future of children in care. Social workers then acted on these decisions. In contrast, the Champagne/Aishihik value continuity of relationships and are prepared to live with chronic parenting problems over long periods of time. It is assumed that change will come as parents mature and healing takes place, and that meanwhile it is the responsibility of the grandparents to ensure the child is cared for.

The problems of applying these different practices were mainly practical. Few social workers could provide the culturally sensitive enabling role required, and the cost of providing service on a daily and intensive basis was high. The economies of scale that could be achieved in a larger organization were not available. In addition, the Champagne/Aishihik agreement did not accord with the minimum-size policies for child welfare agreements contained in the Department of Indian Affairs discussion paper. Nevertheless, without approval or support from DIA the Yukon territorial government has continued to fund the Champagne/Aishihik child welfare agreement.

FIRST NATIONS VIEWS

The Assembly of First Nations is a national body that develops policy and represents Native interests to the federal government. The Assembly regards child welfare as a priority area for policy development and for the exercise of self-government. Its report on child care, issued in 1989, concluded:

> Our most basic recommendations are for immediate funding of community controlled native child-care as part of the enabling process. Such programs would provide First Nations' most precious resources with an early sense of security, stability,

motivation and pride. In the long term complete jurisdiction over the lives of native children must be returned to those First Nations who are ready, and who will be a model for others. (Assembly of First Nations, 1989: viii)

The Assembly held a national child welfare conference in New Brunswick in 1988 (Assembly of First Nations, 1988) and a second conference in Winnipeg in 1991. The second conference focused on the development of a national strategy for First Nations child and family services, including discussion of the issues of:

- *Jurisdiction*: the authority to govern children and families in a system independent of the provincial or federal governments.
- *Interim mechanisms/models*: the development of research, co-ordination, and funding mechanisms to provide the capacity to support First Nations and pursue long-term objectives.
- *Services*: how best to develop and recognize Indian community traditions and approaches to child welfare at both national and regional levels.
- *Funding*: to look at alternative approaches to funding child welfare that avoid or reduce the problems of reinforcing provincial control. (Assembly of First Nations, 1991)

The tripartite child welfare agreements that have been used to obtain Indian management of child welfare were seen by Indian organizations as steps toward the exercise of self-government. It was expected that this would lead to fewer children in care, more culturally appropriate services, and lower costs. The record of achieving these objectives is at best mixed. Services are more culturally appropriate, but there are still many children in care and costs have grown rapidly. Furthermore, it can be argued that the agreements are now becoming a means of governing Indian organizations. These reinforce the Indian Act, section 88 provisions whereby child welfare authority is subject to provincial policy and standards. In the end this could easily lead back to the exercise of policies that integrate Native and non-Native services under provincial jurisdiction rather than contribute to the development of separate institutions of First Nation self-government. Although there has been a reduction of Indian children in care from 63/1,000 (1975-76) to 39/1,000 (1988-89), the number in care remains five times higher than in the non-Native community.

Despite these reservations, the leaders of the First Nations communities are committed to exercising their inherent right to manage their own affairs. The following extracts are from testimony to the National Inquiry into First Nations Child Care (Assembly of First Nations, 1989).

Marguerite Sanderson
The Pas Indian Band/Opasquiak Aboriginal Women's Group
The Pas, Manitoba

As a mother of three, Marguerite Sanderson told the inquiry she was speaking on issues that concern her personally. Children are the native community's greatest resource, and if the native culture is going to survive they must be cared for in a way which reflects the traditional lifestyles.

The Pas Band is preparing a human development plan for the community. A Human Resource Development centre would be established to centralize and expand social programs. Such a plan would include counselling for alcohol and drug abuse, family counselling, an education authority, job training, recreation, social services, and a daycare centre.

The Pas reserve has 1,600 residents, including 650 children between the ages of 0 and 12, but the reserve has no daycare centre. Some band members put their children in daycares in the town of The Pas, but Sanderson said that these centres are full to capacity. As well, band residents would prefer to use a centre on the reserve.

Sanderson said the lack of daycare is one of the main reasons for the high unemployment levels on the reserve. Lack of child care prevents many parents from taking work incentive jobs or job training programs. She pointed out that even if there were daycare on the reserve, social assistance recipients would not receive a government child care allowance to pay for the service. This lack of daycare and lack of employment possibilities contributes to the bleak outlook of many women in the community, since they are in the greatest need of education and skills training. Changes in the Indian Act and the return of many people to the reserve are increasing the pressure on the community for some form of child care.

Sanderson noted that the Opasquiak Aboriginal Women's Group fully supported the band in its efforts to establish a daycare. At the same time she said any band organized daycare would have to be controlled by native people and reflect traditional values. Sanderson listed the necessities of the "Inner Source of Life," which her grandfather had passed on to her. These include kindness, truth and trust, loving one another, caring, sharing, fairness, self-confidence, patience, friendship, responsibility, humility, keeping, respect, and learning.

Sanderson saw the inquiry as a step toward native self-

government, noting it was important to make sure young people do not lose their culture and self-worth.

Chief Gordon Antoine
Coldwater Indian Band
Merritt, British Columbia

The Coldwater Band has been able to take control of its own child welfare programs, but Chief Gordon Antoine explained that formal authority has yet to catch up with the community's informal decision to take action.

While the Coldwater band has no children in the care of the provincial agencies, it does have eleven living with relatives in a total of ten homes. "These placements have only the authority of the Band Council," Antoine said, "and our staff are subject to attack and undermining by both the Province of British Columbia's legislation and the funding the band accesses from the Department of Indian Affairs." The discretionary nature of the funding means that services available to children are extremely limited.

"We would like the force of the national Constitution to acknowledge this process," he said. The Constitution should also ensure sufficient funding "to provide our children the necessary services for their sound development as future citizens."

Antoine made a strong plea for "ourselves as Indian people, and more particularly from people such as ourselves in leadership positions from within Indian country, to eradicate the abuse – sexual, physical, and mental – we tend to foist on our children." He said that this process would call for clear and honest recognition of the extent of the problem itself, as well as an acknowledgement that "the support systems, either in place or being proposed by senior levels of government, are not readily accessible by our members, or [are] designed not to be accessible to our on-reserve population."

"Appreciate that the judiciary systems of this country are punitive in nature and not designed to assist the healing process required by victims, nor [are they] of a nature that is rehabilitative to abusers." Communities must take responsibility for initiating the action needed "in order for our citizens to enjoy a safe and caring environment within which to grow up."

Antoine said investigations into the extent of sexual abuse in his community revealed 497 cases of physical and sexual abuse and forty-nine cases of incest. He talked about the lifelong scars the abuse had left on both the abusers and victims, noting that "we have to acknowledge and own the damn problem."

Since Health and Welfare Canada has failed to fund programs to help heal the situation, he added, "we have to look inside our own resources to equip our front-line workers with the skills and information they need to cope with the problem." "We have to heal the abusers and the victims," he said.

Myrtle Bush thanked him for coming forward on this issue as a chief. It was becoming apparent in the course of the inquiry that abuse is a key child care issue. "We're going to make a very strong reference to all the things you and others have been telling us on this issue," she said, adding that Health and Welfare will have to allocate resources toward solving the abuse problem if child care is to be more than a band-aid solution to a larger problem. She congratulated the Coldwater Band for putting resources into sexual abuse education.

Antoine made it clear that he supports child care and recognizes it as an important need, "but there are unresolved issues that must be addressed. . . . My children need a warm and loving and safe place to grow up in." He again emphasized the importance of treating abusers, as they themselves had been victims. It was impossible for him as a chief "to tell these people they're not welcome in the community. There has to be a rehabilitative process."

Linda Jordan echoed Bush's appreciation of Antoine's remarks and asked whether Coldwater was using any traditional models for dealing with the problem, such as women's and men's circles. A community member appearing with Antoine explained that a new circle had recently been started by two families, and a separate one had been started for young boys. There are plans to start new circles for women, men, and children, based on ongoing discussions with elders.

On the issue of child apprehension, Antoine clarified his view that the law should get the children out of the home, then find them a place within the community that is safe.

Elder Lavina White
Council of the Haida Nation
Vancouver, British Columbia

"I stand before you and our Creator to speak on behalf of those who cannot speak for themselves," said White. "I speak on behalf of the forgotten children in the urban areas." White talked about the need to repatriate adopted children in urban centres back to their home communities, even though the whole concept of reservations was destructive. "We have to think as nations," she said. "We have to think of things holistically."

She talked about the importance of going back to terms such as "village" or "community," and she said that people must begin to name their homelands again. "I am a Haida," she said. "I am from the Haida Nation." "The problem really begins at the cradle," said White. "If we don't have our identity in our home community, we have no identity."

White called for a national First Nations declaration that "we're going to take care of our own children". But she cautioned against taking information and statistics to government or the media, who end up using that information against First Nation people. For the media, she said, the approach must be that "we're dealing with the problems we have, and they are alien to us." White also talked about the need for self-government and the prophecies of a time when First Nations will govern themselves: "If we move toward governing ourselves, we can look after our children."

She emphasized that First Nations leaders must be instructed to go forward and "not be submissive" in their efforts to redress the impact of a residential school system that did not nurture native children. These children, she said, are now parents who lack the necessary teaching to know how to nurture their own children. White called for a healing process to deal with "the boarding school syndrome" and urged First Nations to set up "our own systems of education and justice."

Aboriginal children are neglected for many reasons, White said, and the underlying problems must be dealt with first at the family level and then within the Nation as a whole. But she cautioned against using white systems unless absolutely necessary.

UNRESOLVED PROBLEMS OF IMPLEMENTATION

Independent First Nations family and child welfare organizations promise more appropriate and culturally relevant services. Support for these new approaches is evident both from First Nations and from provincial and federal governments. Despite this enthusiasm and support some unresolved issues of implementation have been encountered.

An example of the form these issues take is provided by Provincial Court Justice Brian Giesbrecht's report (Giesbrecht, 1992) on child abuse on Manitoba's Indian reserves. The report was the result of an eleven-month inquiry into the suicide of a thirteen-year-old boy following a long period of sexual and physical abuse on the Sandy Bay Ojibway Reserve. The justice wrote:

What is clear to me is that Lester Desjarlais had the right to expect more. His family let him down; his community let him down; his leaders let him down; then the agency that was mandated to protect him let him down, and the government chose not to notice.

Testimony to the inquiry had revealed that the continuing abuse of Desjarlais and many other children was known to the Dakota Ojibway Child and Family Services agency responsible for providing child welfare services through an agreement authorized by the Manitoba government. Other examples have occurred where children in care have been returned to reserve communities by provincial child welfare authorities and subsequently have been abused. The provincial agencies have fulfilled their commitment to First Nations child welfare organizations but the welfare of the individual child has not been achieved, and in some cases their wishes have been disregarded.

Three fundamental problems for all welfare services underlie these examples of children who suffer abuse while administrative authorities are reluctant to act.

(1) *The citizenship of First Nations people.* There is now a well-established view that Native Canadians hold a separate and distinct form of membership in our society. However, the form this citizenship takes is by no means clear, and there is a continuing debate concerning the self-government of First Nations communities. The result is that the right of individuals, including children, to equal protection under provincial law is weakened by the wider debate as to whether provincial law should apply to Natives.

(2) *Co-ordination problems between organizations and jurisdictions.* The establishment of independent First Nations family and child welfare organizations has the effect of dividing authority between mainstream provincial agencies and independent First Nations organizations. The result is a diminished accountability in the child welfare system as a whole. At a practical level single accountability for the welfare of children and advocacy for them as individuals is lost because of the fragmentation of authority.

(3) *Deficiencies of knowledge and resources.* Studies by Native communities of the extent of sexual and physical abuse have shown that in some communities most of the children are victims and most of the adults, too, were victims as children. Problems of this scale are of a different order of magnitude to those usually encountered by child welfare agencies. The established models of intervention and the resources that support them are not able to address problems of this scale. When the situation of the individual child is considered a conclusion of service failure is diagnosed, but

the strategies of intervention and the resources to provide services are not, nor have they ever been, adequate to the problem.

CONCLUSION

Family and child welfare measures for First Nations people have been an important part of social policy in each policy period from 1867 until the present day. The form of policy in each period has followed the prevailing understanding of the "Indian problem." Most recently, First Nations are asserting control over child welfare so as to fulfil their ideals of community and cultural appropriateness. Whether or not they will achieve this objective depends on the development of new knowledge and understanding by them, and on the transfer of resources from the control of the non-Native community to the Native community. Canadian public opinion on the case for this transfer and on the desirability of First Nations government remains divided, but each year shows some increase in public understanding for the need to respect the aboriginal rights of the First Nations of Canada.

Native organizations have used arguments based on aboriginal rights to advance their case for programs and services that recognize their unique origins and cultural heritage. Their progress is watched by the members of other minority groups who consider that they, too, should be able to raise their children in accordance with the values and codes of their own culture. Once separate First Nations child welfare policies and practices are established, it will be difficult to resist similar requests from immigrant Canadians. Indeed, provisions for the welfare of all families and children should benefit from a greater knowledge of, and respect for, diversity.

NOTES

1. Although B.C., Manitoba, and the Yukon were chosen so as to illustrate a range of differences in family and child welfare approaches, an additional reason for the choice was the availability of scholarly work on First Nations family and child welfare in each jurisdiction. Professor Brian Wharf, University of Victoria, has documented family and child welfare issues in British Columbia, Professor Ken Coates, University of Victoria, has taken a similar interest in the Yukon, and Professors Peter Hudson and Brad McKenzie, University of Manitoba, have studied family and child welfare policy in Manitoba. Finally, the choice reflects the author's experience in both administration and research in British Columbia and the Yukon.

2. See, for example: (1) Manitoba Metis Federation, *Michif Child and Family Services, Inc.* (Dauphin: North West Metis Council, 1989); (2) Manitoba Metis

Federation, *Submission to the Aboriginal Justice Inquiry* (Winnipeg, 1989); (3) Native Council of Canada, *Native Child Care* (Ottawa, 1990).

3. A visit to Alert Bay confirms the extent of the assault on Indian culture. In the 1920s Alert Bay was a community of 200-300 people. The effect of the trials and imprisonment was doubtless magnified by the building of the school and the effective removal of children from the influence of their parents. The dancing regalia has now been returned and can be seen in a museum. The school, still the only brick building in the community, continues to dominate the reserve, but is now in a partly derelict state, with some sections being used as offices by the Alert Bay Indian band. A road was placed along the Alert Bay waterfront in the 1920s, passing directly through the Indian graveyard.

4. Although King provides a detailed account of the operation of the school at Carcross in the Yukon, the description has many similar features with other accounts of residential school operation. King's account is provided here as a general model of how such schools went about achieving their objectives.

5. Johnston, 1988: 79, cites a letter one of his friends had received.

Dear Son,

This is to let you know we are all fine and hope you are the same. The weather has been real good hear [sic]. We are trying to get you home. I spoke to the priest and the agent and they said they were going help. That's all for now and be a good boy and do what the priest tell you. I pray for you every night for you to come home.

Love Mom.

Johnston writes, "Such a letter gave a boy hope and inspiration and the strength to go on from month to month and year to year."

6. Nuu'Chah'Nulth tribal council (Vancouver Island), Carrier-Sekani tribal council (Prince George), Spallumcheen band (Enderby), McLeod Lake band (McLeod Lake).

Chapter 6

Feminist Approaches: Women Recreate Child Welfare

Marilyn Callahan

Feminist thinking is not very visible in child welfare. Not much has been written from a feminist perspective, and it is rarely taught in schools of social work or fostered in mainstream child welfare. Those entering the field with strong feminist commitments may find that the subtle and not so subtle lack of support for their views causes them to change or leave, to separate their personal views from their professional work, or simply to remain silent and practise in feminist ways where they can.

In many ways, it is surprising that women and feminist thinking have not had more influence in child welfare. Although statistics are difficult to obtain for each province, it is estimated that at least 70 per cent of child welfare workers in front-line child welfare work are women, most of whom have a BSW or MSW degree. The reasons for this lack of influence have not been documented in any methodical way, but it is possible to make some speculations. Since the rapid entry of men into child welfare agencies after the end of World War Two, men have increasingly occupied the supervisory and management positions previously held almost solely by women. A review of the annual reports of the Children's Aid Society of Vancouver from the years 1902-73 supports this contention. Women occupied almost all of the casework and management positions until 1953, when the few men entering the field were quickly elevated to supervisory and administrative posts and had almost complete control of these positions by the time the agency was taken over by government in 1973. Struthers (1987: 140) points out the irony of this male takeover. Women built the social work profession on a fundamental plank: women's skill in nurturing within the family should form the foundation of public child welfare, and by doing so "they ... remained wedded to a social work vision of women's role in society which made their own eclipse by men within the social service sector difficult to challenge."

This trend continued in the seventies and eighties in spite of the strength of the women's movement. Many men who were promoted to management positions in the 1960s remained there and were not yet ready for retirement. Many more married women entered child welfare and stayed after the birth of children. For instance, in 1944, there were twenty-two single women and six married women caseworkers in the Vancouver Children's Aid Society; by 1955 these numbers had changed to thirty-one single women and twenty-three married women, and by 1967 married women caseworkers exceeded single women, sixty-one to forty-five. Married women had to divide their work and home responsibilities and had less opportunity to move up the corporate ladder. (Women in social work with children and other family responsibilities do not evidence less commitment to their work nor do they provide a lower quality of service. There are data to suggest that they have a shorter work history than women with few family responsibilities [Rotman, 1989].) Women attracted to child welfare work may have had more traditional views of family life. Those with an interest in family matters yet with an eye on career advancement may have chosen the widening opportunities in the legal and medical professions.

Another factor affecting women's authority in child welfare was the development of women's services in the sixties and seventies. Rather than reform traditional child welfare agencies, activist women addressed family violence by establishing alternative social service organizations such as transition houses and sexual assault centres. They maintained a clear distance between themselves and mainstream child welfare services to underline the distinction between the two approaches to services and to avoid becoming tarred with the same brush as government workers. They also wanted to distance themselves from the chronicles of women in child welfare that portrayed women as "do-gooders" and "lady bountifuls," which Ursel (1982) has called a movement from private to social patriarchy. As a result, activist women and their reforms have had little influence on child welfare services.

Developments in social work theory and research parallel the exclusion of women and feminist perspectives during the same decades. A recent study examining the feminist identification of a random sample of faculty members in schools of social work concludes that respondents had a very modest commitment to feminism, something of an understatement when the results were examined more closely (Freeman, 1990). A full 20 per cent had no or only marginal identification with feminism, and of those who professed any sort of commitment the vast majority preferred a liberal feminist perspective (73 per cent) as opposed to a socialist or radical feminist perspective. A liberal feminist perspective essentially argues that women's equality can be redressed by legal and social measures that adjust but do not much alter present institutions and values. There was a difference, however, in male and female response: female respondents rated themselves significantly higher than did male respondents on the degree of their feminist identification. However, women have lower representation and status in schools of social work (Gripton, 1974; Walker, 1977).

Feminist thinking, however, has had informal influence on policy and practice in child welfare. Much of this contribution has been made very recently by individual writers and practitioners (Weil, 1988; Smith and Smith, 1990; Swift, 1991; Campbell and Ng, 1991; Schwartz, Gottesman, and Perlmutter, 1988; Bishop, 1992; Costin, 1985) and by those who have left the system entirely and set up their own "feminist child welfare system" in women's services (Chagnon and Robin, 1989; Pennell, 1987; Shepherd, 1990; Vance, 1979).

This chapter will assemble these contributions and propose substantially different directions for child welfare based on this wisdom and experience. This is an important exercise because feminist thinking offers some ways out of the conundrums in child welfare outlined in the first half of this book. It places the experience of women, the major group of consumers and providers in the system, at the centre of the inquiry rather then on the fringes. In doing so, it turns thinking inside out. It then offers a challenge: why not make what are viewed as the exceptions (the way women think and do) the rule (the way the system operates)? In child welfare, this is a particularly important challenge. Women have been viewed as experts in the management and care of children in the private sphere, their homes, when that work is done for no money, but this same expertise has been discounted by policymakers in the public sphere when public expenditures and public scrutiny are involved.

FEMINIST THINKING

Feminism is based on a profound observation. Women are oppressed because they are women; men are oppressed for other reasons but never because they are men. In their manifesto, the radical feminist group, the Redstockings, sums it up as "Men dominate women. A few men dominate the rest" (Roszak and Roszak, 1969, as quoted in Marchant and Wearing, 1986: 43). The concept of the universality of women's oppression gave enormous energy to the "second wave" of feminism in the 1960s. Initially, it provided a common bond of sisterhood for women of different classes and races. It also provided impetus for the massive task of capturing and recording women's experience and knowledge, lost as a result of their oppression.

However, differences soon arose about why women were oppressed and what could be done about it. These differences were given labels. Liberal feminists believed women's oppression was the result of historical inequalities that could be remedied by elimination of sex-role stereotyping and equity policies. In their view, these measures, if well executed, could be comprehensive and sturdy enough to redress inequality in the present patriarchal and capitalist system. On the other hand, radical feminists stated that women's oppression was a result of patriarchal control of their fertility and sexuality and that women's position would not change until fundamental freedoms over reproduction were acquired. Socialist feminists believed that women's oppression was created and maintained by the interaction of the capitalist system, which created class inequalities, and the patriarchal system, which was founded on gender inequalities. Women are exploited both in the marketplace with low-paying jobs and at home with jobs for no pay. Reforms must be significant and must challenge both capitalism and patriarchy.

Problems resulted from these differences in feminist thinking. For one, most feminists were unable to distinguish themselves as purely one or other on the above schema, although most believed that a liberal analysis was eventually self-defeating (Ferguson, 1988). Further, the opportunities for endless and often overlapping divisions occurred: lesbian feminists of colour, working-class lesbian feminists of colour, and so on. The result was a search for differences rather than similarities. Further, internal struggles developed – who was more oppressed than whom – and these conflicts sapped strength from the movement. Middle-class white women, the initial leaders of the movement, became scorned and were scornful in return.

Some changes have occurred in the last decade. Feminist theory grew when it acknowledged that it could incorporate the pleasure that women achieved from serving others, the oppression of women by women, the reality of economic advantages that some women enjoyed, the equality that could exist between some women and men, and yet confirm that the basic fundamental principle of feminism still prevailed: women were oppressed because of their sex.

The acceptance of the heterogeneity of feminist thinking has resulted in another major achievement. Feminists gave up trying to create the one big overarching theory that would bind them together and instead opted for the notion of a cluster of concepts that would change as experience demanded but that would provide the basis for analysing other theories and approaches. And it has proved a useful route. For instance, McLeod and Saranga (1988) offer a feminist critique of the application of family systems theory to child sexual abuse. They state that the real problem of this theory is that it makes family dysfunction the central focus of the analysis. It explains sexual abuse as a coping mechanism for dysfunctional families, in system language a way of maintaining "homeostasis." In doing so, it blurs the fact that family sexual abuse is usually father-daughter incest, that it has a powerful impact on the child, and that fathers are responsible for their sexual behaviour rather than driven by uncontrollable needs. Instead, the mother's ability to manage the emotional needs of family members assumes major importance in the analysis and treatment. By contrast, feminist family systems therapists place the incest as the central problem and the reaction to it as the family dysfunction. They shift the foreground and the background. This analysis in turn demands answers to the question: why do men sexually abuse their daughters? The answers focus on male power and socialization rather than female inadequacy to control that power. Such an analysis also affects how these therapists work with families. Although they might use family systems therapy as a helpful way to deal with disclosure and the feelings of mothers and children, they do not advocate that offenders should be treated within the family systems approach.

Linda Gordon's work (1985) on the analysis of child welfare agency case records in Boston over the past 100 years is another example of how feminist thinking can alter the application of traditional theory. She began her study sympathetic to a Marxist point of view that child welfare agencies serve as vehicles of social control and that their development at the turn of the century was a result of the growing immigrant population, the new middle class of women available to acculturate these foreigners, and the need to restructure the family to serve the interests of the new ruling class of industry and manufacturing. However, while she found evidence that supported this perspective, she also discovered from the case records that the clients sometimes used the agencies to serve their own purposes. In spite of great risks, some women contacted the child welfare agencies themselves to report that their husbands were beating them. They used the power of the agency workers to protect them from their spouses and increase their own power bases within the family. Further, many middle-class women helpers understood and aided in this endeavour. An analysis of class oppression was incomplete if it did not also examine the oppression of women within the family, regardless of class. And the Marxist solution, to overthrow a class society, was useless to women if they were to remain oppressed within their families.

At the heart of the feminist critique is the challenge to theories and practices that ignore an analysis of power and gender. In child welfare, this challenge is reflected in the analysis of the cause of child neglect and abuse. Children suffer because their mothers are assigned their care yet do not have the power to provide for or protect them. Women's behaviour toward their children is better understood in terms of their powerlessness than their perversity. There is no expectation that redefinition of the problem to one of power will lead to a quick fix. Gordon (1986: 63) makes this point clearly when speaking of child sexual abuse:

> Child sexual abuse needs a political interpretation in terms of male power. However, the prosecution of culprits – however necessary – and the breaking up of families that may result do not always benefit the child victims. Especially if they are incestuous sex abuse cases which have something of the tragic about them, because once they arise, tremendous human damage has already occurred, and a politically correct analysis will not ease the pain. Still, that analysis, situating the problem in the context of male supremacy in and outside the family, is the only long term hope for prevention.

One of the most interesting campaigns to gain acknowledgement for the negative impact of power differentials between men and women has emerged from women engaged to end violence against women. These women have argued publicly over a long period of time that sexual assault is an assault by a more powerful person over another; it is not a situation where a lustful man simply couldn't control himself or where "boys will be boys." In redefining the problem as assault, women are hoping to elevate it to the same degree of seriousness as other assaults and to provide some neutrality to the offence so that more women will report assaults and lay charges.

Feminist thinking also includes the notion that a simple redistribution of power between men and women will not suffice; instead, a redefinition of the concept of power is required. Some feminist theorists (Fraser, 1989; Grosz, 1990; Stenstad, 1990; Hartsock, 1990) are challenging traditional definitions of power as a limited commodity, located in hierarchical structures and used to control others. They suggest that women need to examine alternative conceptions of power for several reasons. There are no guarantees that, should women obtain power as traditionally defined, they will wield it more wisely. Moreover, it seems that just as women step into so-called power positions, the power in those positions slips away. As Gunew (1990: 23) states: "It is not simply a question of storming a series of male citadels and of occupying the controls." Instead, women are questioning whether power is not better or also understood as an unlimited process that permeates all relationships, that can be resisted at all levels, and that can release as well as repress. Moreover, resistance is not the only strategy for those with less power. Power moves unevenly throughout the system, creating vacuums as well as points of concentration. Those with little apparent power can make strides, not by taking power away from others, but by moving into these vacuums. This was precisely what women in the sexual assault and transition house movements did in the 1960s. Rather than mutineers who want to seize power, they were like squatters. They created services where none had existed, and from these they developed their own power base.

Recent studies have also examined whether women have different notions of power, perhaps based on their long-standing subordinate position and their responsibility for caregiving. Drawing on the work of McClelland (1982) and Miller (1975), Gilligan (1983) suggests that women are more concerned than men with the notion of interdependence and that they equate power with giving and caring. McClelland, in his studies of male and female fantasies of power, noted that "while men represent powerful activities as assertion and aggression, women in contrast portray acts of nurturing as acts of strength" (1975, as quoted in Gilligan, 1983: 167-

68). Where women child welfare workers were asked to provide examples of powerful and powerless incidents in their work, they presented views of power that contained several common features (see Chapter 3). Workers had the resources and skills to help and knew what should be done. Clients benefited from that help and usually acknowledged the worker. Workers felt that they and their clients were in an authentic as well as a caring relationship. Women are questioning traditional views of power and proposing that the transformation of the concept, as well as its redistribution, is equally important.

In summary, feminist thinking is all about why women are oppressed and what can be done about it. It accepts that there are many answers and degrees of oppression, and even that a few women seemed to have escaped altogether. It rejects answers that do not explore the concept of power and challenge the seemingly inherent right of men to wield it.

THE CASE FOR FEMINIST APPROACHES TO CHILD WELFARE

An argument for feminist approaches to child welfare is not only ideological and theoretical: research supports the notion that there is a link between the status of women and the well-being of children. The following propositions make the argument.

Women are disadvantaged in Canadian society.

It has been well documented that, as a group, Canadian women have less power than Canadian men and that this difference in power is experienced in their homes, at work, at school, and in community and political life. Several reasons have been advanced for this difference in power but most relate in one way or another to the system of patriarchy and its permeation throughout societal structures and discourses. Further, there is general agreement that although the difference in power between men and women is experienced in many ways, economic inequality is the most fundamental, given the values of our culture and the realities of everyday living. Economic inequality does not simply mean unequal pay, although salary is important. It also means not being paid for one's work at all – caring for children and others, managing a household, and working in voluntary organizations. Further, Pateman (1988) has argued that the division between the public work of men for pay and the private work of women for free has created a situation where women do not only lose economic independence but the essence of citizenship as well. Our conception of citizenship is much broader than a legal status and a right to vote. It is fundamentally a concept of independence, the capacity to move freely and safely in the public sphere, to make and spend money, to acquire property, and to be governed by written laws and contracts. Although women ostensibly have such rights of citizenship, the reality of their life in private is often far different. Their own movement and freedom are curtailed and they are governed by unwritten traditions, ties of love, and the vagaries of their partnerships with men who have more power in the private sphere by virtue of their access to the public one.

The position of women in Canadian society has not improved noticeably in the last few decades. Although women have entered the labour market in large numbers during the last twenty years, they are still concentrated in low-paying, female-dominated positions (Parliament, 1990). More women than ever before are employed in part-time and seasonal work (Gunderson, Muszynski, and Keck, 1990). Those women who have entered male professions and occupations fare better but still earn considerably less than their male counterparts (Marshall, 1990).

Women who care for children are more likely to be disadvantaged than those who do not.
The second important issue is that the inequality of women is unequally distributed among women. Poverty, race, culture, marital and parental status, sexual orientation, and disabilities compound the disadvantage of gender and limit even further the opportunities for citizenship. Evans (1991) points out that although Canadian women have always experienced more poverty than their male counterparts, poverty has shifted in the last two decades. While the economic situation of married women has improved, more single-parent women live in poverty than before. Moreover, the economic situation for a married woman is only as good as her marriage. Should it end in separation or divorce, as 40 per cent do, there is a good possibility that she will join the ranks of her poor sisters (National Council of Welfare, 1990).

Women pay a high price for caring for children. An estimated 3.8 million Canadian women have children under the age of sixteen years. The care of children, particularly pre-schoolers, is the single most significant factor in determining the unemployment and underemployment of this group (Akyeampong, 1990). For single-parent women, the risks are considerably greater. Forty-four per cent of such families live below the poverty line. Unless they are able to combine full-time employment with full-time parenting, they are almost certain to live in poverty – 91.4 per cent of non-employed single mothers with children under seven years of age were poor (Gunderson, Muszynski, and Keck, 1990). In a recent report of women and poverty in Canada, the National Welfare Council (1990) concludes:

> The most disturbing finding of this report is the strong link between motherhood and poverty. Very early childbirth too often means a curtailed education and eventual single parenthood. The presence of children increases the risk of poverty of husband-wife families, largely because of the children's impact on the labour force participation of the wives. The impoverishing effect of single parenthood on women is well known.
>
> The link between motherhood and poverty is also clear in the case of older unattached women. Women in their fifties and early sixties who run the greatest risk of being poor are widows and divorced and separated women who spent many years at home caring for their families and are unable to find a place in the labour force. The poorest elderly women are widows who centred their lives on their husbands and children and did not acquire adequate savings and pension income.
>
> The fact that fathers are much less vulnerable to poverty demonstrates that things could be different. If mothers were provided with adequate supports from society, including affordable child care and longer maternity leaves, equal access to well-paying jobs and fairer support payments, and if we had better income security programs for parents and older people, then women would not have to choose between personal financial security and motherhood. (National Council of Welfare, 1990: 130-31)

Those who do child-care work outside the home, mostly women, are also disadvantaged. Day-care workers usually earn only minimum wages and have long and irregular hours of work, limited benefits, and few opportunities for advancement. A recent national study on wages and working conditions for child-care workers presents shocking findings. In spite of the fact that 68 per cent of child-care workers have post-secondary certificates or degrees compared to 41 per cent for the general labour force, the average national wage for child-care "teachers" – those in charge of a group of children, often with staff supervisory duties – was $18,498, a wage that had fallen by 4.5 per cent in the past seven years (*Caring for a Living*, 1992). Ninety-eight per cent of the workers were women.

Child welfare workers fare better but are also underpaid. For instance, the beginning wages for a child welfare worker in B.C. are $1,189-$1,368 biweekly for a social worker with a Master's degree. (By contrast, a highway safety program engineer with a Master's degree in engineering is offered $1,489-$1,654 biweekly.) Female social workers continue to earn less than their male counterparts. The average salary for a male social worker in B.C. in 1985 was $30,334; for a female the average was $27,777, or 91 per cent of her male counterpart. Overall, female social workers were paid less than the average wage for similar professional groups: female teachers earned $32,163; nurses and therapists, $29,033 (British Columbia Ministry of Labour, 1989: 83).

The more disadvantaged the mother or caregiver, the more disadvantaged the child.
This is the crux of the argument. The unequal status of women has two principal consequences for children. They are more likely to live in poverty and suffer the results because their mothers cannot earn sufficient wages and they are at greater risk of violence and sexual abuse because their mothers cannot protect them from likely offenders.

Many Canadian studies have documented the fact that children who live in poverty are more likely to have higher mortality rates, poor health, and poor school records, to be involved with the juvenile justice system, to have mental health problems, and to commit suicide (Trocme, 1991; Canadian Child Welfare Association *et al.*, 1988). Children who are poor and from Native backgrounds are often in double jeopardy, just like their mothers.

Poor children are more likely to come to the attention of child welfare agencies, a fact that is sometimes acknowledged but rarely addressed (National Council of Welfare, 1979; Callahan, 1985; Swift, 1991). In 1986 approximately 49,000 children were in the care of child welfare agencies. Although accurate statistics are difficult to obtain, agencies estimate that 66-75 per cent of such children come from poor families, even though such families constitute only about 20 per cent of the overall population (Canadian Child Welfare Association, 1988; National Council of Welfare, 1979). Novick and Volpe (1989) reported that 83 per cent of families served by a Children's Aid Society in Toronto had incomes below the Statistics Canada low-income cutoff and a further 11 per cent were economically vulnerable. At least half of the children in care come from single-parent families in spite of the fact that single parents constitute about 13 per cent of the families in Canada.

Native children are also disproportionately represented in the child welfare system; more than 20 per cent of children in care are of Native origin, yet Native children make up only 2 per cent of all Canadian children (Wharf, 1986).

The reasons why poor women and children and Native women and children are most likely to come to the attention of child welfare agencies are not hard to imagine. They cannot afford alternative child-care arrangements, professional counsellors, summer camps, boarding schools, and holidays away from their children, all of which form the central planks of a child welfare system for the well-to-do. Nor do they often have the connections, education, and status that would buffer them from inquiries by child welfare agencies. As will be discussed in the next section, child welfare agencies can further endanger the well-being of children, given their modest resources for caring and their inability to enhance the stature of mothers.

A recent study in British Columbia sheds even further light on the situation of women in the child welfare system (J. Campbell, 1991). This study confirms the above statistics: half the children taken into care in B.C. in 1988 came from single-parent families. The other half, the two-parent families, included blended, common-law, and short-term relationships. Nonetheless, the contrast between the female single-parent families and the others was remarkable, as Table 6.1 indicates.

The picture that emerges is striking. A major group of clients whose children are coming into care in the child welfare system are very poor women on social assistance who are charged with neglecting their young children. The same study also notes that children who entered care because of neglect – 70 per cent of all cases of apprehension – were much more likely to be reapprehended in future than those who entered care because of abuse.

The care of children also suffers, not just because their mothers have fewer economic resources but also because mothers are less able to protect them from violence. There is ample evidence that violence against women and children is motivated by deeply held views of the inferiority of women and the rights of men to dominate them. Some men see this as their right because they support their families financially and thus other family members are seen as weaker, as "less than," and as owing something to the one who supports them. In spite of this, many women remain in violent relationships because of their inability to support and protect themselves and their children independently (Barnsley et al., 1980). Many women are no safer and a lot poorer when they leave

Table 6.1

Characteristics of Children and Parents in Child Welfare by Marital Status in British Columbia, 1988

	Single parent (female)	Two parents
Reasons for apprehension		
sexual and physical abuse	17.4%	52%
neglect	52.1%	24.4%
other	30.5%	23%
Age of child		
adolescents	12.7%	52%
under 11 years	77.3%	48%
Income under $20,000	95%	46%
Income Assistance as source of family income	72%	33%

SOURCE: J. Campbell, 1991.

violent partners than if they remain. Further, the reluctance of women to leave violent relationships perpetuates them: from charges not being laid, to further beatings, to children that grow up to batter, and so forth (Price, 1991).

> The prescription for motherhood rips many women apart in terms of deciding to stay in or leave a violent domestic situation. Women report that they often stay because they are fearful of losing custody if they leave alone; because their children are at risk if left even temporarily with the husband; because they worry about inflicting "unnecessary" poverty or deprivation on their children; because they don't want to deny their children a father, or a "family"; because the courts usually grant fathers visiting privileges, thus providing dangerous access to the wife as well as the children; because they know the law provides no concrete protection from domestic male violence. (Levine and Estable, 1981: 18)

The care of children also suffers because of the relative power-lessness of the women social workers and the profession of social work. As noted in Chapter 3, child welfare workers are employed by large government bureaucracies where distances between policy managers, supervisors, and workers are often formidable and the perspectives of each group can differ sharply. It is difficult for workers to influence persons they do not see and argue for needs of clients that differ from prescribed services. Their own professional associations and unions are similarly disadvantaged. Workers report that their public service unions are often developed on a traditional union model, with wages and benefits as the key issues on the agenda. Professional social work associations are small, modestly funded organizations without the clout or the information to make waves.

Child welfare policy and service ignore the disadvantage of women and often exacerbate it.

There are several ways in which women's inequality is maintained through the present child welfare system. First, although most of the women and children are poor, the present system does not address their poverty or the reasons for it. Sometimes the child-care services and homemaker assistance provided to women "at risk" of neglecting or abusing their children can permit these women to seek work outside the home or provide them with needed goods and services. But they are usually time-limited, and when a mother shows some improvement she often loses these services. Further, when children are apprehended and removed from their mothers' care, women can become even poorer. In such circumstances women face the loss of self-esteem, the regard of family and friends, a reduced income assistance allowance, the child tax benefit, and eligibility for social housing. Women must adjust to being single upon the apprehension of the children and then have to begin over again with the children's return: finding a home, reinstating benefits, etc. Moreover, their children may compare them unfavourably with foster mothers who may have had more resources and time to offer children. Poor families receive less from the public purse to care for their children than do those who provide substitute care. It is estimated that in 1987 parents with a family income under $23,500 received $837 in family allowance payments and the child tax credit. By contrast it costs about $5,000 per year for a child in a foster home, $27,000 in a group home, and $54,000 in a special resource (Canadian Child Welfare Association, 1988).

One of the most troubling aspects of child welfare is this separation between poverty and child care. The relationship between these two factors is so self-evident it seems amazing that child welfare services do not make it front and centre in their business. But they do not. Instead, child welfare researchers and policymakers have accepted poverty as the context for the work and within that context have set about to develop other responses. A recent and widely acclaimed study illustrates this phenomenon

(Polansky, Gaudin, and Kilpatrick, 1992). A Maternal Characteristic Scale was applied to poor neglecting mothers and poor non-neglecting mothers, almost half Afro-American. The scale was successful in distinguishing between the two groups on their ability to relate, their impulse control, their confidence, and their verbal accessibility. Examples of such behaviour include "answers with single words," "hard to consider new ways," and "can laugh at herself." The authors suggest that the scale can be used by social workers to distinguish non-neglecting and neglecting mothers, and conclude:

> The MCS emphasizes unresolved schizoid elements and associated problems with forming relationships, communicating, internalizing controls, perceiving reality, self-observation, and empathy. At the level of character traits, we speak of the Apathy-Futility Syndrome and the Impulse-Ridden Character. . . . Review of specific behaviours calls attention to rigidity, withdrawal, flatness of affect, and lack of empathy. (278-79)

It would be equally possible to come to vastly different conclusions. The behaviour of the mothers could be viewed as behaviour typical of powerless people rather than of psychologically inadequate ones. The reasons why some poor mothers and not others exhibited these behaviours could be explained also in terms of powerlessness. The neglecting mothers were rated by child protection workers who had already identified these women as needing assistance. The control group was rated by headstart workers who had made no judgements about the mothers. As the neglecting group was involved in the child welfare system already, that fact alone could have made their behaviour even more typical of powerless people. The whole study could have been reframed to look at poverty, powerlessness, and the child welfare system. Instead, it ignored poverty and attempted to differentiate between mothers' capacity to manage in the face of it.

In a similar way, the fact that women are often unable to protect children from violent or sexually abusive partners is not addressed by child welfare policy and practice. The social worker, usually a woman, investigates the performance of a mother in protecting her child from an abusing man. Given this mandate, it is sometimes difficult for two women to develop a trusting relationship, an essential ingredient in child welfare work. Moreover, social workers work alone under the policies of confidentiality developed by organizations that also divide the work into individual cases assigned to individual workers. In this way, the cumulative experience of mothers living in poverty and violence and of workers who cannot assist women with their defined needs is not collected or broadcast. What is worse, the mother has been identified as inadequate and warned. Her own image of herself may be irrevocably changed from one who is coping to one who has been singled out as inadequate. There is a tendency to internalize this image in the absence of others who can share and support.

In one of the few studies on the operation of the child welfare system across Canada, the following description of practice concludes:

> Thus the non-offending parent, almost invariably the mother, will be left in charge of the victim only if her words and actions indicate that she does not blame the child, that she believes the child's complaint, and that she will be emotionally supportive (e.g., will place no pressure on the child to withdraw or alter his or her complaint). Also, the custodial parent must be willing to abide by any court order that prohibits the offender from having any communication or contact with his family. If the non-offending parent does not fulfil these requirements, it may be necessary to remove the child from the home. (Committee on Sexual Offences Against Children, 1984: 622)

This practice does not recognize the power position of the so-called non-offending parent. For instance, how can she keep away a persistent offender? How can she work outside the home and protect her children at the same time? If she remains at home, how can she support her children? Krane (1990) notes that women in these circumstances have an illusion of choice – between partner and children, between income and poverty, between predictable and unpredictable violence, and they must make their decision at a time when they are most vulnerable and least informed.

Even where mothers are not apparently at fault they can be held responsible. For instance, in her review of research on incest, Wattenberg (1985) notes the overwhelming number of studies that conclude mothers participate explicitly or implicitly in father-daughter incest. She suggests that this theory has developed for a number of reasons, including the availability of mothers and daughters as chief informants and as participants in treatment. She also notes that treating the mother is easier and fits more with professional training than taking strong action against the father. When such an inaccurate diagnosis is made about the mother's responsibility for family problems and "read back" to her, a method of silencing her is created and the theory and practice are self-perpetuating.

One of the most poignant tragedies, which illustrates the depth of the powerlessness of women, is the case of Ethel Mansell, a woman in Victoria, B.C., who burned herself and two of her three children to death. She was sexually abused herself as a child and married a man who was later charged with abusing a neighbourhood child. The charges were stayed for lack of evidence. She believed in her husband's innocence and continued her shift-work job to support the family, leaving him in charge of the children. He abused their daughter and two sons as well as other children and was eventually charged again. However, eight months elapsed between the information and an investigation. This time, he was convicted and imprisoned. Her recovery was slow but not without resources, which included neighbours, church, sexual assault services, counsellors, and psychiatrists.

> So why did she do it? Why did this decent, loving woman do the worst possible thing a human being can do? In tracing the bits and pieces of Ethel Mansell's ordinary life, in particular her last quite-well-documented days, only one reason emerges. Ethel Mansell did not kill herself and her children because she was lonely, divorced, on welfare, living in a basement suite, buying clothes at the Sally Ann, pinching every penny and more or less living every woman's nightmare. She killed herself because she had been sexually abused as a child and never recovered from it. She killed her children because her husband had been convicted of sexually abusing her daughter and her sons also displayed signs of sexual victimization. She had no faith that professionals' skills could undo the damage done, nor any faith whatever in society's ability or even willingness to protect them from the man she now saw as their aggressor – their father. . . . Ultimately, she and her children died because they had lived in a paternalistic society in which child sexual abuse is not only rampant but, to a considerable degree, tolerated. (Birnie, 1991: 22)

Another way in which child welfare perpetuates the inequality of women is in the organization of the work. Should children be removed from their home, they will usually be placed in a foster or group home where the caregivers are underpaid women whose jobs offer not only modest salaries, if any, but few benefits and little job security. The only opportunity for these women to earn more money is to take in an increasing number of difficult children and to ensure that the social worker knows that these children's behaviour does not easily improve. However, these women must also appear capable of coping with such difficulties or risk losing their jobs. Their work usually takes place in their own home or a group home and they are frequently isolated from other workers in similar positions, simply because they are the only caregivers or because they work shifts and rarely see other workers in the same home.

Although social workers are the best-paid workers in the field, their work is equally demanding and highly risky and has limited opportunities for advancement. They frequently work alone, in the homes of their individual clients and with a changing set of colleagues from other organizations, such as police and public health nurses (Callahan and Attridge, 1990). Few female social workers become managers. In a recent study comparing male and female supervisors, Hallett (1989) discovered that male supervisors ranked the following tasks as most important for supervisors: ensuring statutory responsibilities are carried out, giving practical advice, and monitoring standards. Female supervisors, on the other hand, ranked supporting staff in the stresses of the job and helping staff to prioritize work and manage a caseload as the most important tasks. The author concluded that while no one in management suggested directly that women supervisors were not as competent as men, it was evident from the responses of senior management that women's approach to supervision was not valued.

Child welfare as it is presently constituted does not just ignore the poverty and powerlessness of women and exacerbate these, it also perpetuates the division between public and private realms at the heart of women's inequality and their inability to enjoy full citizenship. Child welfare work is concerned with the private lives of families and has a mandate to peep into this world and see how it is getting along. Although pursued through the auspices of a public agency, the work is actually carried out very privately, family by family, woman to woman, confidential case by confidential case, and the work is divided as family work is often divided – women doing the caring; men managing the operations. Instead of seizing the opportunity to make some aspects of private family needs a public business, a public agency often buries them as deeply as private families do.

The child welfare system is concerned with the division of rights and responsibilities for children between parents and the state and between parents themselves. Fundamentally, families are charged with the right and responsibility to care for their children. Although ideologies differ about the degree of state involvement in the care of children, there is general agreement that the state has two roles: to provide care in situations where families are wholly or partially unable to do so and to intervene when parents cannot agree between themselves about who should have custody and care for children. Child welfare is that arm of the state charged with carrying out this mandate.

By contrast, feminist approaches argue that, in reality, it is not families who are responsible for the care of children, it is women both within and outside the family. Feminists have proposed several different but related theories to explain this division of labour and the separation of the sexes into private and public domains. But they agree that women and children have been severely disadvantaged by these arrangements. Thus, feminist thinking on child welfare is not directed at sorting out the boundaries between the rights and responsibilities of parents and of the state for the care of children, between the private world of families and the public world of state services. Instead, it examines how child care has become women's work, both publicly and privately, that is devalued and underpaid. The aim of feminist child welfare is to reveal the importance of child care, wherever it is done, with the purpose of making it an essential, valued enterprise. By doing so, the lot of children, women, and the society as a whole will be improved. Policies and services to accomplish this include pay equity, public child care, domestic labour codes, and parental leaves.

Feminist approaches also suggest that there is no one right child welfare system but that child welfare, like any policy area, is an ongoing process of development and change. However, feminists argue that women's vast experience in caring for children must be central in the development of policy. They also state that women's experience will not be homogeneous but will vary according to the times, the culture, the class, and the individual backgrounds of the women involved. The policy process should be flexible, open, and changing to meet varied needs. Women should also take a principal role in the policy process as a crucial step in gaining their own sense of power and respect.

Clear advantages in refocusing on the inequality of women and connecting child welfare to the women's movement are the prospects of helping clients and workers in the system to emerge and make change and, similarly, the opportunity for the public to learn more about the real workings of the system. Many of the issues in a feminist approach to child welfare – child care, employment equity, violence against women – are already a part of the agenda of women's organizations. But they have not been conceptualized as including an overhaul of the child welfare system. Moreover, because women workers in child welfare may feel guilty about what happens to their women clients and their part in it and because woman clients feel ashamed of themselves, they cannot galvanize support within the women's movement for their cause. A feminist reinterpretation would change this.

There are several dissenting arguments to the one put forward thus far. First, feminists note that the interests of women and children may differ and that connecting child welfare and the advancement of women may not recognize these differing interests. Moreover, when women's and children's interests are combined, women lose out. Second, making a connection between the care of children and the status of women may further the status quo. This is an important issue. On one hand, an argument can be made that, because women have had the responsibility for the care of children historically yet none of the authority for public policy, this latter fact should be reversed. However, if women take over the public power in child care, will it be further identified as a woman's matter and further confined to the responsibility of women? There is another, related argument: that placing emphasis on women's rights will erode further the concept of the family. In this view, women will increasingly raise children without a male partner if the state assumes more responsibility for the breadwinner role. However, Ehrenreich (1983) questions this view. She argues that an increasing number of men have abandoned the "breadwinning" ethic, begining with the *Playboy* and beatnik rebellion of the fifties and continuing through the hippie movement of the sixties and the humanistic psychology notions of the seventies and eighties. Her conclusion is that the family has more to fear from this erosion than from the feminist movement.

The final objection is possibly the most compelling. Feminist perspectives may appear too doctrinaire to have much influence on mainstream child welfare policies, which, like all social policies, represent a series of ideological, theoretical, and practical compromises. The next two sections of the chapter will attempt to address these concerns, first by relating the practical experience of women who have delivered feminist services and then by examining the feasibility of introducing feminist policy and organizational changes into mainstream child welfare services.

THE EXPERIENCE OF FEMINIST SOCIAL SERVICES

The literature on Canadian feminist services is sparse and largely includes descriptive accounts of the history of individual services or organizational strategies to develop and operate such services. Given the recent history of women's services in Canada (the first transition house was developed in 1972), the monumental work involved in maintaining such services, and the difficulty in changing large intractable bureaucracies in child welfare, this modest literature base is not surprising.

Feminist child welfare services could make distinct contributions to our thinking about child welfare in three areas: the development of a compelling mission; a commitment to voluntary programs; and the development of new organizational forms. Each of these will be discussed below.

A Mission – Coming Out on the Side of Clients

Many early child welfare pioneers undertook their duties fervently with a strong sense of purpose: to save children from the ravages of drunken or dispirited parents, godlessness, homelessness, ignorance, and exploitation. In retrospect, this mission has been largely discredited. Instead, these "child-savers" are viewed as taming and transforming the lower classes and improving their own social stature in the process. Yet many of these pioneers cared about children and parents and believed strongly that they could lift them, one by one, to a better life (Morrison, 1976; Mitchinson, 1987). The same sense of commitment to a cause is probably the most important feature of feminist child welfare services. Although the analysis is markedly different, the belief that women and children deserve much better and that improvements can be created from group efforts is similar. Present feminist workers take the analysis for change much further than their foremothers, however.

One of the most interesting aspects of feminist child welfare services is their commitment to creating social change as well as meeting the sometimes overwhelming individual needs of those who come for assistance. There are four particular ways in which women's services have done this. First, individual organizations have focused on one specific aspect of women's oppression: violence toward women or sexual assault or reproductive rights. Thus, the service has a distinct flavour and a manageable mission. Second, organizations have written their commitment to social change into their mission statements and have attracted those with devotion to this mission. Maxwell (1987) compared twenty-five rape crisis centres with other community service organizations and concluded that these centres engage in much more community education and other social change activities than do mainstream human service organizations. Third, most feminist organizations include a structural analysis of client situations in their day-to-day service with clients. Most offer the opportunity for clients to come together and witness that they are not alone but part of a larger issue. Thus the dissemination of knowledge, the development of a movement, and the provision of service are intertwined. The historical development of transition houses is a good example of how service delivery can elevate a private trouble to a public issue. When the Chiswick women came together to form the first transition house in England, they did not do so quietly. Once the women were gathered, once they began to tell their stories to one another, once they illegally occupied a house in downtown London and told why, the private became public and a movement began in earnest (Rose, 1978). Finally, some feminist organizations have developed umbrella organizations without service responsibilities but with a clear social change focus. Many of the provincial associations of transition houses serve such a purpose in Canada.

This focus on change and service is not without difficulties. The sheer demands of a crisis service can overwhelm other activities unless the two are truly woven together. When service and change are combined in the helping process and not done well, as has been reported in a few celebrated cases, there can be serious consequences (Ridington, 1982). Clients may feel the service is merely evangelism and that their individual needs are not heard. Government legislation provides other roadblocks. The societies legislation in most provinces places limits on the rights of voluntary organizations to take a political stance. Similarly, the federal Act that provides for charitable income tax status for service organizations restricts the formal constitutions of these organizations to service goals.

Feminist analysis of child welfare also recognizes that the needs of women and the needs of children will sometimes differ and that these differences are to be acknowledged and accepted. Feminist approaches do not weigh the relative merits of the needs of women, men, and children (Dominelli, 1989). Instead, the emphasis is on finding opportunities for individuals to define their own circumstances and needs as part of the process of gaining control. This analysis includes children and explores ways in which they may participate fully in family and community life. However, child welfare services based on this analysis include responses to the needs of mothers and fathers as well as the needs of children as a legitimate aim of the services. Further, women and men are seen as equally deserving of opportunities, not just in relation to improving their ability to "parent" but as people with the right to full lives. The right of women and men not to be parents is a component of such practice. Clearly, birth control and adoption planning are crucial elements. Thus, feminist approaches challenge the view that parents' needs, particularly the needs of mothers, should take second place.

These principles are often easy to implement in practice because the needs of parents and children are frequently complementary. For instance, as parents feel better about their ability to support their children, they often improve their ability to provide care, their self-esteem improves, and children benefit. Less frequently, these needs are contradictory. A dramatic example occurs when parents' religious beliefs prohibit life-saving medical assistance for their children. A more frequent and difficult instance is the reality that women sometimes abuse and neglect their children, although not in proportion to the time that they spend in caring for them. Some would argue that feminist analysis breaks down at this point. Women may abuse their power with their children; it is not just men that do so. However, an analysis of oppression of women still does apply. It is well demonstrated that those with limited power often do wield it unwisely on those below them. As women feel powerless, they may take out their feelings on those over whom they have some power. The importance of responding to women in these circumstances with attention to their needs apart from those of their children is well documented in the practice of mainstream and alternative child welfare services. It is also important to acknowledge that while feminist perspectives provide a crucial analysis to these situations, they do not constitute all that is needed. Knowledge about behaviour emerges from many theories and many other quarters. Feminist perspectives help to sift that knowledge to ensure that it does not compound the disadvantage of women.

The experience of the Barnardo's Waverly Centre in New South Wales is interesting in its attempts to balance the needs of mothers and children and create a system that acknowledges the importance of caring work (Smith and Smith, 1990). Barnardo's is a voluntary organization with a mandate to place children in foster care and work with their families. Apprehensions are carried out by a state service. Several years ago, the Centre, under the leadership of women with a strong commitment to advance the cause of the clients they served, decided to recast the mission of the organization. As more than 70 per cent of their clients were single-parent women on welfare, they acknowledged that the agency should aim to be a child-minding service for poor women, not unlike the services provided for those who could afford them. As one worker put it, "We say it all the time to the mothers: You are not a failure. I can pay for care. I have a grandmother down the road. You do not have these resources and you deserve them." Natural mothers are viewed as women needing respite child care. They have the right and responsibility to choose that care and to make the major decisions regarding the care of their children with the foster mother and the social worker. Foster mothers are considered workers and are paid double the state rates for foster care. Foster mothers are recruited from the ranks of women who have faced many of the situations confronting natural mothers. As one stated: "You work as a team, not a hierarchy, you don't come from a position of superiority." One of the aims of the service is to create an extended family for women who are alone with their parenting. Foster mothers become like aunts and sisters in some cases and they continue the relationship after the children return home as a part of their job. Barnardo's has tracked its success. Over 90 per cent of children are returned to parents, compared to 57 per cent for state-run services.

Feminist practice is further committed to redefining the notion of family so that it meets the needs of women and children as well as partners and fathers. Indeed, some nuclear families do this very well. And some do not. Alternative family forms, such as second-stage housing projects where women and children live in semi-private accommodations and have opportunities to share responsibilities and offer comfort, provide another option. Stack (1975, as quoted in Gilligan, 1983) investigated an urban black ghetto in the U.S. and saw it very differently from other researchers, who had previously underlined its socially disorganized features. She gained this alternate view by redefining families as "the smallest organized, durable network of kin and non-kin who interact daily, providing the domestic needs of children and assuring their survival," and then could identify crucial networks of domestic exchange that occurred daily.

Voluntary Services and Statutory Funding

Feminists have had mixed views of statutory services. On the one hand, women have argued that state services for women, designed and organized as they are from patriarchal ideologies, actually share much more in common with private family process than with public provisions (Abramovitz, 1988). While laws may be made in public, they are implemented by professionals and bureaucrats who are guided by a labyrinth of policies developed in the privacy of individual offices and confidential communications. Moreover, because the foundation of patriarchal public policies is based on traditional beliefs about women and their place in society, these policies become self-fulfilling; the public continues its belief about women and the individual women consumers become dependent on the services. State provisions for child care make this point. Stingy services are provided by ill-paid women to women and their children, selected because of their inability to provide for themselves. The status quo is maintained.

On the other hand, women have fought to achieve statutory services and their rights to the bounties of the state enshrined in law. Some point out that when the state provides, it does so under public laws that can be challenged and changed, unlike the private customs of individual families. Therefore, women have the opportunity to make their needs known in a public forum and to band together to ensure that they are met.

Most feminist child welfare services are offered through voluntary societies but funded primarily by the state, something of a compromise. Although satisfactory from some points of view, there are well-documented drawbacks, including inadequate funding, inconsistent service from community to community, and lack of access to the government policy process. Becoming a fully fledged government service also offers mixed blessings. Ridington (1982), tracing the development of the Vancouver Transition House from a voluntary organization to a full government service, notes that becoming a government agency provided a more stable funding base and access to clients who might never have been referred to an independent feminist organization. It also meant differential salaries among workers, membership in a large and generally unsympathetic union, and a gradual dissolution of a strong feminist philosophy.

Because a feminist analysis allows for both the potential and danger of state provisions, it encourages feminists to reform state services rather than abandon them or work for their destruction. It also directs attention to those aspects of policy and organization that control rather than empower.

All talk of empowerment fades, however, if a service system is unable to listen to what clients say they need, cannot design flexible services to meet these needs, and refuses to allow clients to select services as they wish, particularly clients who by virtue of age, sex, class, and race are profoundly disadvantaged. Nonetheless, it has proved a daunting task to develop such a flexible service system. In many ways, the development of the shelter movement, while not perfect, has much to offer this discussion.

The development of transition houses was based on the assumption that ill-paid women's organizations could not develop an all-encompassing service and should instead focus on what women needed most: a secure environment, material assistance (food, clothing, shelter), and support of other women in the same boat. What women may also need – money, income assistance, child care, lawyers, safety orders, housing, jobs, and psychiatric help – could not be provided but the organization could serve as a broker and advocate for these. The service was also fluid: women could stay at home and receive counselling and support, refer themselves, define abuse themselves, leave if they wished, work with whom they choose, and so forth. To further promote a commitment of voluntary service, transition houses maintained a clear separation between their services and the legal system and advocated for such a distinction. Offenders were dealt with in court. If women abused or neglected their children in transition houses, workers reported them to child protection authorities. The limits were clear; the needs were most urgent; the service was voluntary.

Although transition houses have aimed for such a program philosophy, in reality there are ongoing problems. Workers have control of resources, which gives them power and sometimes diffuses a client-controlled service. However, clients have the opportunity to create a power base because they know each other and often outnumber the workers (Harmon, 1989). The limiting of services to concrete and vital needs provides focus but at the same time workers often express a sense of working very hard, day after day, to accomplish nothing overall (Vance, 1979). There is a deeply felt sense of ambivalence that can sap strength and commitment (Rose, 1978). Transition houses are, in some ways, like food banks – they blunt the grief.

An interesting outcome of the original transition house movement has been its adaptation to different settings and different client groups. For instance, in rural British Columbia the concept of a transition house makes little sense. Women are too widely scattered to use it easily and it would be impossible to conceal the identity of such a house in a small town. Instead, safe houses, a network of individual homes where residents volunteer to shelter women and children, have been developed. Recent developments in the U.K. and Germany have attempted to apply the transition house model to much younger women, girls who have been sexually assaulted in their homes and do not feel safe. Hamburg's *Madchenhaus* (young women's house) is a refuge for girls ages 13-18 who refer themselves at any time and remain as they wish. (Parents are notified and must consent within forty-eight hours or a court order is obtained.) Most of the young women have been sexually abused, many by their fathers, and the aim is to provide a space and opportunity for women to talk about their lonely experience and find ways to deal with it, usually first with themselves, then with their mothers (O'Hara, 1990).

Innovative Organizations

Feminists have been committed to the development of organizations that reflect their philosophy and aims and that also can be shaped by the ideals and culture of the particular women involved. These organizational forms vary but share two essential qualities: the creation of different alliances within the organization and between the organization and its constituency and the sharing of responsibilities and rights among different constituencies. One of the interesting observations of feminists working from within the bureaucracy to create change (Smith and Smith, 1990; Dominelli, 1989; Hegar and Hunzeker, 1988; Schwartz, Gottesman, and Perlmutter, 1988) is the emphasis on developing alliances among sympathetic policy-makers, managers, and workers. In this view, it is not sufficient simply to elevate women into management positions so that they can make the desired changes. Rather, those at different levels of the organization have their own kind of power, and change is most likely to occur if that power is harnessed at all levels, even if the actual numbers of sympathetic feminists is small. Further, women writing about bureaucracies emphasize the importance of developing alliances between those within the bureaucracy and those in their policy communities: namely social movement members, union members, and academics. In a sense, the boundaries of the organization are drawn differently, not between those at different levels or between those within and those without. Organization members are viewed as those with a commitment to the ideology and aims of the project.

The second characteristic of feminist organizations, most evident in feminist community organizations, is the commitment to break down vertical specialization – the assignment of tasks on the basis of different levels of the organization – and horizontal specialization – the assignment of different aspects of the helping process to different individuals or departments. Thus there are attempts to involve workers, clients, board members, and other experts in policy-making, management, and service delivery. Helping is viewed as a holistic process involving many who share their personal selves and take as well as give.

Participants in feminist organizations have learned a great deal about this ideal of collectivity and how it can best work. When many feminist organizations first began, the commitment to developing new organizational forms was so strong that the collectives that then developed became as rigid as the bureaucracies they were designed to replace. Women were reluctant to demonstrate their expertise in case they were viewed as taking over; others feared doing too much for the same reasons. Collective decision-making included all decisions for all members of the collective. Since many could not commit such time to the endeavour, they dropped out.

However, several important features of collective decision-making have been retained by most feminist organizations. The first is that those who have to implement the decisions should be the ones who make them. House meetings where residents and staff sort out the logistics of their day-to-day living or consumer, volunteer, staff meetings where programs are developed are a common feature. The second is that overall policy-making should be carried out by all because fundamental policy affects everyone. Thus, long-range planning or contentious policy issues are typically sorted out in full collective meetings where all can have a voice. Rose (1978: 257), in reviewing the early U.K. experience, concludes:

> Despite this very unevenness of achievement between and within the separate refuges, the whole is characterised by a continuous and painstaking attempt to find the precise shape of these social forms which speak of a new society while at the same time providing a framework within which the struggle against the injustice of the present society can be waged. The juxtaposition, between the enforced dependency and powerlessness of women enshrined within the assumptions and legislation of the Welfare State, and the conception of women as equal and independent beings, which infuses the work of Women's Aid, could not be more complete.

The Los Angeles County Department of Children's Services, a large, complex bureaucracy with the usual funding and operational constraints of public child welfare organizations, provides an interesting example of a public agency that attempted to incorporate some of these overall features of feminist organizations (Weil, 1988). In 1978 the agency established a special child sexual abuse unit with the mandate to provide services for crisis, protection, court investigations, supervision, and individual and family therapy. Interestingly enough, the unit was to work with Parents United, a self-help organization that had supported the initial development of the unit. Not unexpectedly, it was a tall order. Workers were soon overwhelmed. Rather than hire more personnel or control intake, the staff decided to take another tack, based on a feminist analysis of the problem and its possible responses. They developed group programs for parents, victims, and siblings as the method of choice and referred elsewhere those who required long-term individual treatment. They removed protection investigations from staff responsibility and referred these to the regular protection units. Volunteers from Parents United were trained to provide the crisis services. They ensured that the needs of fathers, mothers, victims, and siblings were met by assigning them to separate programs and different workers where appropriate. To manage this rapidly changing organization, they developed what they called a feminist matrix management model. Each worker in the unit was simultaneously in charge of one self-help group and served on the committee for another program area. The leadership was committed to this shared management model and to ensuring that the unit survived in the uncertain political climate of a large and harried bureaucracy. Although specific outcomes are not reported, the evaluation emphasizes the high degree of staff satisfaction and the ongoing involvement of Parents United.

Another interesting example of innovation within statutory government services is emerging on Vancouver Island, where women supervisors of child protection units are changing the distribution of the work (Bishop, 1992). Instead of assigning caseloads to individual workers, supervisors are forming teams and developing group caseloads. Each team is responsible for organizing the work as they see fit and for identifying methods of accountability. Benefits to workers include a shared sense of responsibility, colleagues who can support and advise, and an increased feeling of control over the amount and flow of the work. As a team, workers feel that they can argue more forcefully for a reasonable workload. Benefits to clients include more accessibility and continuity of service and some degree of choice of workers. In recent months, the B.C. Ministry of Social Services has taken the recommendations of this chapter and initiated a pilot project to determine how child welfare services can be delivered by women child welfare workers, in concert with clients and with a focus on economic as well as social responses. Although this work is just beginning, it provides a concrete example of the resonance that feminist arguments are beginning to make in child welfare.

One of the interesting overall comments about women's services is that, while they are bone clear on the cause and remedy of women's inequality, they allow for contradictions and try to avoid the usual dichotomies: service or change; women or children; government or voluntary; professional or self-help. Pennell (1987) has analysed the ideological statements of a transition house and has concluded that the refusal to engage in these debates is functional: it avoids distraction from the main issues and allows women from various backgrounds to engage in a common struggle. It also allows women to reframe the issues as they see them rather than in terms defined for them, in itself a powerful activity.

POLICY RECOMMENDATIONS FOR CHILD WELFARE

It is not the intent here to present a detailed blueprint of policy, programs, and organizational design to implement a feminist perspective on child welfare. In fact, this would be contrary to the basic notions of feminist process: that those involved should create changes and that there is no one best way or product. On the other hand, some logical changes for mainstream child welfare emerge from the above analysis. The policy planks for building feminist approaches to child welfare include the following.

Rekindling and Reformulating a Mission

The women's service experience directs attention to the value of helping clients and workers develop a common analysis of problems and a common vision for change that is on the side of clients. The linchpin of this analysis is a feminist critique of patriarchy and its impact on the family. Given the enormous barriers – the present philosophy of government, the indifference of the public, the traditional structures of child welfare organizations, the privacy of the casework process, and the sense of shame of many clients – changing ideological orientations is not an easy task.

One method would be to do as Native people have done: seize authority and simply create independent child welfare services, begin to practise in more communal ways, and, in the process, gain legitimacy for the work. As noted above, another approach is for like-minded workers and managers to reform small units of child welfare offices based on feminist thinking. On a day-to-day basis workers within traditional child welfare organizations can challenge those policies and procedures that obscure a feminist analysis. They can, for instance, refuse to apprehend children from homes where the mother seems unable to protect her children from a male offender and demand that she be provided with assistance in maintaining security. Within the women's movement, feminists could make ongoing connections between child welfare and violence, poverty and powerlessness, and use the public voice of the movement to broadcast the issues. Schools of social work could make changes in their curricula, as some are doing, to include class, race, and gender analyses (Moreau, 1990). Scholars have a particular obligation to challenge the androcentric bias in much of their theories. A concerted effort on several fronts is required.

Another strategy for reformulating the mission of child welfare is to develop pride in our heritage and connect the contributions of heroines, long dismissed or forgotten, to present practice. The history of child welfare is an illustrious one, and many of the pioneers were women who took great risks and were determined to bring about changes for women and children. While their efforts can look simplistic today to those with a managerial frame of reference, or naive and even oppressive to radicals, their actual accomplishments were astonishing for mostly unmarried, middle-class women with little encouragement to attend university or make careers for themselves. Their deep commitment to a cause is evident in the following anecdote from Bessie Snider, a single woman employed as a general welfare worker in northern B.C.

> I did an interesting little piece of research of my own. I was able to get an Indian family on one of the islands down the Skeena River on Mother's Allowance and I had to fight very hard with our supervisors who received our reports at head office to make this happen. You see, you got more on Mother's Allowance for a while. And I was so pleased. . . . Her husband had been a fisherman and had drowned. . . . When I would visit her, and I would have to go with the Indian agent on his boat to visit this family, I had said to the mother, you know, we do have some of our Mother's Allowances recipients . . . keep a record of what it costs for them to buy certain things. And I had to explain to mothers when I was asking them [to do] this . . . how it would be helpful if I had this information so that I could get it back to our office to get the allowance revised. So I had said to this mother

in the presence of her teenage boy, who would be about twelve, no more, we have a column for miscellaneous. If you can't remember everything and anything that you do have to spend money on, you put it in the miscellaneous. So the boy said to me, "How do you spell miscellaneous," and I spelled it out for him. Well, when I came back the next time, they had this beautifully outlined in a scribbler and the boy had done this and he was so pleased about this. . . . they never saw these books that the mothers were keeping, though I would send down reports telling them how inadequate the allowance was.

[Later while working at headquarters in Victoria] I was a member of the federal-provincial committee on Indians and I was the chief representative of our department, and Shirley Arnold who was the head social worker for the federal department of Indian Affairs and the co-chairman and we had one of our district supervisors on the committee. We had a couple of Indian agents on that committee. . . . We met once a month, and it took us ten years to get a similar amount of social assistance to Indian peoples as to non-Indians. We went all over the province, we talked to municipal people and so on and so on. We talked to our regional administrator and finally we convinced them that these people were people, Indian children were like our children and they could not subsist on the amount of Indian relief. And for sure, Shirley Arnold, who's still living and a very great friend of mine, would concede that was the one thing that we did, probably the only thing we did, after ten years of meeting. (Hill, 1990: 24-25, 28-29)

Women such as Snider had a clear sense of purpose and a commitment to social change that placed them on the margins from their contemporaries, yet this commitment sustained them even though they had been marginalized and sometimes ridiculed.

Creating a Manageable Mandate

The child welfare system cannot be responsible for tackling the massive problem of the inequality of women and meeting all of the needs of families and children. However, it can do its part in making change. No government departments speak for the status of mothers and the care of children in a comprehensive fashion, and the new child welfare system could fill such a void. The mission could focus on advocacy, service, and research. Advocacy could aim to develop a compatible policy system for mothers and children. Given the above analysis, the bundle of compatible policies would include primarily those concerned with the economic status of mothers: child tax benefit, child tax credit, a mother's allowance, spousal support, social assistance, child care, employment equity, family housing, and those having to do with family violence. In this latter mission, child welfare might link closely with the transition house and sexual assault movements.

The services co-ordinated and offered by this system at the local level would primarily concern the care of children overall and the special needs of children and caregivers who by virtue of income, race, handicaps, parenting difficulties, and other variables require a different range of services. Day care would be the central program of child welfare, but other essential services are pre- and postnatal health, family planning, and women's resource services. These services would be developed with the founding principle that improving the status of mothers and the care of children are not contradictory aims. The crucial lesson from feminist services, that long-term change is a day-to-day activity, would be important to incorporate in any new system. The method of working with women and children would closely parallel that in existing feminist services.

Separation of Services

All of the above examples of feminist child welfare services have separated the mandate of child apprehension from voluntary services to families and have distinguished between behaviours more appropriately dealt with by courts and needs more appropriately dealt with by services. According to this experience, crimes should not be ignored and people cannot be empowered through force. It is timely for those in mainstream child welfare services to re-examine this issue. As noted at the beginning of this chapter, the impact of a rising number of abuse reports on child welfare organizations has been to turn them into quasi-judicial services. The needs of voluntary clients with less defined legal needs invariably assume a lower priority.

In implementing such a separation, several models could be explored. In any model, the so-called crime of neglect should simply disappear from the child welfare statutes. Instead, child welfare statutes could be reframed to define the caring services to be provided and the circumstances under which they will be provided. If chronic neglect is primarily a matter of poverty, frequently the poverty of disadvantaged women, then it should be dealt with as a resource issue rather than a personal, individual problem. If situational neglect occurs, such as the abandonment of children, then such problems can be dealt with by providing care and resources to children, locating parents, and helping them make plans for their children. Proving them unfit to care for their children in either case is irrelevant, as it wastes court time and damages parent-child relationships. Voluntary care orders would remain. In any event, neglect could remain within the Criminal Code for those difficult cases where serious neglect occurs yet help is refused.

Such a change may seem like an impossible task, but it is interesting to consider that another long-standing and similar offence, incorrigibility, was removed from many child welfare statutes without fanfare and without apparent problems almost two decades ago. The reasoning then was similar to the case for removing neglect as a cause for protecting children now. Incorrigibility was an imprecise term and often included children with a host of mental, physical, and behavioural problems. The court process frequently alienated parents and children further, one blaming the other, and the care provided by the state frequently did not change the child or improve the family relationships. At present, most of these cases are dealt with outside of court as voluntary care agreements or family service cases. The new child welfare legislation in Ontario, which, along with the Alberta statute, makes the most concerted attempt to identify specific reasons for child apprehension, does not include neglect as a possible reason. Instead, severe emotional harm, serious mental, emotional, or developmental conditions, and abandonment, possible indicators of neglect, are identified as reasons for apprehension.

It is more difficult to consider the ramifications of removing abuse investigations from the mandate of child welfare organizations and charging the criminal justice system to deal with such offences. This measure is a highly controversial one and has been debated frequently by child welfare specialists. The Committee on Sexual Offences Against Children (1984) identified two particular approaches to child sexual abuse prevalent in child welfare systems in Canada: *the child-centred approach*, where sexual crimes were referred to the criminal justice system and the focus of effort was on supporting the victim and punishing the offender; and *the family-centred approach*, where attempts were made to minimize the criminal justice system and use family counselling methods to help families deal with sexual abuse. The findings of the study indicate that, given what is known now, the child-centred approach appeared to be preferable in protecting children and providing support to them and the non-offending members of their families. In effect, those child welfare systems that emphasized distinctions between crimes and service seemed to be doing a better job.

There are several arguments against the sole use of the criminal justice system. First, the police are viewed as unsuitable investigators of the murky issues of family problems. The uncertainties of many such situations may lead them to avoid such cases, dismiss them, or to charge parents unnecessarily. In some cases, the mere presence of the police may make unfounded complaints even more traumatic for the family and children. Second, opponents suggest that those carrying out investigations should have some knowledge of and commitment to what happens to families and children afterwards. Otherwise they may prosecute cases without due consideration to the consequences and leave others to pick up the pieces. The third objection is perhaps the most compelling. The standards of evidence in criminal cases are far higher than those for civil cases tried under protection legislation. Given the difficulty in proving many child abuse cases, a higher standard of evidence would make the problem of obtaining a conviction that much worse.

There are several ways in which these arguments could be addressed without abandoning the case for a separation of functions. Some child welfare agencies have developed separate protection and family service units, although this is usually only possible in larger centres and there are still obvious connections between units. Although workers may understand the separation of functions, clients often do not. Another approach is to assign the authority for child abuse investigations under present child welfare legislation and the Criminal Code to a separate body, perhaps the police or the Crown prosecutor's office. These organizations could hire social workers to carry out the investigations and co-ordinate the responses. Both these approaches maintain the current child welfare legislation and allow civil as well as criminal proceedings. A third approach would be to rescind civil proceedings in child abuse and turn such prosecutions over to the police, who again could hire special personnel for the job.

My preference is for the second alternative. It provides for genuine separation and maintains civil as well as criminal proceedings. Child abuse work could be combined with the family violence sections of police departments or prosecutors' offices, providing a more comprehensive service with more clout within the department. There will be ongoing overlap between child welfare agencies and police or other investigating bodies, as there is now. Some preliminary work may still be better (or inevitably) carried out by child welfare. However, it is important to ensure that the whole service philosophy and organization are not defined by the minority of situations that do not fit in. This issue requires further debate but does not undermine the argument for separation of services.

In separating mandatory from voluntary services in child welfare, at least two outcomes are expected. Consumers will be more willing to go for help if they do not think they are in danger of losing their children, and thus more cases, which are now dealt with in court, will now be handled through a voluntary process. Women will be more likely to achieve and maintain control of the voluntary service system because it fits more with a feminist philosophy and their long-standing experience with working with one another.

Organizational Reform

Many of the suggested reforms emanating from feminist services are not unique but have been identified in the literature on quality of work life and in Japanese management approaches. Some suggestions include that child welfare services should be controlled by women and collaboratively organized and they should offer open connections between private and public work.

In terms of control, women should be represented at all levels of the system in proportion to their responsibilities for caring for children and their presence in the child welfare work force. The system should model its message.

Women's organizations are relatively flat structures, with movement among positions. They also stress the importance of connecting with other like-minded organizations and social movements and building services on models of self-help. Self-help services do not exclude professional helping but allow for the development of client connections so that they can both help each other and have a power base from which to be more informed consumers of professional services. A self-help model also provides a clear structure for consumers to speak publicly about their needs.

Finally, women's organizations do not sharply divide work life and private life. Organizations can encourage workers to harmonize their private and public responsibilities, for example, by organizing work so that it can be done at flexible times and places, by providing on-site child care, and by developing flexible sick leave and parental leave policies. In effect, this ethos illustrates the mission of child welfare: child care is public business for child welfare workers as well as their clients.

CONCLUSION

The present child welfare system is concerned with identifying unacceptable behaviours of children and/or parents and changing them. This work may be done after so-called bad behaviour occurs, the residual approach, or before, the preventive approach. It may be done with the individual, with small groups, or with identified communities. The work may primarily involve counselling, education, and the provision of time-limited resources, or it may be pursued by more coercive measures such as apprehension of children and criminal charges. It may use approaches that are sensitive to gender, race, and class or it may not. But overall, the aims remain the same.

A feminist approach suggests that we suspend all this activity and think again. Instead, we should examine the disempowering impact first of womanhood, then of motherhood, and then of motherhood, class, and culture. It suggests that the true aim of child welfare should be to seek to ensure that mothers become citizens with the rights and responsibilities of citizenship. Through this process, their lives will be enriched and the lives of most of their children will similarly improve. Moreover, focusing on caregivers and caregiving will put value on an enterprise that has been sorely discounted. The lot of all caregivers and children can only benefit. This argument does not exclude the use of civil and criminal actions to redress crimes against children and women. In fact, it encourages them.

A feminist approach also demands a rethinking of the language and concepts that have been the building blocks of the present child welfare system. As long as parents, in particular mothers, are viewed as having the prime responsibility to provide for and protect their children, then terms like child neglect and child abuse discredit them. The issues that feminist child welfare addresses require other terms: caring work, community safety, hungry kids, women's wages, and many more.

One of the other conclusions is that by focusing on behaviour and by making the whole business a confidential one, the child welfare system has no logical social movement to connect with and a limited capacity to attract a constituency. Social movements need a cause, one deeply felt by those in the movement, usually based on their own experiences. Most sexual offenders cannot campaign against such offences, most neglected children cannot organize. Instead, the few groups that advocate for child welfare are often dominated by professionals and are sometimes viewed as self-serving. In many ways, child welfare systems are like isolated families. Consequently, the needs of women and children in the system receive low priority on the public policy agenda. An expanded child welfare agenda, particularly one that includes the care of middle-class children, will invariably receive more attention.

It may be that all of these changes seem too impractical ever to occur and that entrenched ideologies, organizations, and professionals would never give up their present ways of viewing the world. In many ways, the practicalities of implementing the reforms suggested in this paper have been tackled already by feminist social services and occasional changes in mainstream services. Recently, this paper was reviewed by a thoughtful supervisor of child welfare services in a government bureaucracy. He said that twenty years ago we thought nothing about how Native children and their parents were treated by the child welfare system. We had no perspective. Yet when we look back now on what happened to these people and our part in it, we feel ashamed. He said that we may feel the same sense of shame when we look at what we are doing now to women, twenty years hence.

Chapter 7

Rethinking Child Welfare

Brian Wharf

The chapters in the first section of the book described the development of child welfare policy from the child-saving era to the period when professionals sought to improve services by placing a professional stamp on practice, to the current era where residual policies and the corporate management approach dominate the child welfare scene. The chapters in the second section presented a critique of residualism and corporate management based on the views of feminists and First Nations people and on the need to develop a variety of constituencies for child welfare.

The objective of this concluding chapter is to rethink the objectives and purpose of child welfare. The rethinking and the proposals for reform that flow from this examination are anchored in the fundamental proposition that child welfare policy represents an extreme case of cultural lag. Even in jurisdictions with modestly progressive legislation, such as the Yukon and Ontario, child welfare policy fails to recognize that child care is performed by women in their roles as mothers, foster mothers, child-care workers, and social workers and that this work is either unpaid or poorly paid. It fails to recognize the impact of poverty on the capacity of families to care for their children. It fails to acknowledge the importance of cultural values and traditions, although, as noted in Chapters 4 and 5, there are some encouraging signs with respect to First Nation control of child welfare. It fails to recognize and take into account the fundamental changes that have occurred in Canadian families, including the high rate of divorce, the employment of women both in and outside the home, and the awareness of the existence of long-standing violence against women and children. It fails with respect to the structural and administrative arrangements established to develop policy and deliver services – arrangements that exclude the contributions of clients, concerned citizens, child welfare workers, and staff of voluntary agencies in making policy and in developing innovative approaches to service delivery. As emphasized repeatedly throughout this book, the exclusion has resulted in policy for child welfare becoming a closed and closeted affair dominated by a few with a very particular and narrow understanding of the needs of the people being served.

The cultural lag has the profound consequence that child neglect and abuse are attributed solely to the failure of parents rather than being recognized as emanating from a complicated web of factors including the powerlessness of women, the lack of status and adequate rewards for caregiving roles, and the effect of other social policies that condemn one-sixth of Canada's children to live in poverty. It is not a coincidence that the child welfare population is made up of women and children who are poor and are members of minority racial groups. As the previous chapters have argued, an accurate and regrettable generalization is that child welfare in Canada consists of a set of poorly funded, residual programs designed to assist only when families cannot cope. Child welfare policy represents a reflection of the consequences of a society that has consistently shrunk from the task of distributing power and income between men and women, between races, and between classes in a fair and equitable fashion.

We recognize that changing the distribution of power and income would constitute a fundamental challenge to Canadian society. It challenges the existing values that celebrate private property, the right of individuals to accumulate wealth and to transfer their money and property to succeeding generations and thereby preserve the unequal distribution of wealth and power. In Lindblom's terms "the distribution of power, wealth, and corporate prerogatives" constitutes the grand issue of social policy – an issue that represents a veritable Catch-22 since the change involves overcoming the opposition of those who currently hold positions of power (Lindblom, 1979).

One challenge to the grand issues is posed by the social development approach to social policy that was briefly discussed in Chapter 2. In common with the institutional approach, social development begins by accepting that social services are a necessary social provision that should be available to all families. It leaves the institutional approach behind by elevating social policy to an equal place with economic policy and by insisting that those affected have a say in developing social policies. In effect, the social development approach calls for changes in the grand issues of social policy by interfering in present economic arrangements and by increasing the numbers of people who participate in governing. While the social development approach does not call for the destruction of the market economy, it insists on managing the economy in such a way that social policies are given equal consideration to economic ones and in distributing the benefits of the economy in a much more equal fashion than prevails at the present time. Pateman argues:

> One necessary condition for the creation of a genuine democracy in which the welfare of all citizens is served is an alliance between a labour movement that acknowledges the problem of patriarchal power and an autonomous women's movement that recognizes the problem of class power. Whether such an alliance can be forged is an open question. (Pateman, 1988: 256)

To Pateman's alliance of the social movements of women and labour should be added others such as the First Nations and environmental movements with their concerns for social and environmental justice. These social movements face a common enemy: the inequities they seek to remove are founded in the same institutions and preserved by a small group of the captains of industry and their political friends. An alliance of these social movements could provide solid backing for a political party committed to social justice.

While our intention at the outset was to concentrate on reforming the child welfare system, writing this book has been a voyage of discovery. We have discovered that rethinking child welfare requires attention not only to the governance and practice of child welfare, but also, in a much more fundamental fashion, to the very objectives of child welfare. In turn, this rethinking of objectives bumps into some grand issues of social policy, notably the definition of work and of payment for work. Hence the following proposals for reform reflect our interest in both the ordinary and the grand issues and the connections between them. Four proposals are presented: developing policy communities, transforming the role and status of caregivers, changing the mandate of child welfare, and adopting diversity as the policy of choice in providing child welfare services. While conceptually distinct these changes do connect and reinforce each other. Thus if policy communities were established they could advocate for other proposed changes. Similarly, transforming the caregiving role would ease the prospects of reforming the mandate of child welfare, and a new mandate would greatly facilitate the otherwise difficult task of implementing diversity as the policy of choice in governing services.

DEVELOPING POLICY COMMUNITIES

Policy communities consist of those government agencies concerned with a particular field together with their attentive publics. These latter include institutions, pressure groups, specific interests and individuals – including academics and journalists – who are affected by or interested in the policies of specific agencies and make it their business to follow and attempt to influence these policies.

The policy community includes . . . many who have no capacity to decide policy but who do have sufficient interest in the field to want to influence it. Often these people – whether interested group members, bureaucrats or independents – will be quite opposed to current policy trends and will exert what efforts they can to change it. (Pross, 1980)

As discussed in Chapter 4 there are only a few fairly fragile policy communities in child welfare, but they contain the potential to make a number of important contributions. First, they represent a way of extending the range of information provided to policymakers. Thus, rather than policies being restricted to the information supplied by senior bureaucrats and politicians, the process is enriched by information from sources such as clients, academics, representatives of concerned social movements, and citizens and professionals from the voluntary sector.

Second, policy communities afford a vehicle for social learning. At the present time information about the complex interplay of public issues and private troubles that bring about the conditions of child neglect and abuse is limited to a relatively few professionals in child-serving agencies. As a consequence the public has no awareness of the success stories in child welfare, is horrified by the failures that are given headline treatment by the press, and is unable to understand the need for substantive reforms.

In some policy fields such as agriculture, forestry, industry, trade and banking, policy communities are well defined and are a key part of understanding how policy is made. The presence of such a community can greatly facilitate policy action while its absence may make coherent policy impossible. Such communities have a sense of policy history, are repositories of technical knowledge and have dealt with each other over many years. (Doern and Phidd, 1992: 77)

Doern and Phidd make the point that some policy communities have become "clubs composed of tiny bands of experts." In these instances policy again becomes a closed affair where no differing opinions are raised. However, at the present time in social policy and particularly in child welfare, we do not have to worry about closed clubs. Where they exist at all, policy communities in child welfare are loose, *ad hoc* arrangements whereby provincial policy-makers seek advice from the voluntary sector and from staff on very specific issues and problems. As discussed in Chapter 4 only the Association of Children's Aid Societies in Ontario, which represents the interests of local societies, comes close to the notion of a policy community.

Another exception to the usually restricted nature of child welfare policy occurs when provincial ministries decide to revise legislation and seek opinions during the course of the review. However, there is no guarantee that the results of reviews will be implemented. For example, the recommendations of the Royal Commission on Family and Children's Law (1975), perhaps the most comprehensive inquiry into family and children's law ever conducted in Canada, were largely ignored by a Social Credit government determined to set its own stamp on child welfare policy (Callahan and Wharf, 1982).

Given the size of the potential membership of policy communities in any given province, a number of organizational structures will be required. Our suggestions include the establishment of advisory councils at the provincial level and the incorporation of policy communities into the governing bodies at the community level. Discussion of the latter structures is reserved for the concluding section of the chapter.

The overall purpose of provincial advisory councils would be to provide ministers with advice that is independent of the bureaucracy. Councils require a small secretariat and a budget adequate for meetings and for funding research projects. The terms of reference and composition of provincial councils must be established in legislation and must ensure representation from women, voluntary agencies, clients and former clients, and citizens at large. Indeed, parents could and should participate, particularly if a parental wage came into effect and legitimized their participation. In our view it is of the utmost importance that councils be given the right in legislation to add their own objectives and agenda to that of providing advice to the minister and to express their views in the public domain even if these differ from those of the minister. In other words, the model to follow is that of the National Council of Welfare.

TRANSFORMING THE ROLE AND STATUS OF CAREGIVERS

The second change to emerge from our rethinking of child welfare is to recognize the crucial significance of caregiving roles. If the importance of children for the future of society is to be given anything other than platitudinous recognition by politicians and other policy-makers, rewards and status must be attached to people who care for children. In specific terms this means that caregivers in the home must receive an adequate wage and that the inadequate wages now paid to such caregivers as foster mothers, day-care staff, homemakers, and social workers be increased.

Such reform may sound, in Lessing's term, "screwball" since it constitutes an affront to the notion that caring for children is the private responsibility of parents, and in particular of women (Lessing, 1991). However, the lessons of history are useful. Until the present century parents were responsible for the health, education, and recreation needs of children. But the introduction of public education, health care, recreation programs, and other forms of public assistance have had the profound consequence of diminishing the parental role and sharing the responsibility of raising children between parents and the state. Few now advocate returning these responsibilities to parents, even though at the time of introduction these programs were seen as a radical intrusion into the parental role.

In addition, paying for work from the public purse both in the human services and in industry is commonplace. Communities compete with each other for federal and provincial funds for a wide variety of purposes – from building schools to equipment for the armed forces. In our view the former projects are necessary and socially desirable, but the same cannot be said for building destroyers, tanks, fighter planes, and other instruments of destruction. While an argument can be mounted for a Canadian armed force for peacekeeping purposes, such a force does not require sophisticated and expensive equipment.

The argument is nicely captured by the following letter to the

Ottawa Citizen from the president of the Canadian Association of University Teachers.

You have carried stories in recent weeks about how the federal government plans to spend 4.3 billion on military helicopters, a demand originally generated by the military to combat the now non-existent Soviet menace. At the same time Ottawa has cut 4.7 billion from its cash payments for post-secondary education for the period 1986-1993. When it comes to the choice I am sure that most Canadians would prefer to have state of the art universities rather than state of the art military helicopters. The consequence of the choice the government has apparently made means that the students, their parents and staff across the country will, in effect, be paying for the military helicopters through reductions in the quality and accessibility of university education. Government means choices as editorial writers and politicians keep saying. The choice on the part of this government is clear and wrong. (Andrews, 1992)

A similar position is developed in a recent article, "Dismantling the Cold War Economy":

In the debate about the Seawolf submarine, no one in Congress seriously argued that the vessel was critical to the nation's security. Instead the emphasis was on the more than 10,000 workers in southeastern Connecticut whose livelihoods depended on the Seawolf and who, without it, have no apparent work alternatives. Seawolf submarines and B-2 bombers have become, pure and simple, jobs programs and the worst possible kind. (Markusen, 1992)

The decisions of the governments of Canada and the U.S. to allocate funds for job creation programs "of the worst possible kind" symbolize their attachment to ruling practices that are another example of cultural lag. We acknowledge that reducing or even eliminating funds now allocated to the military would be insufficient to eliminate child poverty, but the change would signify a fundamental shift in public policy and would at least begin the war on child poverty.

Shifting funding from defence to social purposes will require changing the definition of work, a fundamental change for the reforms advocated here. We suggest that a decent wage to caregivers would not only reduce poverty among single and low-income parents but that it would also alter their status in society. As discussed in Chapter 6, we concur with Pateman's observation that "paid employment has become the key to citizenship and the recognition of an individual as a citizen of equal worth to other individuals is lacking when a worker is unemployed" (Pateman, 1988: 237). The argument can be extended to low-paid work. Since mothers in the home and caregivers in day care, foster homes, and other settings are either unpaid or poorly paid, their worth as contributors to the economy and as citizens is minimalized. But definitions of work vary and are laden with contradictions. Exposing these contradictions may help to change the definitions.

> The way a society defines the concept "work" has important consequences for the circumstances of living of individuals. . . . By excluding certain functions and contexts from the social and economic definition of work, persons assigned to these functions are deprived of economic rewards. By defining other functions and contexts as "voluntary" work, symbolic and psychological rewards are substituted for economic ones which is another mechanism for economic exploitation. It should be noted that women are constantly urged to engage in voluntary work. Business executives who entertain prospective customers are "working," and so are professional ball players who are throwing balls, but volunteers who "entertain" patients in a hospital, or tutor slow learning children in schools or women who clean their families' home, prepare meals and care for children are "not working." (Gil, 1990: 103)

There have been many past and recent proposals to eliminate or reduce child poverty, including expanding family allowances into a substantial universal payment for children – a strategy favoured by the Child Poverty Action Group – and the targeted Child Benefit Plan selected by the federal Minister of Health and Welfare. However, little attention has been given to the strategy of paying caregivers an adequate wage. Such payment would reward a valuable role and thereby enhance its status and at the same time provide funds that for poor families would mean the difference between an adequate income and poverty. Taxing wages as income would also mean that families not requiring additional funds would pay back the caregiving wage in the form of income tax. Hence, this proposal has the potential not only to change significantly the role of women, since they represent the majority of caregivers, but to reduce child poverty and to make some progress in altering the distribution of income.

The notion of a parental wage may disturb many readers since it alters the employer/employee relationship characteristic of wage arrangements since the beginning of industrial economies. The arrangement is based on the time-honoured practice of paying a wage only for satisfactory performance and for terminating the relationship in the event of unsatisfactory performance. The questions raised by the parental wage include who would be the employer and how performance would be judged. To be sure, the notion of a parental wage is unsettling, but innovations by definition upset the status quo and require alterations in existing structures, roles, and relationships. Indeed, they are dedicated to the task of challenge and reform.

Further, parental performance should not be subjected to continual scrutiny; rather, the operating assumption should be that parents will both "care about and care for" their children and that the parental wage will assist them in the "caring for" function (Swift, 1991). Since some parents will experience difficulties from time to time, the range of supports suggested in previous chapters should be available and criminal proceedings would be launched against parents who abuse their children.

In conclusion, the parental wage is preferable to alternatives such as child and parental allowances since the former clearly places caring for children in the context of work and thus elevates the status of both the work and the workers.

CHANGING THE MANDATE OF CHILD WELFARE

The third reform advocated here requires relinquishing the current focus of child welfare on the investigation of child neglect and abuse and adopting the objective of providing support to parents and advocating with them when they lack the necessary resources. Callahan, in Chapter 6, puts the point clearly:

> . . . the so-called crime of neglect should simply disappear from the child welfare statutes. Instead, the child welfare statutes could be reframed to define the caring services to be provided and the circumstances under which they will be provided. If chronic neglect is primarily a matter of poverty, frequently the poverty of disadvantaged women, then it should be dealt with as a resource issue rather than a personal, individual problem. If situational neglect occurs, such as the abandonment of children, then such problems can be dealt with by providing care and resources to children, locating parents, and helping them make plans for their children.

Striking neglect from the statutes would be a feasible proposition if a parental wage was in place. Further, this conception of child welfare views the abuse of children as a crime like any other abusive act against the individual. As such, the investigation of child abuse would become a responsibility of the police, the courts, and the offices of attorneys-general.

This rethinking is reinforced by referring to the concept of affinity. Although postulated many years ago, the concept has had little influence in guiding the development of the social services, but it has much to commend it. Affinity refers to the need for

> potential users to assess their state of personal identity with the provider as a condition for using their service. Areas where affinity judgements are made often involve the more intimate areas of personal need. Affinity is the perception that a provider possesses a unique set of characteristics which are important to the consumer. (Social Planning Council of Metropolitan Toronto, 1976; 106.)

Given the intimacy of child welfare there can be few other areas of service where the concept of affinity is of such importance. Support for the concept comes from projects in the U.S. designed to prevent the out-of-home placement of children and carried out by voluntary agencies and by units within state governments. They have been awarded the explicit responsibility of providing assistance to families without the latter worrying that involvement with the agency might lead to apprehension of their children. Reviews of these projects reveal that the key ingredient in preventing out-of-home placement was a philosophy of service that emphasized the dignity and worth of clients and the match between needs and services: agencies clearly advertised their services as being concerned with helping families and not with the investigation of neglect and abuse. With affinity between agency objectives and client needs, clients can view agencies as a source of assistance and not as agents of control. (For reviews of these projects, see Jones, Magura, and Shyne, 1981; Jones, 1985; Nelson, Landsman, and Teitelbaum, 1990; Wharf, 1991.)

Reshaping child welfare from investigation to support has implications for the structure and philosophy of agencies providing services. A fundamental position taken throughout this book is that the heart and soul of child welfare is the interaction between practitioner and client. It follows, then, that legislation, policies, and agency structures must be configured to promote and enhance this interaction. Chapters 2 and 3 have argued that the precise opposite has happened in recent years with the result that the wisdom of practitioners is not supported and legitimized, nor are structures created to incorporate this wisdom into the policy-making process.

Support-focused child welfare agencies would be characterized by a low level of bureaucratization and would reject the corporate approach to management. Services would be provided in a user-friendly fashion and through geographic locations that wherever possible conform to the notion of accessibility within "pram-pushing distance" (Committee on Local Authority and Allied Social Services, 1968).

Support for our position is long-standing and flows from the work of such pioneering organizational theorists as Douglas Mac-Gregor and has continued more recently in the now classic *In Search of Excellence* (1982) by Thomas Peters and Robert Waterman. The most recent confirmation of the importance of staff and client participatory governance comes from Canadian studies conducted by the Auditor General and discussed in Chapter 3.

We are finding three aspirations that people at all levels and locations consistently express. People value making a contribution; they want to make a difference, have an influence, and master some task or activity. People value being recognized and rewarded for their contribution; they look for respect and appreciation. People value belonging to a group especially if they consider the group to be successful. (Brodtrick, 1991: 22)

The studies of Peters and Waterman and their many followers and of the Auditor General are supported by work in the implementation of policy. There is general agreement in the literature on policy implementation with the conclusions of Michael Lipsky's research on front-line staff such as teachers, social workers, and police officers, staff Lipsky describes as street-level bureaucrats. "Fundamentally at issue is the reality that street-level bureaucrats determine policy implementation, not their superiors" (Lipsky, 1980: 207). Since line workers control implementation they determine the success or failure of policy. In turn, this conclusion argues for the involvement of practitioners in all stages of the policy process.

An important cornerstone of our reframing of child welfare is therefore to create organizations in which the experience of practitioners and clients is taken into account in making policy and in providing services.

TOWARD A POLICY OF DIVERSITY

The final change builds on the previous reforms and focuses on service delivery. Chapter 2 contained a review of the legislative and administrative arrangements in place at the present time and of proposals advanced to overcome the deficiences of existing arrangements. One popular proposal is that child welfare services should be folded into an integrated system of services.

Given its dominant place in discussions of reform, the concept of integrated services is reviewed in detail here to determine its utility for carving out a new direction for child welfare. According to this argument child welfare should become part of those social provisions that serve all children, such as day care, health, and education. Further, this integrated pattern of services should be provided by a single ministry or department in order to eliminate the confusion that currently exists in most provinces as to which ministry is responsibile for services to children and families – Education, Social Services, Health, or the Attorney-General. It is argued that clients of child welfare agencies experience a multitude of problems, ranging from poverty and poor housing to difficulties in marital and other personal relationships, and hence no single service will suffice to meet their needs. Rather, they require a set of comprehensive services, such as adequate financial assistance and housing, access to education, training, and employment, day care, support services such as mothers' time out and respite programs, and counselling and therapy. A basic assumption underlying the call for integration is that sufficient and appropriate services exist but that these are scattered and unco-ordinated. The solution is to reorganize agency structures, to bring order out of chaos, and to create a systematic and controlled pattern of services.

In Canada the preoccupation with co-ordination of social and health services can be traced back to the influential report of the Commission on Emotional and Learning Disorders in Children, known as the CELDIC report. Sponsored by seven national organizations, this study took five years to complete and concluded with 144 recommendations. Without doubt the issue that most troubled the investigators was the absence of a co-ordinated approach: "the multiplicity of unrelated services seems to us to be the number one problem in providing services to children with emotional and learning disorders" (CELDIC, 1970: 294).

More recent calls for service co-ordination come from an investigation into children's services by the Office of the Ombudsman in B.C. (British Columbia Office of the Ombudsman, 1990b), from a comprehensive study in Ontario (Advisory Committee on Children's Services, 1990), and from previous writings by the authors (Armitage, 1989; Wharf, 1985).

Strategies To Achieve Co-ordination

Three of the most prominent strategies to achieve the elusive goal of a well-co-ordinated pattern of services are multi-service centres, service protocols, and the amalgamation of government departments or agencies. These strategies are briefly reviewed below.

The multi-service centre concept represents the human service counterpart of the "one-stop shopping centre." Agencies are located together in the same building to reduce confusion for clients and to promote co-operation among service providers. However, as Kahn noted many years ago, the concept is "an understandable strategy tied to a lost cause" (Kahn, 1976: 40). It is a lost cause if integration at the local level is achieved in the absence of integration at the policy and management levels. Under this arrangement personnel in the multi-service centre report to their own agencies rather than the centre. A not unusual consequence of this arrangement is that co-operation among service providers is thwarted or contradicted by the policies and management practices of the different agencies.

We should note, too, that an initial promise of multi-service centres was that they would become "blending machines" where the services of different agencies and professionals would mesh smoothly together (Clague *et al.*, 1984). But the downside of blending is that it can squeeze out uniqueness and the capacity for innovation.

In essence the multi-service centre strategy relies on promoting co-operation between service providers and on the assignment of case managers to manage the affairs of clients whose needs spill over between agencies. While none would quarrel with the intent of enhancing co-operation, the question is raised as to whether these well-intentioned efforts can offset, and indeed might distract attention from, the larger issues affecting clients of child welfare – issues of poverty, poor housing, and services displaced from their original intent of helping to one of investigation. Rein's review leads him to conclude that "the sense of the literature is that few coordination projects have made an important contribution to client well-being" (Rein, 1983: 74).

Overcoming the deficits of co-operation requires more drastic measures. One such attempt is reflected in the establishment of service protocols. As noted in Chapter 2, these protocols define the boundaries of responsibility between ministries involved in the welfare of children. Protocols are favoured by policy-makers and managers committed to the philosophy of corporate management and represent an attempt to specify clearly the roles and responsibilities of staff of different agencies, and, indeed, to control the interaction between clients and line workers. However, as already mentioned, research and experience suggest that worker/client relationships are largely determined by these actors. Attempts to regulate this interaction through service protocols represent yet another strategy tied to a lost cause. In addition, like the multi-service centre strategy, service protocols cannot alter the larger issues facing clients. It makes little difference if service boundaries are clearly delineated if none of the agencies involved possesses the mandate or the resources to provide the kind of assistance required by families.

The third and most ambitious attempt to co-ordinate services is to amalgamate ministries of education, health, and social services into a single ministry. However, the consequence of such radical reorganization is the creation of a human service ministry of mammoth proportions, particularly if both the legislative/policy and direct service responsibilities are brought together. As noted in Chapter 4, our view is that bigness is a recipe for disaster in the human services.

In addition, a characteristic of all bureaucracies is a hierarchical structure that concentrates power in the hands of a few individuals. Hence, in a comprehensive human service ministry, policy and practice will be dictated by a very few individuals, primarily the minister and deputy minister. The very nature of hierarchical arrangements guarantees that contrary voices will not be heard, and a surer strategy for ensuring that Lord Acton's dictum – "power corrupts and absolute power corrupts absolutely" – will prevail can scarcely be imagined.

Indeed, calls for structural reform mask the reality that the basic problem in child welfare is not the lack of co-ordination but poverty and ineffective/inappropriate services. It is much easier to point to an apparent abundance of resources manifested by the existence of a number of independent community agencies serving families than it is to acknowledge that more fundamental reasons for the need for service are poverty and the lack of affinity between the needs of parents and the "services" provided.

Structural reforms alter only the formal arrangements of child welfare. They do not address the fundamental issues of poverty, the role of women, and the need for services based on affinity. Our argument in favour of a policy of diversity and community governance unfolds in the following fashion. Diversity represents the policy of choice regardless of the changes discussed above. Thus, even if parental wages are not provided and the mandate of child welfare remains unchanged, we still opt for diversity and community governance. That said, there is no doubt that these policies would be more attractive and indeed compelling if parents had sufficient funds and if neglect disappeared from the statutes.

Toward a Policy of Diversity in Providing Services

Chapter 4 developed the position that it is time for provincial departments to get out of the business of delivering services. Rather, a partnership approach between province and community is required, whereby the province retains responsibility for establishing legislation, allocating funds, setting and monitoring standards, and operating specialized services. This partnership arrangement contains the distinct advantage that provincial departments would be decreased in size since they would no longer have the responsibility of providing services. Given a considerable reduction in size, it would then be possible and even desirable to integrate human service ministries for legislative, policy, budget, and standard-setting functions.

Without repeating the discussion from Chapter 4, it is pertinent to summarize the advantages of community governance in order to connect the case with the reforms discussed above. It is also important to add that the concept of community as used here refers to communities of interest as well as geographic areas. Thus constituencies devoted to the welfare of children are considered as communities.

The first advantage of community governance is that it provides an opportunity for social learning – for citizens to gain some understanding of the complexities of child neglect and abuse and some appreciation of the impact of factors such as poverty and the lack of affordable housing. Second, community governance requires that communities *own* child welfare. Rather than being seen as the exclusive responsibility of a provincial bureaucracy that is supposed to solve all problems, and that is subject to severe criticism when it fails to do so, child welfare becomes a community concern and challenge. Third, community governance allows for the possibility of tuning services to meet local needs, for experimenting with local innovations, and for involving citizens in a variety of voluntary activities. Fourth, community governance spells the end of large and cumbersome provincial bureaucracies.

A policy of diversity would allow a number of community-level structures to govern child welfare services. Chapters 5 and 6 made the point that First Nations and feminist organizations have the capacity to govern services, and in fact have done so in a more appropriate and effective fashion than large provincial bureaucracies. In a field of service as riddled with complexity as child welfare there is no one best structure or approach to providing service. Hence, we argue against the notion of shaping a uniform pattern of services across provinces. Our resolution calls for diversity in auspices rather than provincial monopolies. In addition to First Nation band councils and feminist organizations, other appropriate structures include locally controlled health and social service agencies, particularly those devoted to health promotion and community development.

There are, to be sure, some downsides to a policy of diversity and community governance. In the first place, we expect such proposals to be severely criticized by those who favour the corporate approach to management and the creation of comprehensive human service ministries to provide services. Such individuals desire neat and tidy organizational structures and will recoil in dismay from a policy of diversity. But as Brodtrick and others have argued, attempts to impose clean organizational patterns on an essentially chaotic world are artificial and doomed to fail: "The world is messy. Hence, to manage well we need to develop managers who can perform productively in work environments that are messy, uncertain and unpredictable" (Brodtrick, 1991: 20).

We have emphasized repeatedly throughout this book that the world of child welfare is messy and unpredictable. It is therefore important to prepare child welfare workers who are comfortable with uncertainty. A teamwork approach to practice can offset the troubling insecurities that come from messy work situations, as can opportunities for study leave and the time to reflect on policy and practice.

Another potential source of criticism of the policy of diversity is that it would not resolve the current dilemmas experienced in serving the hard-to-reach client and the multi-problem family. As Callahan acknowledges in Chapter 6, reversing the priority of child welfare to focus on prevention and support will not eliminate all neglect and abuse. Who, then, is to serve the families for whom the provision of resources and a variety of supports are not sufficient?

It is irresponsible to dismiss this criticism by pointing out that the existing child welfare services, focused as they are on protection and crisis intervention, fail the hard-to-reach and multi-problem families as well as the larger number of families who could be aided by the appropriate resources and services. In our view the reforms recommended here would better serve the larger group, and it makes no sense to construct policies on the basis of the needs of the residual few. Further, it is entirely possible that staff in the judicial/correctional system would be better able to work with these parents than child welfare workers. While parents might have previously spurned offers of help on the grounds that they did not require assistance in caring for their children, the impact of having been found guilty of the offence of neglect or abuse might be sufficient to bring about a change of mind. In addition, probation and parole officers and family court counsellors are accustomed to working with people who have broken the law. They are experts in working with difficult and recalcitrant clients and are comfortable in a work environment characterized by the exercise of authority.

A final criticism is that it will be difficult to construct information systems in diversified and community-based services. Information systems have been developed within and because of the needs of large bureaucracies. Finding ways to collect and accumulate information across a number of agencies without violating the privacy of clients will not be easy. But the challenge might allow child welfare organizations to revisit the need for information. Who requires information and who uses it? The research of Campbell and Ng suggests that information is collected primarily to meet the needs of managers, not front-line workers (Campbell and Ng, 1991). Is this desirable and should it continue?

ARE THERE ANY GLIMMERS OF HOPE?

It is clear that we are calling for a return to the days when child welfare was distinguished by commitment to a mission. The pioneers in child welfare approached the task of "saving children" with all the fervour of zealous missionaries. Over time, this zeal came to be regarded as an embarrassment that had to be replaced by professional knowledge and the application of detached professional skills. (The same process of discrediting a mission occurred in public health, where the early public health officers who engaged in social reform were seen as mucking about in the social environment – a task not suitable for the medical profession [Higgins, 1992].) While knowledge and skills are necessary, these contributions should enhance rather than reduce commitment to a mission.

Some glimmers on the public-sector horizon support our call for reform. But these are faint and dim at the federal level, where the current government is committed to dismantling Canada's universal social programs and to establishing a residual course for the future. For example, the government discontinued the family allowance program in January, 1993, in favour of a selective child benefit program. The stated intent of the new program is to eliminate the waste incurred by providing family allowances to all Canadian families regardless of income and to increase benefits to poor families. In its brief to the parliamentary committee responsible for reviewing the new legislation, the Canadian Council on Social Development (CCSD) pointed out that

> it excludes a large number of the working poor, for example, couples without children and unattached families. And a significant number of working poor families will receive no benefit at all. Perhaps the greatest shortcoming is that two-thirds of poor single-parent families will receive no benefit at all. (Canadian Council on Social Development, 1992: 4)

The CCSD brief further noted that the cost of the new program, some $400 million, does not even begin to compare with revenues forgone by the 1988-89 budget, which raised the limit on RRSP contributions from $7,500 to $15,000. In 1989 this resulted in lost revenues to the tune of $4.5 billion. As the brief acidly asked, "Why are Canadian taxpayers subsidizing the private pensions of bank presidents and many other upper income earners who do not need help from the state?" (ibid.: 13).

While the federal government has moved away from a universal position with respect to income security it has supported the move to self-government for First Nations. There is, then, some federal support for the directions espoused here, but the most promising encouragement comes from several provincial governments. Given the commitment of the New Democratic Party to social justice, it will come as no surprise that the reforms are taking place in provinces where the NDP is in power.

Following the recommendations of a Royal Commission on Health Services and Costs to decentralize health services, the provincial government in B.C. has created a Capital Health Council in Victoria to take on the responsibility of governing all in- and out-patient health services in the capital region. While the members of the first board have been appointed, the intent is to elect members in the future in a fashion similar to that for election of members of school boards. Although the Council is in its infancy, its early work has placed the issues of poverty, unemployment, and the lack of affordable housing as the highest priorities. The Council is seen as a possible prototype for the rest of the province, although it is recognized that communities will wish to develop their own and different governing structures. Given a broad definition of health and a mandate to pursue health promotion and prevention activities, it is entirely possible that health councils will in time be assigned responsibility for both social and health services.

In a similar vein the provincial government in Saskatchewan has amalgamated three ministries – health, social services, and the environment – and has awarded governance of these services to locally elected boards at the community level.

The provincial government in Ontario is considering measures that will directly affect the role of women. Included in a package of radical reforms are a $1 billion program of pay equity for women, legislation that will compel employers to hire and promote more women, non-whites, and the disabled, and advocacy legislation designed to protect the rights of children.

It is possible, therefore, that the "screwball ideas" advanced here will be supported by the actions of provincial governments in B.C., Saskatchewan, and Ontario. Certainly community-governed agencies with a mandate to prevent child abuse and neglect will provide a congenial work environment for child welfare workers. Freed from the responsibility of investigation and apprehension, workers will be able to make visible the kind of invisible work discussed in Chapter 6. From the critical incidents described in that chapter there is no doubt that some workers will welcome the opportunity to change their practice to support and advocate for clients. But not all will want to do so, and some will cling to the safety of an environment where regulations rule practice. Brodtrick addresses the issue of the acceptance of change in organizations:

Is it possible to move the public service from the era of control and compliance to an era of collaboration, cooperation and commitment? In Washington about thirty years ago they used to talk about the "noble conspiracy." The idea was that you have to create spaces where you plant this thing and let it grow. And you nourish it and you foster it and eventually YOU TAKE OVER. This idea has been taken up and added to by Professor Dror who came up with the term "islands of excellence." We each have to create our own islands of excellence and hope that they grow and eventually pervade our organizations. (Brodtrick, 1991: 22)

Some "islands of excellence" are being created in First Nation child and family agencies in many provinces, in the projects currently under way in the Ministry of Social Services in B.C. and described in Chapter 6, and by numerous other innovative projects. Child welfare workers need to know about these islands, and some bridges must be found to connect them. This book may serve as one bridge. A national child welfare journal is sorely needed in Canada and could serve as another connector, as can conferences and local computer networks.

To conclude, it is our conviction that child welfare services cannot remain in their currently unsatisfactory state. The present child welfare system does not meet the needs of women, single-parent families, First Nation families, or, for that matter, any families, and some radical shifts are required to lift child welfare out of the cultural lag in which it now languishes. The present work represents an effort to rethink the fundamental assumptions that have shaped child welfare and has outlined a number of reforms based on that rethinking. These reforms would transform child welfare from a crisis intervention system to one concerned with prevention of neglect and abuse. Thus we have suggested that (1) policy communities be established to promote the cause of the welfare of children and that these communities are sufficiently important to be supported by the public purse; (2) the role of caregiver should be redefined and paid a wage; (3) the purpose of child welfare should be to support and assist parents; (4) services are most appropriately provided in agencies governed by locally elected boards and characterized by a high degree of participation by staff and a low level of bureaucratization.

Some of these suggestions may be too "screwball" to permit acceptance in the near future. But our proposals may provoke others concerned with child welfare to undertake similar explorations. For example, many schools of social work now include the exploration of gender, class, and race issues as required content in the curriculum, and consideration of these issues will spur faculty and students to challenge the existing conceptions of child welfare. And as we have noted throughout the work at hand, definitions of roles and of problems do change. The justice system has discarded the definition of incorrigibility and, similarly, illegitimacy is no longer accorded the stigma it once received. In time the caregiving role may be defined as a job requiring adequate pay from the public purse. Such a definition recognizes the importance of this role and would distinguish Canada as a society dedicated to the welfare of children.

It is appropriate to conclude by pointing out that Canada's reputation on the international scene has been largely secured by providing leadership in peacekeeping activities. While this is a laudable reputation, our preference would be for Canada to be known for its commitment to the welfare of children. Instituting an adequate parental wage to honour the House of Commons resolution to eliminate poverty by the year 2000 would be a great beginning.

Bibliography

Abramovitz, Mimi (1988). *Regulating the lives of women: Social welfare policy from colonial times to the present.* Boston: South End Press.

Advisory Committee on Children's Services (1990). *Children First.* Toronto: Queen's Printer.

Akyeampong, Ernest (1990). "Women wanting to work but not looking due to child care demands," *The Labour Force,* 71001, Ottawa, Statistics Canada.

Albert, Jim (1985). "Child Welfare," in *The Canadian Encyclopedia.* Edmonton: Hurtig Publishers.

Alinsky, Saul (1969). *Reveille for Radicals.* New York: Vintage Books.

Alinsky, Saul (1971). *Rules for Radicals.* New York: Vintage Books.

Andrews, Alan (1992). Letter to the Editor. *Ottawa Citizen.*

Armitage, Andrew, ed. (1989). *The Future of Family and Children's Services in British Columbia: An Agenda for Action and Research.* Victoria: University of Victoria, School of Social Work.

Armitage, Andrew, Elizabeth Lane, Frances Ricks, and Brian Wharf (1988). *Evaluation of the Champagne/Aishihik Child Welfare Pilot Project.* Victoria: University of Victoria.

Assembly of First Nations (1988). *Strengthening the Family, Building the Community: Final Report on the First Canadian Indian-Native Child Welfare Conference.* Fredericton, New Brunswick.

Assembly of First Nations (1989). *Report of the National Inquiry into First Nations Child Care.* Ottawa.

Assembly of First Nations (1991). *For Discussion: National Strategy on First Nations Child and Family Services.* Ottawa.

Assu, Harry, and Joy Inglis (1989). *Assu of Cape Mudge: Recollections of a Coastal Indian Chief.* Vancouver: University of British Columbia Press.

Auditor General of Canada (1988). "Attributes of well-performing organizations: A study by the office of the Auditor General of Canada," *Annual Report, 1988.* Ottawa.

Baines, Carol (1991). "The Professions and an Ethic of Care," in Carol Baines, Patricia Evans, and Sheila Neysmith, eds., *Women's Caring: Feminist Perspectives on Social Welfare*. Toronto: McClelland & Stewart.

Bala, Nicholas C., and Kenneth L. Clarke (1981). *Child and the Law*. Toronto: McGraw-Hill Ryerson.

Barman, Jean (1986). "Indian and White Girls at All Hallows School," in Barman, ed., *Indian Education in Canada*, Vol. 1.

Barnhorst, Richard F. (1986). "Child Protection Legislation: Recent Canadian Reform," in Barbara Landau, ed., *Children's Rights in the Practice of Family Law*. Toronto: Carswell.

Barnsley, Jan, Helga Jacobson, Jean McIntosh, and Jane Wintemute (1980). *A review of Monroe House: Second stage housing for battered women*. Vancouver: Women's Research Centre.

Barr, Douglas (1979). "The Regent Park Community Services Unit: Partnership Can Work," in Brian Wharf, ed., *Community Work in Canada*. Toronto: McClelland and Stewart.

Beltrane, Julian (1985). "Incest haunts the lives of poor hillbillies," *The Vancouver Sun*.

Birnie, Lisa Hobbs (1991). "Mother love," *Saturday Night*, 106, 2.

Bishop, Arlene (1992). "Managing caseloads by teams: a new look at caseload management," University of Victoria, unpublished paper.

British Columbia Ministry of Labour (1989). *Women in the B.C. Labor Market*. Victoria, B.C.

British Columbia Office of the Ombudsman (1990a). *Report No. 22, Public Services to Children, Youth and Their Families in British Columbia: The Need for Integration*. Victoria.

British Columbia Office of the Ombudsman (1990b). *1988 Annual Report*.

Brodtrick, Otto (1991). "A Second Look at the Well Performing Organization," in James C. McDavid and D. Brian Marson, eds., *The Well Performing Government Organization*. The Institute of Public Administration of Canada.

Bullen, John (1990). "J.J. Kelso and the 'New' Child Savers: The genesis of the Children's Aid Movement in Ontario," Proceedings of a Multidisciplinary Workshop on Historical Research Concerning Children and Youth in Canada, Winnipeg, February, 1990.

Burnham, Rebecca (1990a). "The Child Snatchers," *British Columbia Report*, September 10.

Burnham, Rebecca (1990b). "Subjectivity and Abuse," *British Columbia Report*, December 17.

Burt, Sandra (1990). "Canadian Women's Groups in the 1980s: Organizational Development and Policy Influence," *Canadian Public Policy*, XVI, 1.

Callahan, Marilyn (1985). "Public Apathy and Government Parsimony: A Review of Child Welfare in Canada," in Ken Levitt and Brian Wharf, eds., *The Challenge of Child Welfare*. Vancouver: University of British Columbia Press.

Callahan, Marilyn (1988). "British Columbia," in Jacqueline S. Ismael and Yves Vaillancourt, eds., *Privatization and Provincial Social Services in Canada*. Edmonton: University of Alberta Press.

Callahan, Marilyn (1989). "Child Welfare Policy Since 1980 in British Columbia," in Andrew Armitage, ed., *The Future of Family and Children Services in British Columbia: An Agenda for Action and Research*. Victoria: University of Victoria, School of Social Work.

Callahan, Marilyn, and Carolyn Attridge (1990). *Women in Women's Work: Social Workers Talk About Their Work in Child Welfare*. Victoria: University of Victoria.

Callahan, Marilyn, and Brian Wharf (1982). *Demystifying the policy process: a case study in the development of child welfare legislation in B.C.* Victoria: University of Victoria School of Social Work.

Campbell, Jim (1991). "An Analysis of variables in child protection apprehensions and judicial dispositions in British Columbia child welfare practice," M.S.W. thesis, University of British Columbia.

Campbell, Jim (1992). "Children and Youth: Ministry of Social Services Child Protection and the Legislative Review," *Perspectives*, Vancouver.

Campbell, Marie (1992). "Administering child protection: A feminist analysis of the conceptual practices of organizational power," *Canadian Public Administration*, 35, 4.

Campbell, Marie, and Roxana Ng (1991). "Report of the participatory research project on empowerment and equity in Catholic Children's Aid Society of Metro Toronto," unpublished paper.

Canadian Child Welfare Association (1986). *Mission Statement*. Ottawa.

Canadian Child Welfare Association *et al.* (1988). *A Choice of Futures; Canada's Commitment to Its Children*. Ottawa.

Canadian Council on Children and Youth (1987). *Poor Now, Poor Later*. Ottawa.

Canadian Council on Children and Youth (1988). *Wasting Our Future: The Effects of Poverty on Child Development*. Ottawa.

Canadian Council on Children and Youth (1988a). *Caring For Our Children*. Ottawa.

Canadian Council on Children and Youth (1988b). *Eight Years Later*. Ottawa.

Canadian Council on Social Development (1991). *Mission Statement*. Ottawa.

Canadian Council on Social Development (1992). *Child Benefit Proposals*. Ottawa.

Canadian Welfare Council and Canadian Association of Social Workers (1947). *Joint Submission to the Special Joint Committee of the Senate and House of Commons Appointed to Examine and Consider the Indian Act*. Ottawa: Canadian Welfare Council.

Cantrell, Debbie (1988). "Front-line turnover," *Journal of the Ontario Association of Children's Aid Societies,* 32, 9.

Cardinal, Harold (1969). *The Unjust Society*. Edmonton: Hurtig.

Caring for a Living: A national study on wage and working conditions in Canadian child care (1992). A joint study of the Canadian Day Care Advocacy Association and the Canadian Child Day Care Federation. Vancouver: Karyn Communications.

Cassidy, Frank (1991). "Organizing For Community Control," *The Northern Review*, No. 7

Cassidy, Frank, and Robert L. Bish (1989). *Indian Government: Its Meaning in Practice*. Lantzville: Oolichan Books.

Cebotarev, E.A. (1986). "Women's invisible work," *Women's education des femmes,* 4, 3.

Chagnon, L., and M. Robin (1989). "Nouvelle group: An example of feminist intervention," *The Social Worker,* Summer, 57, 2.

Child Poverty Action Group (1986). *A Fair Chance for All Children: The Declaration on Child Poverty*. Toronto.

Child Poverty Action Group (1990). *Poor People Are Not the Problem, Poverty Is*. Toronto.

Child Poverty Action Group and Social Planning Council of Metropolitan Toronto (1991). *Unequal Futures*. Toronto.

Christenson, Carole Pigler (1989). "Protecting our youth: Cultural issues in the application and administration of the Youth Protection Act," *Intervention*, November, no. 84.

Clague, Michael, Robert Dill, Roop Seebaran, and Brian Wharf (1984). *Reforming Human Services: The Experience of the Community Resource Boards in B.C.* Vancouver: University of British Columbia Press.

Coates, Kenneth (1988). "Best Left as Indians," in Robin Fisher and Ken Coates, eds., *Out of the Background: Readings on Canadian Native History*. Toronto: Copp, Clark and Pitman.

Cole, Douglas, and Ira Chaikin (1990). *An Iron Hand Upon the People*. Seattle: University of Washington Press.

Commission on Emotional and Learning Disorders in Children (1970). *One Million Children*. Toronto: Leonard Crainford.

Committee on Local Authority and Allied Social Services (1968). *Report*. London: Her Majesty's Stationery Office.

Committee on Sexual Offences Against Children (1984). *Sexual Offences Against Children*. Ottawa: Minister of Supply and Services.

Considine, Mark (1987). "Turning the guns on the public service," *Australian Society,* April.

Coopers and Lybrand (1990). Assessment of Services delivered under the Canada/Manitoba Indian Child Welfare Agreement, Winnipeg, Manitoba.

Costin, Lela B. (1985). "Toward a Feminist Approach to Child Welfare," *Child Welfare*, LXIV, 3.

Cruickshank, David (1985). "The Berger Commission Report on the Protection of Children: The Impact on Prevention of Child Abuse and Neglect," in Ken Levitt and Brian Wharf, eds., *The Challenge of Child Welfare*. Vancouver: University of British Columbia Press.

Daley, M.R. (1979). "Burnout: smouldering problem in protective services," *Social work,* 24.

Dedyna, Katherine (1992). "Victoria man heads up chapter for victims of child abuse laws," *Times Colonist*, Victoria, May 11.

Department of Indian and Northern Affairs (1897). *Annual Report*. Ottawa.

Department of Indian and Northern Affairs (1989). *Indian Child and Family Services Management Regime: Discussion Paper*. Ottawa.

Doern, G. Bruce, and Richard W. Phidd (1992). *Canadian Public Policy: Ideas, Structure, Process*, Second Edition. Scarborough, Ontario: Nelson Canada.

Dominelli, Lena (1989). "Creating a feminist statutory social work," in Lena Dominelli and Eileen McLeod, eds., *Feminist Social Work*. London: Macmillan.

Ehrenreich, Barbara (1983). *The hearts of men*. London: Pluto Press.

Eichler, Margrit (1989). "Family Policy in Canada: From Where to Where," in Virginia Carver and Charles Ponee, eds., *Women, Work and Wellness*, Toronto: Addiction Research Foundation.

Evans, Patricia (1991). "The Sexual Division of Poverty: The Consequences of Gendered Caring," in Baines, Evans, and Neysmith, eds., *Women's Caring: Feminist Perspectives on Social Welfare*. Toronto: McClelland & Stewart.

Falconer, Nancy, and Joseph Hornick (1983). *Attack on burnout: The importance of early training*. Toronto: Children's Aid Society of Metropolitan Toronto.

Ferguson, Evelyn (1988). "Liberal and socialist feminist perspectives on child care," *Canadian Social Work Review*, 5, Winter.

Fraser, Nancy (1989). *Unruly practices: Power, discourse and gender in contemporary social theory*. Cambridge: Polity Press.

Freeman, Miriam (1990). "Beyond women's issues: Feminism and social work," *Affilia,* 5, 2, Summer.

Fryer, G., J. Poland, D. Bross, and R. Krugman (1988). "The child protective service worker: a profile of needs, attitudes and utilization of professional resources," *Child Abuse and Neglect,* 12, 4.

Gage, Robert (1976). "Integration of Human Service Delivery Systems," *Public Welfare,* Winter.

Germain, Carel (1985). "Understanding and Changing Communities and Organizations in the Practice of Child Welfare," in Joan Laird and Ann Hartman, eds., *A Handbook of Child Welfare: Context, Knowledge and Practice.* New York: The Free Press.

Giesbrecht, Brian (1992). *Report on the Death of Lester Desjarlais.* Winnipeg: Office of the Chief Medical Examiner, Queen's Printer.

Gil, David (1990). *Unravelling Social Policy,* Revised Fourth Edition. Rochester, Vermont: Schenkman Books.

Gilligan, Carol (1983). *In a different voice: Psychological theory and women's development.* Cambridge, Mass.: Harvard University Press.

Gilroy, Joan (1990). "Social Work and the Women's Movement," in Brian Wharf, ed., *Social Work and Social Change.* Toronto: McClelland & Stewart.

Giovannoni, Jean (1991). "Book Review: For Reasons of Poverty," *Children and Youth Services Review,* 13, 3.

Goffman, Erving (1961). *Asylums.* New York: Doubleday.

Gordon, Linda (1985). "Child abuse, gender, and the myth of family independence: A historical critique," *Child Welfare,* LXIV, 3.

Gordon, Linda (1986). "Feminism and social control: The case of child abuse and neglect," in J. Mitchell and A. Oakley, eds., *What is feminism? A Re-examination.* New York: Pantheon Press.

Goreau, Wayne (1986). *Native Child and Family Services in Manitoba.* Winnipeg: Department of Community Services.

Grant, Foster (1984). *The Moon of Wintertime.* Toronto: University of Toronto Press.

Gripton, James (1974). "Sexism in Social Work: Male takeover of a female profession," *The Social Worker,* 42, 2, summer.

Grosz, Elizabeth (1990). "Contemporary theories of power and subjectivity," in Snego Gunew, ed., *Feminist knowledge: Critique and construct.* London: Routledge.

Guest, Dennis (1985). *The Emergence of Social Security in Canada,* second edition, revised. Vancouver: University of British Columbia Press.

Guillemette, Rev. André-M. (1961). "Welfare organization and services in the Province of Quebec," in *Proceedings* of the Ninth Annual

Program Meeting, Council on Social Work Education, Montreal, Quebec. New York: Council on Social Work Education.

Gunderson, M., L. Muszynski, and Jennifer Keck (1990). *Women and labour market poverty*. Ottawa: Canadian Advisory Council on the Status of Women.

Gunew, Snego, ed. (1990). *Feminist knowledge: Critique and construct.* London: Routledge.

Hall, D.J. (1971). "Clifford Sifton and Canadian Indian Administration 1896-1905," *Prairie Forum*, 2.

Hallett, Christine (1989). *Women and social services departments.* Hemel Hampstead: Harvester Wheatsheaf.

Harmon, Lesley (1989). *When a hostel becomes a home: experiences of women.* Toronto: Garamond Press.

Harris, Michael (1990). *Unholy Orders: Tragedy at Mount Cashel.* Toronto: Penguin Books.

Harrison, David (1980). "Role strain and burnout in child protective service workers," *Social Service Review,* 54.

Hartsock, Nancy (1990). "Foucault on power. A theory for women?" in Linda J. Nicholson, ed., *Feminism/Postmodernism*. New York: Routledge.

Hawthorn, H.B., chair (1966). *A Survey of the Contemporary Indians of Canada: A Report on Economic, Political, Educational Needs and Policies*. Ottawa: Supply and Services.

Health and Welfare Canada (1990). *Reaching For Solutions*. Ottawa: Minister of Supply and Services.

Hegar, Rebecca, and Jeanne M. Hunzeker (1988). "Moving toward empowerment based practice in public child welfare," *Social Work*, 33, 6 (Nov-Dec).

Higgins, Joan Wharf (1992). "The Healthy Community Movement in Canada," in Brian Wharf, *Communities and Social Policy in Canada*. Toronto: McClelland & Stewart.

Hill, Elizabeth (1987). *Urban Models for Native Child Welfare: Progress and Prospects*. Winnipeg: University of Manitoba, School of Social Work.

Hill, Karen (1990). *Final Report: Pioneers in Social Progress: oral history of social work in Canada*. Ottawa: Canadian Council on Social Development.

House of Commons (1989). Resolution: This House Seeks to achieve the goal of eliminating poverty among Canadian children by the year 2000. Ottawa.

Hudson, Peter, and Brad McKenzie (1987). *Evaluation of the Dakota Ojibway Child and Family Services*. Winnipeg: Department of Northern and Indian Affairs.

Hudson, Peter, and Sharon Taylor-Henley (1987). *Agreement and Disagreement: An Evaluation of the Canada-Manitoba Northern Indian Child Welfare Agreement*. Winnipeg: University of Manitoba.

Hudson, Peter, and Sharon Taylor-Henley (1992). *Interactions Between Social and Political Development in First Nations Communities*. Winnipeg: University of Manitoba, Faculty of Social Work.

Ismael, J., and Y. Vaillancourt (1988). *Privatization and Provincial Social Services in Canada*. Edmonton: University of Alberta Press.

Jayaratne, S., W.A. Chess, and D.A. Kunkel (1986). "Burnout: its impact on child welfare workers and their spouses," *Social work*, 31.

Johnston, Basil (1988). *Indian School Days*. Toronto: Key Porter.

Johnston, Patrick (1983). *Native Children and the Child Welfare System*. Toronto: James Lorimer and Canadian Council on Social Development.

Johnston, Patrick (1991). Letter to Brian Wharf.

Jones, Andrew, and Leonard Rutman (1981). *In the Children's Aid: J.J.Kelso and child welfare in Ontario*. Toronto: University of Toronto Press.

Jones, Mary Ann (1985). *A Second Chance for Families*. New York: Child Welfare League of America.

Jones, Mary Ann, Stephen Magura, and Ann W. Shyne (1981). "Effective Practice with Families in Protection and Prevention Services: What Works?" *Child Welfare*, LX, 1.

Kahn, Alfred (1976). "Service Delivery at the Neighborhood Level: Experience, Theory and Fads," *Social Service Review*, 50.

Karger, H.J. (1981). "Burnout as alienation," *Social Service Review*, 55.

Kendrick, Martyn (1990). *Nobody's children: The foster care crisis in Canada*. Toronto: Macmillan.

Kimelman, Edwin C., *et al.* (1985). "No Quiet Place," *Report of the Review Committee on Indian and Metis Adoptions and Placements*. Winnipeg: Department of Community Services.

King, Richard (1967). *The School at Mopass*. Stanford: Holt, Rinehart and Winston.

Kramer, Marlene, and Claudia Schmalenberg (1988). "Magnet hospitals: Institutions of excellence," *Journal of Nursing Administration*, 18, 1.

Krane, Julia (1990). "Explanations of child sexual abuse: A review and critique from a feminist perspective," *Canadian Review of Social Policy*, 25.

LaForest, Gerald V. (1983). "The Canadian Charter of Rights and Freedoms: An Overview," *The Canadian Bar Review*, 61.

Laidlaw Foundation (1988). *Children at Risk: Preliminary Report*. Toronto.

Laidlaw Foundation (1990). *Children at Risk: Prospectus Report*. Toronto.

Laidlaw Foundation (1991). *National Report*. Toronto.

Laidlaw Foundation (n.d.). *Children at Risk: Application Procedures and Guidelines*. Toronto.

Landau, Barbara (1986). *Children's Rights in the Practice of Family Law*. Toronto: Carswell.

Latouche, Kenneth (1985). "Quebec," in *The Canadian Encyclopedia*. Edmonton: Hurtig Publishers.

Lesemann, Frederic (1987). "Social Welfare Policy in Quebec," in Shankar Yelaja, ed., *Canadian Social Policy*. Waterloo: Wilfrid Laurier University Press.

Lessing, Doris (1991). University Lecture Series, University of Victoria, as quoted in the *Ring*, 12, 18.

Levine, Helen, and Alma Estable (1981). *The power politics of motherhood: A feminist critique of theory and practice*. Ottawa: Carleton University.

Lindblom, Charles (1979). "Still Muddling, Not Yet Through," *Public Administration Review*, Nov./Dec.

Lipsky, Michael (1980). *Street Level Bureaucracy*. New York: Russell Sage Foundation.

Littner, Ner (1957). *The strains and stresses on the child welfare worker*. New York: Child Welfare League of America.

Maines, Joy A. (1959). "Through the years in C.A.S.W.," *The Social Worker*, 27, 4 (October).

Ma Mawi Wi Chi Itata (1985). *First Annual Meeting Report*. Winnipeg.

Manitoba Tripartite Committee (1980). *Manitoba Indian Child Welfare Sub-Committee Report*. Winnipeg.

Marchant, Helen, and Betsy Wearing, eds. (1986). *Gender reclaimed: Women in social work*. Sidney: Hale and Ironmonger.

Markusen, Anne (1992). "Dismantling the Cold War Economy," *World Policy Journal*, Summer.

Marron, Kevin (1988). *Ritual Abuse*. Toronto: Seal Books.

Marshall, Katherine (1990). "Women in male-dominated professions," in Craig McKie and Keith Thompson, eds., *Canadian social trends*. Toronto: Ministry of Supply and Services and Thompson Educational Publishing.

Maslach, Christina (1982). *Burnout: the cost of caring*. Englewood Cliffs N.J.: Prentice-Hall.

Maxwell, Margaret (1987). "Rape crisis centres as feminist movement organizations: Comparisons with mainstream human service organizations on community education and services," Dissertation abstracts international A: The Humanities and Social Sciences, 48, 4 (October).

McCall, M.L. (1990). "An Analysis of Responsibilities in Child Welfare Systems," *Canadian Journal of Family Law*, 8.

McClelland, David (1982). *Motivation and Society*. San Francisco: Jossey-Bass.

McDonald, Jack (1985). "The Spallumcheen By-Law," in Levitt and Wharf, eds., *The Challenge of Child Welfare*. Vancouver: University of British Columbia Press.

McEachern, Allan, The Honourable Chief Justice (1990). *Reasons for Judgment*. The Supreme Court of British Columbia, Vancouver, The Smithers Registry.

McEachern, Colin, and D.L. Harris (1973). "Community Action," *Journal of the Ontario Association of Chidren's Aid Societies*.

McKenzie, Brad (1991). "Decentralization in Winnipeg: Assessing the Effects of Community Based Child Welfare Services," *Canadian Review of Social Policy*, No. 27.

McKenzie, Brad (1992). Reviewer's comments. Winnipeg, Faculty of Social Work.

McKenzie, Brad, and Peter Hudson (1985). "Native Children, Child Welfare and the Colonization of Native People," in Levitt and Wharf, eds., *The Challenge of Child Welfare*. Vancouver: University of British Columbia Press.

McLeod, Mary, and Esther Saranga (1988). "Challenging the orthodoxy: Towards a feminist theory and practice," *Feminist Review*, 28.

Meyer, C.H. (1985). " A feminist perspective on foster family care: redefinition of the categories," *Child Welfare*, 54, 3.

Miller, Jean Baker (1975). *Towards a new psychology of women*. Boston: Beacon Press.

Miller, J.R. (1989). *Skyscrapers Hide the Heavens: A History of Indian-White Relations in Canada*. Toronto: University of Toronto Press.

Ministry of Community and Social Services (1979). *Child Welfare in Ontario: Past, Present and Future*. Toronto: Queen's Printer for Ontario.

Ministry of Community and Social Services (1986). *The Child Health Study: Summary of Initial Findings*. Toronto: Queen's Printer for Ontario.

Ministry of Community and Social Services (1988). *Investing in Children: New Directions in Child Treatment and Child and Family Intervention*. Toronto: Queen's Printer for Ontario.

Ministry of Community and Social Services (1990). *Foster Care as a Residential Family Resource*. Toronto: Queen's Printer for Ontario.

Mitchinson, Wendy (1987). "Early women's organizations and social reform: Prelude to the welfare state," in Allan Moscovitch and Jim

Albert, eds., *The Benevolent State: The growth of welfare in Canada.* Toronto: Garamond Press.

Montgomery, John (1979). "The Populist Front in Rural Development: or Shall We Eliminate the Bureaucrats and Get on the Job?" *Public Administration Review,* Jan/Feb.

Moore, Scott (1987). "The theory of street-level bureaucracy," *Administration and Society,* 19, 1.

Moreau, M. (1990). "Empowerment through advocacy and consciousness-raising: Implications of a structural approach to social work," *Journal of Sociology and Social Welfare,* 17, 2.

Morris, R., and I. Lescohier (1979). "Service Integration: Real Versus Illusory Solutions," in R. Sarri and Y. Hassenfeld, eds., *Management of the Human Services.* New York: Columbia University Press.

Morrison, T.R. (1976). "'Their proper sphere': feminism, the family, and child-centered social reform in Ontario, 1875-1900," *Ontario History,* LXVIII, 1-2.

Nathan, Holly (1992). "Watts filling in as Alberni native leader after Chief jailed for abuse," *Times Colonist,* Victoria, September 27.

National Council of Welfare (1975). *Poor kids.* Ottawa.

National Council of Welfare (1979). *In the best interests of the child.* Ottawa.

National Council of Welfare (1990). *Women and poverty revisited.* Ottawa.

Nelson, K., M. Landsman, and W. Teitelbaum (1990). "Three Models of Children's Placement Prevention Programs," *Child Welfare,* LXIX, 1.

Nova Scotia Department of Social Services (1987). *Report of the Task Force on Family and Children's Services.* Halifax.

Novick, Marvyn (1992). Letter to Brian Wharf.

Novick, M., and R. Volpe (1989). *Perspectives on social practice: Children at risk project,* Vol. 1. Toronto: Laidlaw Foundation.

O'Hara, Maureen (1990). "Refuge for young women in crisis," *Childright,* 71.

Ontario Association of Children's Aid Societies (1973). *Brief to the Task Force on Community and Social Services.* Toronto.

Ontario Association of Children's Aid Societies (1990a). *Strategic Plan,* prepared by F.J. Galloway Associates. Toronto.

Ontario Association of Children's Aid Societies (1990b). *Fact Sheet #2.* Toronto.

Ontario Association of Children's Aid Societies (1991). *OACAS Advocacy Inventory.* Toronto.

Parker, Roy (1990). "The Immigration of Unaccompanied Children from

Britain to Canada, 1870-1914," Lansdowne Lecture, University of Victoria.

Parliament, Joanne B. (1990). "Women employed outside the home," in McKie and Thompson, eds., *Canadian social trends*. Toronto: Minister of Supply and Services and Thompson Educational Publishing.

Parton, Christine, and Nigel Parton (1989). "Women, the family and child protection," *Critical Social Policy*, Spring.

Pateman, Carol (1988). "The Patriarchal Welfare State," in Amy Gutmann, ed., *Democracy and the welfare state*. Princeton, N.J.: Princeton University Press.

Peikoff, Tannis, and Stephen Brickey (1990). "Creating precious children and glorified mothers: A theoretical assessment of the transformation of childhood," *Proceedings*, Multidisciplinary Workshop on Historical Research Concerning Children and Youth in Canada, University of Manitoba.

Pennell, Joan T. (1987). "Ideology at a Canadian shelter for battered women: a reconstruction," *Women's studies international forum*, 10, 2.

Peters, R. DeV. (1988). *Children's Mental Health: An International Perspective*. Kingston: Queen's University.

Peters, Thomas, and Robert H. Waterman (1982). *In Search of Excellence*. New York: Warner Books.

Pitsula, James (1979). "The emergence of social work in Toronto," *Journal of Canadian Studies*, 14, 1.

Polansky, N., J. Gaudin, and A. Kilpatrick (1992). "The maternal characteristics scale: A cross validation," *Child Welfare*, LXXI, 3 (May/June).

Popham, Rosemary (1992). Letter to Brian Wharf.

Popple, Philip R. (1983). "Contexts of Practice," in Aaron Rosenbeath and Diana Waldfogel, eds., *Handbook of Clinical Social Work*. San Francisco: Jossey-Bass.

Price, Lisa (1991). "A violent legacy: exploring the link between child sexual abuse and wife assault," *Vis-à-Vis: A national newsletter on family violence* (Canadian Council on Social Development), 9, 2.

Pross, Paul (1980). *Duality and Public Policy: A Conceptual Framework for Analysing the Policy System for Atlantic Canada*. Halifax: Dalhousie University, Institute of Public Affairs.

Provincial/Municipal Social Services Review (1990). Toronto: Queen's Printer for Ontario.

Quebec (1987). *Statement of Orientations and Administrative Structure of the Quebec Government's Family Policy*. Quebec: Ministry of Social Affairs.

Rawls, John (1973). *A Theory of Justice*. Oxford: Oxford University Press.

Reckart, Josephine (in press). *Public Funds, Private Provision: The Role of Voluntary Sector Social Services in the 1980's*. Vancouver: University of British Columbia Press.

Rein, Martin (1972). "Decentralization and Citizen Participation in the Social Services," *Public Administration Review*, No. 32.

Rein, Martin (1983). *From Policy to Practice*. New York: M.E. Sharpe.

Reitsma-Street, Marge (1986). *A Feminist Analysis of Ontario Laws for Delinquency and Neglect: More Control than Care*. University of Toronto, Faculty of Social Work, Working Papers on Social Welfare in Canada.

Report of the British Columbia Commission on Health Care and Costs (1991). *Closer To Home*. Victoria: Crown Publishers.

Ridington, Jillian (1982). "Providing services the feminist way," in Connie FitzGerald and Margie Wolfe Guberman, eds., *Still Ain't Satisfied: Canadian Feminism Today*. Toronto: Women's Press.

Romanyshyn, John (1971). *Social Welfare: Charity to Justice*. New York: Random House.

Rooke, P.T., and R.L. Schnell (1988). *No Bleeding Heart: Charlotte Whitton, a feminist on the right*. Vancouver: University of British Columbia Press.

Rose, Hilary (1978). "In practice supported, in theory denied: an account of an invisible urban movement," *International Journal of Urban and Regional Research*, 2, 3.

Ross, Murray, and Ben Lappin (1967). *Community Organization: Theory, Principles and Practice*. New York: Harper and Row.

Rothman, Jack (1974). "Three Models of Community Organization Practice," in F. Cox *et al.*, eds., *Strategies of Community Organization*. Itasca, Illinois: Peacock Press.

Rotman, Ann (1989). "Female Social Workers: Career or Family," *Affilia*, 4, 4.

Royal Commission on Family and Children's Law (1975). *Fifth Report: The Protection of Children*. Vancouver.

Royal Commission on Family and Children's Law (1975). *Tenth Report: Native Familes and the Law*. Vancouver.

Rycraft, Joan (1990). "The survivors: a qualitative study of the retention of public child welfare workers," Ph.D. dissertation, University of Denver.

Schwartz, Allyson, Eve Gottesman, and Felice Perlmutter (1988). "A case study in feminist administration," *Administration in Social Work*, 12, 2.

Scott, Duncan Campbell (1913). "Indian Affairs 1867-1912," in Adam Shortt, ed., *Canada and Its Provinces*. Toronto: University of Toronto Press.

Shackleton, Doris (1977). *Power Town: Democracy Discarded*. Toronto: McClelland and Stewart.

Shepherd, J.E. (1990). "Evolution of organizational structure in a shelter for battered women: a case study," Ph.D dissertation, University of Illinois.

Smith, B., and T. Smith (1990). "For Love and Money: Women as foster mothers," *Affilia*, 5, 1.

Social Planning Council of Metropolitan Toronto (1976). *In Search of a Framework*. Toronto.

Society for Children and Youth of British Columbia (1991). *Strategic Plan/Working Paper*. Vancouver.

Society for Children and Youth of British Columbia (n.d.). "A short history of SCY," unpublished paper, Vancouver.

Stenstad, Gail (1990). "Anarchic thinking," in Ann Garry and Marilyn Pearsall, eds., *Women, knowledge and reality*. Boston: Unwin Hyman.

Strong-Boag, Veronica (1977). "'Setting the Stage': National Organization and the Women's Movement in the late 19th Century," in Susan Mann Trofimenkoff and Alison Prentice, eds., *The Neglected Majority: Essays in Canadian Women's History*. Toronto: McClelland and Stewart.

Struthers, James (1987). "Lord give us men: Women and social work in English Canada, 1918-1953," in Moscovitch and Albert, eds., *The Benevolent State: The growth of welfare in Canada*. Toronto: Garamond Press.

Sutherland, Neil (1985). "History of Childhood," in *The Canadian Encyclopedia*. Edmonton: Hurtig Publishers.

Swift, Karen (1991). "Contradictions in Child Welfare: Neglect and Responsibility," in Baines, Evans, and Neysmith, eds., *Women's Caring: Feminist Perspectives on Social Welfare*. Toronto: McClelland & Stewart.

Technical Assistance and Family Planning Associates (1979). *A Starving Man Doesn't Argue: A review of community social services to Indians in Canada*. Toronto.

Todd, James (1991). "School for Shame," *Vancouver Sun*, April 26.

Trocme, Nico (1991). "Child Welfare Services," in Richard Barnhorst and Lavia Johnson, eds., *The State of the Child in Ontario*. Toronto: Oxford University Press.

Ursel, Jane (1982). "The State and the Maintenance of Patriarchy: A Case Study of Family, Labour and Welfare Legislation in Canada," in Arlene McLaren, ed., *Gender and Society*. Toronto: Copp, Clark Pitman.

Ursel, Jane (1992) *Private Lives, Public Policy: 100 years of state intervention in the family*. Toronto: Women's Press.

Vance, Joanie (1979). "The experience of rape crisis centres,"*Atlantis*. 4, 5 (Spring).

Vanier Institute of the Family (1986). *Child Care Options For Canadian Families*. Ottawa.

Victorian Family and Children's Services Council (1990). *One Year Later: Review of the Redevelopment of Protective Services for Children*. Melbourne, Australia.

Vinokur-Kaplan, Diane, and Ann Hartman (1986). "A national profile of child welfare workers and supervisors," *Child Welfare*, LXV, 4.

Vogle, Robin (1991). "Initial Involvement," in N. Bala, J. Hornick, and R. Vogle, eds., *Canadian Child Welfare Law*. Toronto: Thompson Educational Publishing.

Waerness, Kari (1984). "Caring as women's work in the welfare state," in H. Holter, ed., *Patriarchy in a welfare society*. Oslo: Universitetsforlaget.

Walker, Gillian A. (1977). *The Status of Women in Social Work Education*. Ottawa: Canadian Association of Schools of Social Work.

Walker, Gillian A. (1986). "Burnout: From metaphor to ideology," *Canadian Journal of Sociology*, 11.

Walker, Gillian A. (1990). *Family Violence and The Women's Movement*. Toronto: Women's Press.

Wasserman, Harry (1970). "Early careers of professional social workers in a public child welfare agency," *Social Work*, 15.

Watson, Nettie (1960). "Historical Background," in *A Summary and discussion of the History and Problem of Child Welfare Services in Vancouver with Particular Reference to Temporary Foster Home (Non-Ward) Care and Its Costs*, prepared by E.F. Watson, Family and Child Welfare Division, Community Chest and Councils of The Greater Vancouver Area.

Wattenberg, Esther (1985). "In a different light: a feminist perspective on the role of mothers in father-daughter incest," *Child Welfare*, 54, 3.

Weil, M. (1988). "Creating an alternative work culture in a public service setting," *Administration in Social Work*, 12, 2.

Weiss, Janet (1981). "Substance Versus Symbol in Administrative Reform: The Case of Human Services Coordination," *Policy Analysis*, 7, 1.

Wharf, Brian (1985). "Preventive Approaches to Child Welfare," in Levitt and Wharf, eds., *The Challenge of Child Welfare*. Vancouver: University of British Columbia Press.

Wharf, Brian (1986). "Social Welfare and the Political System," in J.C.

Turner and F.C. Turner, eds., *Canadian Social Welfare*. Toronto: Collier Macmillan.

Wharf, Brian (1989). *Toward First Nations Control of Child Welfare*. University of Victoria, Victoria, B.C.

Wharf, Brian, ed. (1990). *Social Work and Social Change*. Toronto: McClelland & Stewart.

Wharf, Brian (1991). "Preventing Out of Home Placements," *Children Australia*, 16, 3.

Wharf, Brian (1992). *Communities and Social Policy in Canada*. Toronto: McClelland & Stewart.

Whittaker, James (1983). "Social Support Networks in Child Welfare," in James Whittaker, James Garbarino and associates, eds., *Social Support Networks: Informal Helping in the Human Services*. New York: Aldine Publishing.

Wilensky, Harold, and Charles Lebeaux (1965). *Industrial Society and Social Welfare*. New York: Macmillan.

Wilson, James Q., and George L. Kelling (1989). "Making Neighbourhoods Safe," *The Atlantic*, 263, 2.

Wood, Chris (1986). "The Scars of Poverty," *Maclean's*, March 10.

Zigler, Edward (1986). "The Family Resource Movement: No Longer the Country's Best Kept Secret," *Family Resource Coalition Report*, 5, 3.

About the Authors

ANDREW ARMITAGE received his doctorate from the University of Bristol and is currently Director of the School of Social Work at the University of Victoria. He has previously taught at U.B.C. and Calgary and was an assistant deputy minister in the British Columbia government. He is the author of *Social Welfare in Canada* (1988).

MARILYN CALLAHAN is currently completing doctoral studies at the University of Bristol and teaches at the University of Victoria, where she has served as director of the School of Social Work.

EWAN MACINTYRE earned his Ph.D. from the University of Southern California and presently teaches in the School of Social Work at McMaster University, of which he formerly was the director.

BRIAN WHARF received his Ph.D. from Brandeis University and currently teaches in a multidisciplinary policy/practice program in the Faculty of Human and Social Development at the University of Victoria. His numerous works include *Social Work and Social Change in Canada* (1990) and *Communities and Social Policy in Canada* (1992).

Acknowledgements

We wish to acknowledge the help of colleagues and friends who helped us at various stages of writing this book.

Janet Eibmer assisted Ewan in conducting library research for Chapter 1 and Brenda Orgar aided in formatting this chapter.

Chapter 4 benefited from the information and reviews provided by the following individuals: Bob Glossop (Vanier Institute for the Family); Valerie Fronczak (Society for Children and Youth for B.C.); Patrick Johnston (Canadian Council on Social Development); Murielle O'Hara (Children * Enfants * Jeunesse * Youth); Mary McConville (Ontario Association of Children's Aid Societies); Marvyn Novick (Children at Risk Program, The Laidlaw Foundation); and Rosemary Popham (Child Poverty Action Group).

We are particularly grateful to Brad McKenzie of the Faculty of Social Work, University of Manitoba, for his detailed and perceptive review of the manuscript. Brad challenged us to revise and improve the manuscript. We hope the final version reflects his comments.

Finally, we wish to acknowledge the help of Barbara Egan for compiling and revising the bibliography and formatting the work of four authors and for doing so in such a cheerful fashion. Carol Gamey once again undertook the painstaking tasks of proofreading and index construction and Richard Tallman provided the finishing touches with his exemplary editing.

Index